D0571019

Better Homes and Gardens®

505

QUILT BLOCKS

Plus 36 beautiful projects

Better Homes and Gardens® Books
Des Moines, Iowa

505 QUILT BLOCKS

Better Homes and Gardens® Books
An imprint of Meredith® Books

Editor: Carol Field Dahlstrom
Contributing Writer: Sylvia Miller
Technical Editor: Susan M. Banker
Designer: Angela Haupert Hoogensen
Technical Assistants: Judy Bailey, Staci Bailey
Copy Chief: Terri Fredrickson
Copy and Production Editor: Victoria Forlini
Editorial Operations Manager: Karen Schirm
Managers, Book Production: Pam Kvitne, Marjorie J. Schenkelberg, Rick von Holdt
Contributing Copy Editor: Margaret Smith
Contributing Proofreaders: Chardel Blaine, Julie Cahalan, Cindy McLeod
Photographers: Scott Little, Andy Lyons Cameraworks, Peter Krumhardt
Technical Illustrator: Chris Neubauer Graphics, Inc.
Electronic Production Coordinator: Paula Forest
Editorial and Design Assistants: Kaye Chabot, Mary Lee Gavin, Karen McFadden

Meredith® Books
Publisher and Editor in Chief: Linda Raglan Cunningham
Design Director: Matt Strelecki
Executive Editor, Food and Crafts: Jennifer Dorland Darling

Publisher: James D. Blume
Executive Director, Marketing: Jeffrey Myers
Executive Director, New Business Development: Todd M. Davis
Executive Director, Sales: Ken Zagor
Director, Operations: George A. Susral
Director, Production: Douglas M. Johnston
Business Director: Jim Leonard

Vice President and General Manager: Douglas J. Guendel

Better Homes and Gardens® Magazine
Editor in Chief: Karol DeWulf Nickell

Meredith Publishing Group
President, Publishing Group: Stephen M. Lacy
Vice President-Publishing Director: Bob Mate

Meredith Corporation
Chairman and Chief Executive Officer: William T. Kerr

Chairman of the Executive Committee: E. T. Meredith III

All of us at Better Homes and Gardens® Books are dedicated to providing you with information and ideas to create beautiful and useful projects. We welcome your comments and suggestions. Write to us at: Better Homes and Gardens Books, Crafts Editorial Department, 1716 Locust Street—LN112, Des Moines, IA 50309-3023.

If you would like to purchase any of our crafts, cooking, gardening, home improvement, or home decorating and design books, check wherever quality books are sold. Or visit us at bhgbooks.com. Permission is granted from Meredith Corporation to photocopy the quilt patterns for personal use only.

505 BLOCKS...
thousands of possibilities

When we started this book, *we knew it would be fun* to choose the 505 new quilt blocks all stitched in beautiful fabrics. What a delight it was to work with fabric companies and quilters from all over the country as we made the decisions about picking the designs and then the fabrics to complement each new block.

We knew it would take time to decide which quilt block designs you would love most. We asked experienced quilters, beginning quilters, young quilters, and not-so-young quilters what projects they liked to quilt. We talked with quilters who loved patchwork and some that preferred appliqué. We visited with quilters who made quilts for their beds and those that made smaller pieces to keep or give away as gifts.

We knew it would be amazing to see all 505 blocks come together into one book, complete with clever projects to make. We even added dozens of graphics to show how the blocks might look when they were pieced together.

And now *we know that you'll love* the *Better Homes and Gardens® 505 Quilt Blocks* book and that you'll find thousands of possibilities to use your amazing quilting talents.

Carol Field Dahlstrom

CONTENTS

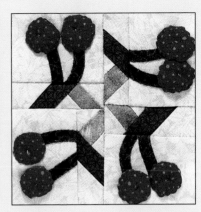

BLOCKS~

When you have 505 block designs from which to choose, the sky is the limit! Combine your favorite pieced and appliquéd designs to show off your quilting talents.
pages 50–305

~TIPS & TECHNIQUES

Whether you're new to quilting or have mastered many projects and techniques, you're sure to find helpful guidance in this section. From how to make a template to creating fun yo-yos, from rotary cutting to mitering corners, you'll discover a wealth of information to help you achieve quilting success.
pages 306–315

MITERED BORDER CORNERS

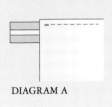
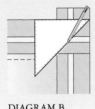
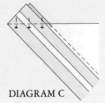

DIAGRAM A

DIAGRAM B

DIAGRAM C

INDEX~

Use this handy, extensive index to quickly locate a particular quilt block or project.
pages 316–319

~SOURCES

Check out this page to locate materials. These sources will help you find the tools and quilting products you're looking for.
page 320

HOW TO USE THIS BOOK

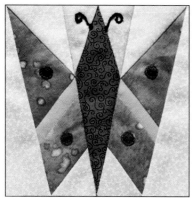

ABOUT THE BLOCKS

A ll 505 blocks in this book are 4 inches square when finished, which makes it easy to interchange the blocks in any of the projects. **All blocks are sewn together with ¼-inch seam allowances.** If you prefer to work with larger blocks, photocopy and enlarge the designs to the size desired. Permission for photocopying the patterns for personal use is on *page 2.* For help with making a template, see *page 312.*

For easy reference, the quilt blocks are grouped by subject, such as patriotic and floral, and listed in the block index, *pages 316–319.*

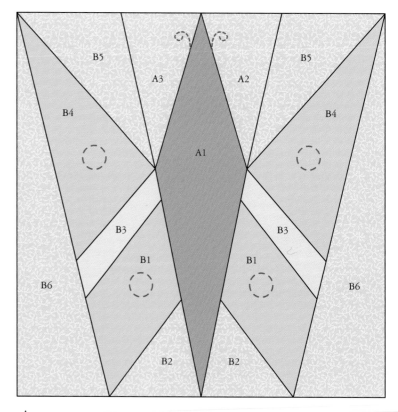

ABOUT THE PATTERNS

A neutral-tone pattern is shown next to each block photo. The pattern pieces are labeled with letters that correspond to the references in the instructions. Dotted lines indicate hand-embroidery, such as the butterfly wing spots and antennae, *above,* or where pieces overlap, such as on appliqué blocks.

ABOUT THE INSTRUCTIONS

To ensure your stitching success, each block is accompanied by instructions for the block construction. Some blocks are pieced; others are appliquéd. For quilting instructions and tips, see *pages 306–314*. For specialty stitch diagrams, see *page 315*.

BRIGHT BUTTERFLY

A9 Make A section by joining pieces in numerical order. Make 2 B sections and sew to each side of the A section. Embroider circles on the wings using satin stitch outlined with stem stitch. Use stem stitch for antennae.

LOOK AGAIN

Occasionally we include a "Look Again" bar near a quilt block. Here you'll find four blocks arranged to call your attention to a new or unusual pattern that develops. To play with block arrangement, make several photocopies of your stitched blocks (or the patterns) and experiment with various combinations.

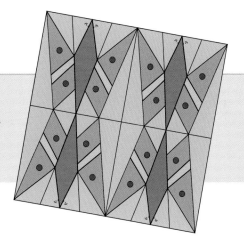

Look Again

Create a field of diamonds by combining pairs of Bright Butterfly blocks. Joining blocks mirror fashion often creates interesting repetitive shapes.

ABOUT THE PROJECTS

The projects on *pages 10–49* are created using the 4-inch blocks from the Blocks section of the book. Each project lists the blocks used; however, because the blocks are interchangeable, you can choose your favorites to personalize each project.

All of the projects include a supply list for materials needed in addition to the blocks and step-by-step instructions. When helpful, diagrams are included.

PROJECTS

Show off your quilting talent by sewing inspiring and creative projects. From easy-to-make tote bags, toys, and towels to keepsake curtains, pillows, and quilts—you'll find more than thirty projects to piece and quilt. So choose your favorite blocks from the following chapters to incorporate into stunning projects to display, use, and give to those dear to your heart.

Gather your things in this roomy tote that celebrates the fall season with colorful appliquéd leaf blocks. Use the same concept to make a holiday bag or to showcase your favorite blocks.

MATERIALS

½ yard fabric for back, sides, bottom, and borders
¼ yard fabric for sashing and handles
½ yard fabric for lining
15×21-inch piece of fabric for backing
15×21-inch piece of batting
4 yards cotton-covered cording
Twelve ¾-inch buttons

Finished size:
19 inches wide, 13 inches high, 4 inches deep

Block patterns:
6 leaf blocks 06–010 and 012, pages 302–305

CONSTRUCTION

1 From fabric for borders, cut 12—1×4½-inch strips. Sew a strip to the top and bottom of each leaf block. Cut 12—1×5½-inch strips; sew a strip to each side of the leaf blocks.

2 From fabric for sashing and handles, cut 9—1½×5½-inch strips. Join blocks in vertical pairs by sewing a strip between the top and bottom of pairs of leaf blocks; sew a strip to the top and to the bottom of each pair.

3 From the same fabric, cut 4—1½×13½ inch strips. Join the block pairs with these strips. Sew a strip to each end to complete the tote front.

4 Layer the backing, batting, and the pieced panel. Pin or baste layers together. Machine-quilt around the leaves. Quilt in-the-ditch around the borders and sashing. Trim the backing and batting even with the pieced panel. Sew cording from the top down one side, around the bottom, and up to the top of the opposite side.

5 For the tote back, cut 1 rectangle 13½×19½ inches or the same size as the pieced panel. Sew cording to the sides and bottom in one continuous strip, as with the front.

6 For the sides and bottom, cut 2 strips 4½×13½ inches and 1 strip 4½×19½ inches. Sew a short strip to each narrow end of the long strip for a continuous length. Press. Sew the strip to the pieced front panel and the back. Sew cording along the top opening.

7 From fabric for handles, cut 2 strips 3½×17 inches. Wrong sides together, fold the strip in half; press. Fold the raw edges toward the center; press. Topstitch close to both folded edges. Raw edges even, baste the handles to the right side of the front and back of the tote bag, lining them up with the sashing.

8 For lining, cut 2 pieces 13½×19½ inches, 2 side panels 4½×13½ inches, and 1 bottom panel 4½×19½ inches. Sew sides to bottom piece; join front and back pieces. Wrong sides together, sew lining to tote along the top edge stitching along cording stitching, and leaving an opening for turning. Turn to right side and hand-stitch opening closed. Sew 12 buttons in place, as shown in the photo, *opposite.*

ASSEMBLY DIAGRAM

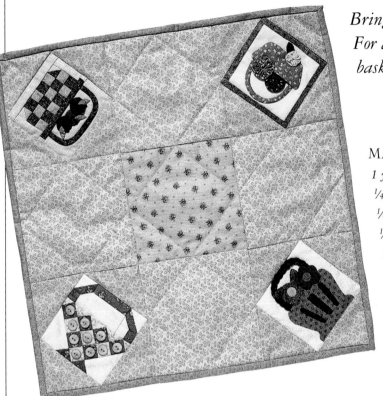

Bring baskets to the table to share.
For a bountiful display, set off your handmade
baskets in big block style.

MATERIALS

1 yard fabric for backing and binding
¼ yard fabric for blocks
¼ yard fabric for center block
¼ yard fabric to complete basket blocks
19-inch square of batting

Finished size: 17 inches square

Block patterns:
4 basket blocks B8, B11, B13, and B16, pages 73, 75–77

CONSTRUCTION

1 Cut 4 triangles (pattern, *bottom right*) for each basket block. Sew triangles to the 4 sides of each completed basket block to make 6-inch blocks.

2 Cut 4—6-inch-square blocks, from one fabric and one 6-inch block from a coordinating fabric.

3 Assemble blocks into 3 rows of 3 blocks each with basket blocks on the corners, and the contrasting block in the center. Join the rows; press.

4 Cut backing 2 inches larger than the pieced top. Layer and baste backing, batting, and top.

5 Using the diagram, *right,* as reference, quilt the piece.

6 Cut enough 2½-inch-wide binding strips to equal 74 inches length; piece for a continuous strip. Fold in half lengthwise, press, and sew raw edges to the quilt top. Fold binding to the back and hand-stitch in place.

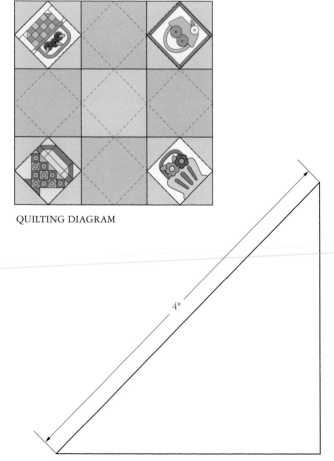

QUILTING DIAGRAM

4"

FULL-SIZE PATTERN (ADD ¼ INCH SEAM ALLOWANCE)

Prairie point flowers bloom beautifully on this pieced and stipple-quilted background.
The fresh color scheme blends with the decor of many rooms.

MATERIALS

¼ *yard (or fat quarter) fabric for flowerpot*
⅛ *yard fabric for flowerpot tray and rim*
¼ *yard dark blue fabric for bottom strip*
½ *yard dark green fabric for stems and leaves*
⅛ *yard each of 4 additional green fabrics for leaves*
¼ *yard (or fat quarter) each of 4 or 5 light blue fabrics*
1 *yard light blue fabric for backing*
33×42-*inch cotton batting;* 9—⅝- *or* ⅞-*inch buttons*

Finished size: 31×40 inches

Block patterns:
Prairie Point Flower blocks F27, page 125, plus 2 half-blocks and
1 *partial block*

CONSTRUCTION

1 Using the same light blue background color, make 6 prairie point flower blocks (*page 125*). Make 2 half-blocks with 3 prairie points (*page 313*). Make 1 partial block using darker fabric (to be used on bottom strip) with one prairie point.

2 Referring to illustrations, *page 16,* for each section, cut and piece the wall hanging. Note: Seam allowances are NOT included in measurements; add ½ inch to each measurement for seam allowance.

SECTION A

Using darker fabric for the bottom section, join 2×4-inch partial prairie point block to A1 piece; join to A3 and A4 pieces to complete the section.

SECTION B

Use 2 flowerpot fabrics for B1, B4, and B7. Use an assortment of light blue fabrics for background pieces. Join pieces in numerical order to complete the B section. Note: Sew only outside edges of seam along top of B7, joining to background B10–B15 blocks, leaving center open to sew in appliqué stems. After stems and leaves are appliquéd on, remaining part of seam may be sewn shut.

SECTION C

Use 2 complete prairie point flower blocks and 1 half-block in this section. Cut background from assorted light blue fabrics. Join pieces in numerical order to complete the section.

SECTION D

Use 3 complete and 1 half prairie point blocks for this section. Cut remaining sections from assorted light blue. Join pieces in numerical order to complete the section.

SECTION E

Use 1 complete prairie point flower block; cut background pieces from assorted light blue fabrics. Join pieces in numerical order to complete the section.

ASSEMBLE QUILT FRONT

Join section B to section C; join section D to section E. Join section A to the B-C unit. Join the A-B-C unit to the D-E unit.

APPLIQUÉ

From dark green fabric cut ¾-inch bias strips to make flower stems. Using the photo of the wall hanging as a guide, appliqué curving ¼-inch stems from the flowerpot to each prairie point flower block.

Using patterns provided, add seam allowances, and cut leaves from assorted green fabrics. Using photo as a guide, appliqué leaves along the stems.

COMPLETE QUILT

Layer backing, batting, and pieced top. Baste or pin together. Machine-quilt using straight stitching on flowerpot. Stitch a vein in the center of each appliquéd leaf.

Machine-stipple-quilt the background.

For the binding, from assorted light blue and dark fabric cut enough 2½-inch-wide binding strips to equal 160 inches when joined in a continuous length. Fold strip in half lengthwise matching long raw edges; press. Align raw edges; sew binding to the quilt top, matching the dark fabric to the lower border.

Trim the backing and batting even with the quilt top. Turn binding to back and hand-stitch in place.

Sew buttons to the center of each prairie point flower.

continued on page 16

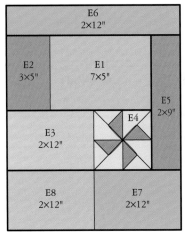

Section E

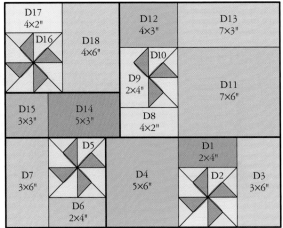

Section D

Full-Size
Patterns

3 LEAF PATTERNS

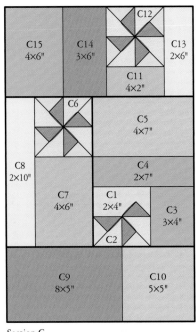

Section C

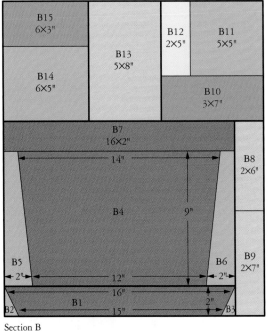

Section B

PRAIRIE POINT HALF-BLOCK

PRAIRIE POINT PARTIAL BLOCK

Section A

WALL HANGING SCHEMATIC

Fabrics that resemble the vintage fabrics of yesterday make this tiny quilt seem lovingly used. The method used for this quilt can also be applied to place mats and other decorative home accents.

DOLLY'S QUILT

MATERIALS

½ yard fabric for backing
12×16-inch piece of batting; floss to tie

Finished size:
12×16 inches

Block patterns:
6 Two Squares blocks N41, page 288
6 Four Triangles blocks N46, page 290

CONSTRUCTION

1 Alternating block patterns, stitch 4 pieced blocks in a row. Make 3 rows. Sew rows together in checkerboard pattern.
2 Layer the backing and top with right sides together. Layer batting on top. Stitch layers together around edge, leaving an opening for turning. Turn to right side and hand-stitch the opening closed.
3 Tie with floss at the center of each pieced block and at the block intersections.

NOSTALGIA TODAY

*A little mirror and a fancy pincushion, crazy quilted in satin
and embellished with embroidery stitches, make a lovely gift. Make this
nostalgic pair using two of the 4-inch quilt block patterns.*

MATERIALS

Mirror made for 3½-inch needlework insert

Strawberry emery from purchased pincushion

4½-inch square of satin for back of pincushion

Small pieces of satin to cover strawberry emery and button

Small piece of suede or felt to cover top of strawberry emery

1⅛-inch covered button form

Small flat button

⅓ yard twisted cord

1 yard ⅝-inch satin ribbon

Pearl cotton

Polyester fiberfill and polypellets

4-inch square of batting

Finished sizes:

Mirror: 4×8 inches

Pincushion: 5 inches square

Block patterns:

1 Crazy Patch block N13, page 274

1 Victorian Heart block H44, page 184

CONSTRUCTION

Pincushion:

1 From satin, cut a 4½-inch square for backing.

2 Gather 1 yard of ribbon to fit edge of crazy-quilt block; stitch in place. Right sides together and ribbon ruffle toward center, join backing and pieced block leaving an opening to turn and stuff. Fill cushion with a combination of fiberfill and pellets. Hand-stitch the opening closed.

3 Using a strawberry emery from a purchased pincushion, cut a cone-shape piece of satin to cover the emery. Stitch in place. From suede or felt, cut a top for the emery and tack in place. Attach a pearl cotton cord to emery and to center of cushion.

4 Make embroidery stitches on a circle of satin and use it to cover a button following directions with the button form. Sew button to the top center of the cushion, pulling thread to back side and securing with a small flat button.

Mirror:

1 Piece a crazy-quilt heart block as desired to fit mirror insert; trim edges to fit. Back with batting.

2 Follow manufacturer's directions to mount insert in mirror. Glue cording around edge.

PICTURE THIS

Very special handiwork deserves to be framed. Display these delicate quilt blocks with fabric mats, buttons, and a golden frame.

MATERIALS

6×8-inch single or double frames
¼ yard fabric for covering mats
Fabric to back blocks
Eight ⅝-inch buttons
Sixteen ⅜-inch buttons
2 pieces cardboard, each 6×8 inches
Fabric glue; small pieces of batting

Finished size:
6×8-inch frame

Block patterns:
2 sunbonnet blocks N61 and N62, page 298

CONSTRUCTION

1 Cut backing pieces for each block. Place backing and block wrong sides together. Stitch an outline around each figure on each block. Cut slits in the backing pieces to stuff small pieces of batting between the layers, giving dimension to the sunbonnet figures. Hand-stitch openings closed.

2 Make a 4-inch square template with curved corners. Use the template to cut openings in 6×8-inch cardboard. Fit the cardboard into the frame and mark the edges of the frame.

3 Cut fabric 7×9 inches for each picture mat. Using cardboard for a guide and ½-inch allowance to be turned to the back, mark corner button placement. Sew 3 buttons in each of the four corners. Cut a 3-inch square opening in center of each fabric piece.

4 Cover cardboard with fabric, turning ½ inch to the back of the board. Trim corners, clip curved edges, and secure with fabric glue.

5 Place padded block behind opening in picture mat and mount in frame.

State flowers for all 50 states make a
bloomin' pretty quilt. Here is a lovely way
to salute our country in the soft colors of
nature's blossoms.

STATELY BLOOMS

MATERIALS

4½ *yards print fabric for outer border, binding,*
  and backing

¾ *yard lavender fabric for sashing strips*

1 *yard rose fabric for sashing strips*

½ *yard soft green print fabric for squares*

¼ *yard gold print fabric for inner border*

⅛ *yard soft blue print fabric for 4 corner*
  blocks

52×70-*inch batting*

Finished quilt:
47½×65½ *inches*

Block patterns:
50 *state flower blocks F33–F82,*
pages 128–152

CONSTRUCTION

1 For sashing, cut 1½-inch strips from
   lavender print and 1-inch strips from
   rose print. Stitch rose strips to each
   side of the lavender strips. (See
   illustration, *page 22.*) Cut pieced
   sashing strips into 4½-inch lengths.
   You will use 123 sashing strips.

2 From soft green print fabric, cut
   70–2½-inch corner post squares.

3 Using pattern, *page 22*, make
   4 corner blocks from soft green
   and soft blue prints.

4 Assemble blocks as desired or
   alphabetically by state (see page
   22) and sashing in rows 6 blocks wide and
   9 blocks long.

5 Join squares and sashing strips for first row. Join sashing
   strips and blocks for second row. Repeat to assemble all
   rows. Join the rows.

6 Cut 1¼-inch strips from gold print for inner border. Piece
   strips for a total of 200 inches. Stitch strips to sides of quilt
   and then to top and bottom. Trim even.

7 Cut 4½-inch strips for outer border. Stitch to top, bottom,
   and sides of quilt top, mitering corners.

8 Cut and piece backing.
   Layer backing, batting, and quilt top. Baste or pin.
   Machine-quilt in-the-ditch as desired around blocks.

9 For binding, cut and join 2¾-inch strips to equal 240
   inches. Fold strip in half; press. Raw edges together, sew
   binding to the quilt top, mitering corners. Turn binding
   to the back and hand-stitch in place.

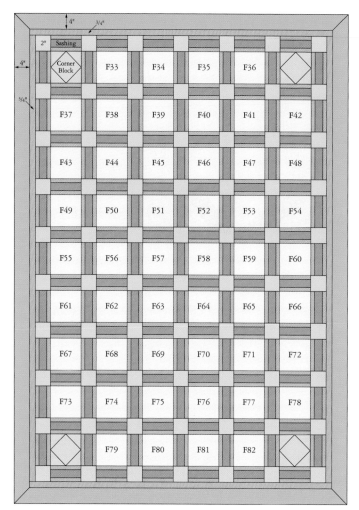

4"
3/4"
2" Sashing
4"
3/4"

Corner Block

F33	F34	F35	F36	
F37	F38	F39	F40	F41	F42
F43	F44	F45	F46	F47	F48
F49	F50	F51	F52	F53	F54
F55	F56	F57	F58	F59	F60
F61	F62	F63	F64	F65	F66
F67	F68	F69	F70	F71	F72
F73	F74	F75	F76	F77	F78
	F79	F80	F81	F82	

ALPHABETICAL
(BY STATE)
ASSEMBLY
DIAGRAM

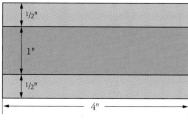

1/2"
1"
1/2"
4"

SASHING STRIP

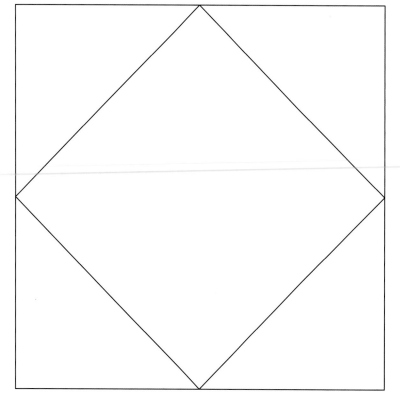

FULL-SIZE
CORNER
BLOCK
PATTERN

Show off your masterpiece blocks. Make a small wall hanging or keep stitching until you have a king-size quilt! Choose fabric for sashing and corner posts to frame your handiwork as a piece of art.

FRAMED COLLECTION

MATERIALS

¼ yard fabric for corner posts

¼ yard fabric for sashing

1½ yards fabric for backing and binding

23×28-inch piece of batting; baby rickrack

Finished size:
21×26 inches or size desired

Block patterns:
20 blocks of your choice (or number desired)

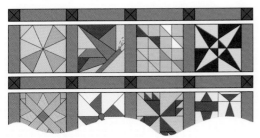

ASSEMBLY
DIAGRAM

CONSTRUCTION

1 For sashing, cut strips 1½×4½ inches; cut corner posts 1½ inches square.

2 Assemble pieced blocks in rows of 4 blocks each by stitching a sashing strip between each block and at each end of the row. Make 5 rows.

3 Assemble a sashing and corner post row by joining sashing strips with 1½-inch squares. Join rows of blocks with sashing units.

4 Layer backing, batting, and quilt top. Baste or pin. Machine-quilt in-the-ditch around each 4-inch pieced block. Stitch a X in each corner post.

5 Cut 2¾-inch binding strips, fold strips in half, wrong sides together, and press. Baste rickrack in place around quilt edges, ¼ inch in from raw edge. Stitch raw edge of binding to front, mitering corners. Trim backing and batting even with quilt top. Turn binding to back and hand-stitch in place.

BUTTERCUP CHECKERBOARD

MATERIALS

½ yard light color fabric (white)

1 fat quarter contrasting fabric (yellow)

Finished size:

11 inches square

Block pattern: 4 Pretty Reverse Flowers blocks, F26, page 124, in two colors (reversing colors)

CONSTRUCTION

1 Cut:

    4—⅞×12-inch light color strips

    4—1⅜×12-inch dark color strips

    2¼×45-inch light color strips for binding

2 Join the four blocks as shown and press seams open.

3 For the border, sew together a ⅞-inch-wide strip and a 1⅜-inch strip; press seam toward dark color. Make 4 strip sets, mark center of each and mark every 4 inches on each side of center on light edge. Sew one border to each side of the pieced quilt. Miter each corner, check for accuracy and trim seam allowance. Press seam to side.

4 Layer backing, batting, and quilt top; quilt as desired.

5 To quilt the leaf design in the dark border, make a scallop guide and mark one edge, then reverse guide and mark again.

Appliqué bold floral designs in two tones for a sunshine-fresh table mat. Here, yellow and white are used, but you can choose any two colors you like to bring cheer to the table.

These kitchen towels, great for giftgiving, showcase delicious fruit blocks. Selecting the towels, ribbon, and trims to complement the blocks is half the fun!

FRUIT OF THE KITCHEN

MATERIALS

1 finished kitchen towel for each block
²⁄₃ yard of ³⁄₈-inch-wide grosgrain ribbon for each towel
Rickrack or other trim to fit each towel width

Finished size:
Kitchen towel 16×26 inches or larger.

Block patterns:
1 Cherries block G3, page 154; 1 Lemon block G5, page 155
1 Orange Slice block G6, page 155; 1 Strawberry block G10, page 157

CONSTRUCTION

1 Center block on front of selected towel. Baste grosgrain ribbon over raw edges of block, mitering corners. Topstitch ribbon along inner and outer edges.

2 Topstitch rickrack or other trim along towel hem.

An appliquéd animal block is the center of attention on each soft baby building block. Stack up your quilting talents for a delightful baby shower gift.

BABY'S BLOCKS

MATERIALS

4-inch foam cube for each block
Cotton batting to wrap each cube
Pearl cotton to tie sides

Finished size:
4-inch cube

Block patterns:
1 baby animal appliqué block for each block: A21–A26, pages 62–64
5 Square-in-a-Square blocks for each block: N43, page 289

CONSTRUCTION

1 Stitch 3 pieced Square-in-a-Square blocks and 1 animal appliqué block into a row. Stitch the row into a loop.

2 Stitch a pieced square-in-a-square block to the loop on each side to form the top of the block, starting and stopping ¼ inch from each corner.

3 Pin remaining pieced block to the bottom and stitch two adjacent sides.

4 Wrap foam cube with a layer of batting and insert into the cube of blocks. Hand-stitch the two open sides closed.

5 With pearl cotton, tie a knot at the midpoint of each side of the cube. (For a baby or toddler, you may wish to omit the ties.)

Celebrate the tradition of saving bits and pieces of fabric and memories. This slip-on album cover is an honor to your family.

PATCHWORK SCRAPBOOK

MATERIALS

Album with 12½-inch cover
½ yard fabric for backing and lining
2½ yards covered cording
13×28-inch piece of batting

Finished size:13×14-inch album

Block patterns:
6 pieced 9-patch blocks: variation of N11, page 273
1 "A" block I1; 1 "B" block I2; 1 "C" block I3, pages 194–195

CONSTRUCTION

Note: The size of the cover can be adjusted to fit a different size album by adjusting the size of the back of the cover and borders on pieced blocks. Cut lining and pockets to fit the front cover.

1 Assemble pieced blocks in
   3 rows of 3 blocks each as follows:
   Row 1: "A" block, red patchwork block, yellow
      patchwork block
   Row 2: Red patchwork block, "B" block, red
      patchwork block
   Row 3: Yellow patchwork block, red patchwork block,
      "C" block.

2 Join the 3 rows to make album cover front.

3 From red fabric, cut 2—1×12½-in strip and 1—1×14-inch strip. Stitch to top, bottom, and right side of the album cover front.

4 Cut a 13½×15½-inch piece of fabric for album back cover; stitch to the left side of the album front cover.

5 Cut 2 pockets, 6×13½ inches. Cut lining 13½×26 inches.

6 Stitch a ½-inch hem along one 13½-inch side of each pocket.

7 Assemble album cover by placing a piece of batting on the back of the cover. Right sides together, place a pocket on each end. Pin or baste in place. Right sides together, place lining piece over the cover and pockets. **Note:** The lining piece is shorter than the cover and will not be stitched at either end.

8 Stitch the lining, pockets, and cover together with cording inserted into the seam. Turn to right side through the open ends of the lining. Place the cover on the album, using the pockets to hold it in place.

ALPHABET COLLECTION

Add cheer to a little one's room with bright curtains showing off an alphabet border. To personalize the effect, use the quilt blocks to spell the name of the child.

WINDOW TREAT

MATERIALS

Desired length of fabric for each panel
Lining fabric equal to panel length plus 4 inches
1¼ yard covered cording for each panel

Finished curtain panel:
41-inch panels made to desired length

Block patterns:
24 alphabet blocks I1–I26, pages 194–206

CONSTRUCTION

1 Cut 1½-inch sashing strips. Join alphabet blocks in a row of 8 with sashing strips between each block and at ends.
2 Cut a 3-inch strip of fabric and stitch to the bottom of the row of blocks.
3 Stitch panel of fabric to desired length (plus amount for rod pocket and heading) to top of blocks.
4 Cut lining piece to fit. Right sides together and stitching cording into bottom seam, join the lining to curtain front along bottom and sides. Turn to right side.

5 For heading, turn 4 inches to the back. Stitch a heading and rod pocket across the top.

desired length

1"

1/2"

ASSEMBLY DIAGRAM

This cover-up is designed to keep youngsters clean as a whistle.
Alphabet block pockets provide useful fun as well as artful design.

APRON ART

MATERIALS

¾ yard fabric for apron
½ yard fabric for bias binding
¼ yard fabric for sashing strips; two ⅝-inch buttons

Finished size:
Child's size 8–10

Block patterns:
3 alphabet blocks 124–126, pages 205–206

CONSTRUCTION

1 Join 3 alphabet blocks in a row by sewing 1¼-inch sashing strips to block sides. Sew a 1-inch strip to the bottom of the block row.

2 Cut a 2½-inch strip to bind the top of the row with a 1-inch binding. With right sides together, stitch 2½-inch strip to top of blocks, turn to back and press with ¼ inch pressed under at back bottom edge. Topstitch in place.

3 Using measurements from diagram provided, make a pattern and cut 1 front piece, 2 back pieces, and 2 side plackets.

4 Cut and join 1-inch bias binding strips to total approximately 4½ yards.

5 Bind the top of two placket pieces; topstitch binding on the front of each placket.

6 Turn under 1 inch and stitch a ¾-inch hem along each center back.

7 Place quilt block pocket along bottom front; pin or baste in place. Topstitch through the center of the sashing strips to make 3 pockets.

8 Join plackets to each side of front piece, seams wrong sides together. Join back pieces to side plackets in the same manner. (Binding will cover these seams.) Join shoulder seams right sides together.

9 Bind sides, neck, and bottom of the apron; topstitch binding strips. Sew 2 buttonholes and buttons to back opening.

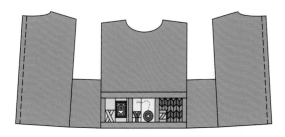

APRON ASSEMBLY DIAGRAM

APRON POCKET SCHEMATIC

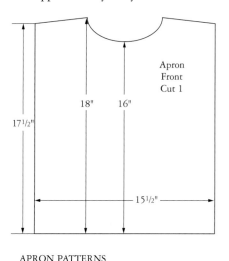
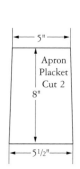
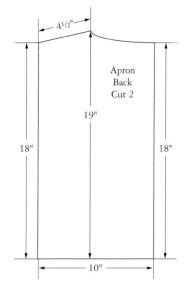

APRON PATTERNS

MATERIALS

½ yard fabric for backing
1 yard fabric for sashing strips and binding
⅛ yard fabric for corner posts blocks
19×25-inch piece of batting

Finished quilt:
17×22¼ inches

Block patterns:
12 retro blocks from K1–K12, pages 241–246

CONSTRUCTION

1   From sashing fabric, cut 1¾-inch strips. You will need 31 strips 1¾×4½ inches. From contrasting fabric cut 20—1¾×1¾-inch squares for corner posts.
2   Follow the assembly diagram to assemble sashing strips and retro blocks in rows. Join the rows.
3   Cut fabric for backing to fit. Layer backing, batting, and quilt top. Machine-quilt in-the-ditch along each sashing strip and corner post. Quilt an X in each sashing strip.
4   Cut 2¾-inch binding strips, piecing as necessary to make an 84-inch length. Fold strip in half wrong sides together. Stitch binding to the front of the quilt, mitering corners. Turn binding to the back and hand-stitch in place.

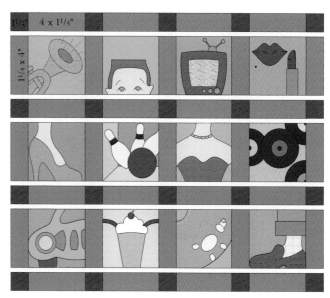

ASSEMBLY DIAGRAM

Celebrate the '50s when records were 78s and flat tops, poodle skirts, and hot cars were in. This nostalgic collection will bring smiles wherever it hangs out.

CHANGE OF SEASONS

Celebrate the seasons by sharing your quilting talents! Bind 4 finished blocks to attach them to this "Welcome" greeting. Switch from February hearts to March kites to April showers.

MATERIALS

¾ yard fabric for backing and hanging pocket

½ yard dark fabric for wall hanging front

¼ yard light fabric for "welcome" background

⅛ yard fabric for "welcome" letters

Small pieces of 20 or more colorful fabrics for piecing

¼ yard lightweight fusible webbing

20×29-inch batting

12×18-inch cardboard or foamcore board

Small hook-and-loop tape, such as Velcro

Plastic rings for hanging

Finished quilt:
18×27 inches

Block patterns:
4 heart blocks H41–H44, pages 183–184 (or other favorites)

CONSTRUCTION

1 From dark fabric, cut a 12½-inch square. From assorted bright fabrics cut 52—1½-inch squares.

2 Make 2—14-square strips and 2—12-square strips. Stitch 12-square strips to each side of center piece; stitch 14-square strips to the top and bottom.

3 From dark fabric, cut 4 strips 2½×14½ inches; from selected color, cut 4—2½–inch squares. Join 1 strip to each side of the center section. Join square to each end of remaining 4½-inch strips; join border to top and bottom.

4 Using pattern, *opposite,* and adding seam allowances, cut and piece the 10-piece multiwedge section using 10 assorted bright fabrics.

5 Make a pattern for the "welcome" background piece by drawing a 3¼-inch-radius half-circle and a 7¼-inch-radius half-circle. The outer border for the top section is made by drawing a 6¾-inch-radius half-circle and a 9¼-inch-radius half-circle. Join these 2 arcs to the multiwedge section.

6 Trace patterns for "welcome" letters onto fusible webbing (reversing images). Fuse to selected fabric and cut out letters. Arrange letters on background piece and fuse in place. Machine satin-stitch over raw edges of the letters.

7 Join top section of the wall hanging to the lower section. Cut backing piece to fit the joined sections. Cut a separate backing piece the same size as the top section; set aside.

8 Layer backing, batting, and pieced top. Machine-quilt, outlining borders, wedge section, and letters. Stipple-quilt the rest of the piece.

9 For the hanging pocket, baste the top section backing to the back of the quilted piece.

ASSEMBLY DIAGRAM

10 Piece a multicolor 2¾-inch binding strip. Fold in half, wrong sides together. Stitch raw edges to front of wall hanging. Turn binding to the back; hand-stitch in place.

11 Cut a piece of cardboard or foamcore board to fit the back pocket; insert in the pocket. Tack the lower edge of pocket to hold cardboard in place. For hanging, sew 2 small plastic rings at an equal distance from bottom edge to the pocket near the top curve.

12 Back and bind 4 blocks for display. Arrange blocks on center square. Attach hook-and-loop tape to the back of each block and at a matching point on the wall hanging.

LETTER PATTERNS

1 SQUARE = 1 INCH
(ENLARGE AT 400%)

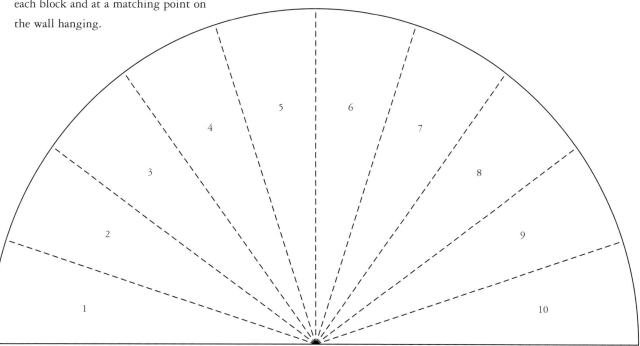

FOUNDATION PIECING DIAGRAM

35

WATCHED POTS

Boiling pots do not burn when handsome hot pads are handy.
This set of 3 is bound to inspire more for great kitchen gifts.

MATERIALS

¼ yard each of fabrics for backing and binding
⅛ yard each of fabrics for piecing fronts
3 pieces of cotton batting, each 7 inches square
1 yard loop trim
Three ½-inch diameter plastic rings
Pearl cotton

Finished hot pads:

7 inches square

Block patterns:

1 Teakettle block E1, page 107
1 Pot block E2, page 107
1 Cookie Jar block E3, page 108

CONSTRUCTION

1 For the square-in-a-square cookie jar hot pad, cut
 4 triangles, *below,* and join triangles to the 4 sides of the
 appliquéd block (see Diagram 1, *right*).

2 Cut 1-inch sashing strips and sew to sides, top, and bottom
 of the block, making a ½-inch finished border.

3 Stitch loop trim to front of block. Place batting behind
 block and backing on top of the block (right sides
 together). Stitch around block, leaving an opening for
 turning. Turn; hand-stitch opening closed. Machine-quilt
 in-the-ditch around borders and designs.

4 For boiling pot and teapot hot pads, cut 4—2×4½-inch
 sashing strips, one for each side of the center block (see
 Diagram 2). Cut 4—2-inch corner post squares. Stitch a
 sashing strip to two sides of the center block. Make 2 units
 by joining a corner post to each end of a sashing strip. Sew
 a unit to the top and bottom of the block.

5 Layer backing, batting, and pieced top. Machine-quilt
 in-the-ditch. Cut 2¾-inch binding strips. Fold strip in half
 lengthwise and stitch raw edges to front of hot pad, mitering
 corners. Turn binding to back and hand-stitch in place.

6 Using pearl cotton, single crochet to cover hanging ring.
 Sew ring to top corner of hot pad.

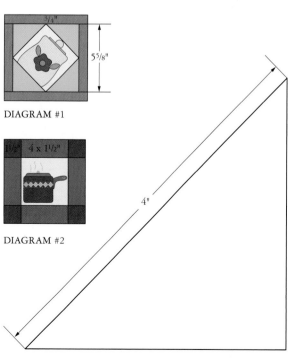

5/4"

5⅝"

DIAGRAM #1

1½"   4 x 1½"

DIAGRAM #2

4"

FULL-SIZE PATTERN (ADD ¼ INCH SEAM ALLOWANCE)

TREE TRIO

This pine tree accent pillow can be dressed for the holidays or made to complement your decor for year-round enjoyment.

MATERIALS

½ yard red fabric for backing and outer border
⅓ yard fabric for backing pillow front
⅛ yard green fabric for sashing
⅛ yard gold fabric for inner border
12×23-inch piece of batting
Fabric and polyester fiberfill to make pillow form
Pearl cotton; 3 buttons

Finished size:
11½×22½ inches

Block patterns:
3 tree blocks 03–04, page 301; and H18, page 171

CONSTRUCTION

1 Using pattern *right,* cut four triangles. Set the center tree block as a square-in-a-square by joining a triangle to each side of the pieced block.

2 Cut 4 green sashing strips 1¼×4½ inches. Join these strips to the top and bottom of the other two tree blocks.

3 Cut 4 green strips 1¼×6 inches. Join the tree blocks using these strips; then add one strip to each end.

4 Cut 2 gold strips 1×17 inches. Join to top and bottom of the tree block row. Cut 2 gold strips 1×7 inches; join to each end of the tree block row.

5 For outer border, cut 2 strips 3×18 inches; join to top and bottom of panel. Cut 2 strips 3×12 inches; join to each end of the panel.

6 Cut a 12×23-inch piece of backing fabric for pillow front. Place batting between front and back. Machine-quilt in-the-ditch around each tree block and along gold and red borders.

7 Make button-on pillow back by cutting 2 pieces 12×13½ inches. Make a 1½-inch hem along one 12-inch side of each piece. Make 3 buttonholes in one hem. Overlap the 2 pieces with buttonholes on top to make back measure 23 inches.

8 Right sides together, stitch pillow front to pillow back. Turn to right side.

9 Topstitch around pillow cover ½ inch from the outside edge. Using pearl cotton add blanket stitch trim to this outside edge. Sew on 3 buttons to match buttonholes. Insert pillow form.

4"

FULL-SIZE PATTERN (ADD ¼ INCH SEAM ALLOWANCE)

ASSEMBLY DIAGRAM

Santa will love to
fill this stocking on
Christmas Eve.
Stitch it in no time
using motifs from
his wardrobe.

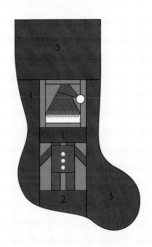

PIECING DIAGRAM

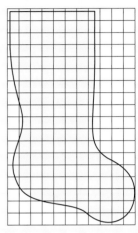

PATTERN   1 SQUARE =
1 INCH
(ENLARGE AT 800%)

ST. NICK SOCK

MATERIALS

½ yard fabric for stocking back and trim

¼ yard fabric for piecing stocking front

¼ yard fabric for cuff; ½ yard fabric for lining

1½ yards covered cording; 10×18-inch piece of batting

10×18-inch piece of muslin; 6 buttons (⅝-inch or size desired)

Finished size:
10×18 inches

Block patterns:
1 Santa's hat block H15 and 1 Red Long Johns block H16, page 170

CONSTRUCTION

1 Using stocking diagram, *above right,* make a paper pattern.
Cut stocking back; cut front and back linings.

2 Follow illustration, and using paper pattern for shape, cut
piecing strips to make stocking front. Add ¼-inch seam
allowances to each piece.

3 Join Santa blocks with a 1¼×4-inch sashing strip. Join
shaped strip to the bottom of the block unit. Join toe and
heel pieces to each side of the block unit. Join unit to top.

4 Cut muslin to fit stocking front. Place batting between
stocking front and muslin. Machine-quilt in-the-ditch
around the blocks.

5 Make bias cording to match stocking back (or use purchased
cording); stitch to sides and bottom of stocking front. Right
sides together, join stocking back to front, leaving top open.

6 Join lining front and back, turn; slip inside stocking.

7 Cut a 9½×16½-inch strip for stocking cuff. Stitch 9½-inch
ends to make a loop. Fold cuff in half and press.

8 Make a band for the cuff by cutting a 2½×16½-inch bias
strip of fabric. Join short ends to make a loop. Fold in half,
lengthwise, wrong sides together; press. Stitch raw edges to
stocking band 1½ inches above lower edge of cuff. Turn band
over seam; topstitch. Sew buttons evenly spaced on band.

9 Make a ½×4-inch hanging loop. Join hanging loop as you
join cuff to stocking and lining.

39

PAIR OF PILLOWS

These bright-as-a-summer-day pillows cheer any corner of your home.
While the pillows are made similarly, note the difference created by
wider sashing strips on the flower pillow.

MATERIALS

Butterfly pillow:

⅔ yard fabric for backing and ruffle

⅛ yard each of 2 fabrics for piecing pillow front

1½ yards covered cording; 3 buttons; pillow form

Flower pillow:

¾ yard fabric for backing, ruffle and sashing strips

⅛ yard each of 3 fabrics for piecing pillow front

1⅔ yards covered cording; 3 buttons; pillow form

Finished size:

Butterfly pillow: 12½ inches square

Flower pillow: 14 inches square

Block patterns:

4 butterfly blocks A5–A7,

pages 54–55; A9, page 56

4 flower blocks F6, page 114;

F14, page 118; F15, page 119;

F28, page 125

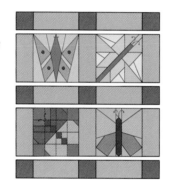

ASSEMBLY DIAGRAM

CONSTRUCTION

Butterfly pillow:

1 Cut 12—2×4½-inch sashing strips. Cut 9—2-inch squares. Join each pair of pieced butterfly blocks with a sashing strip; join a sashing strip to each end. Make 3 strips by joining squares and sashing strips as shown. Join strip and block rows as shown to complete pillow front panel.

2 For button-on pillow back, cut 1—13×11-inch piece and 1—13×5-inch piece. Hem a 13-inch side of the larger piece by folding back 1 inch; make 3 buttonholes along this edge. Hem one 13-inch side of the smaller piece by folding back 1 inch. Overlap pieces to make a 13-inch square; sew on buttons to match buttonholes.

3 For the ruffle, cut 4-inch strips, piecing to equal 100 inches. Fold strips in half, wrong sides together, and press. Gather strip to fit pillow front, placing cording between the front and the ruffle. Stitch to pillow front.

4 Right sides together, stitch pillow front to pillow back. Turn to right side through button opening.

Flower pillow:

1 Cut 12—2½×4½-inch sashing strips. Cut 9—2½-inch squares. Join each pair of pieced flower blocks with a sashing strip; join a sashing strip to each end. Make 3 strips by joining squares and sashing strips as shown. Join strip and block rows to complete pillow front.

2 For pillow back, cut 1—14½×13-inch piece and 1—14½×5-inch piece. Hem a 14½-inch side of the larger piece by folding back 1 inch and make 3 buttonholes along this edge. Hem one 14½-inch side of the smaller piece by folding back 1 inch. Overlap pieces to make a 14½-inch square, and sew buttons on shorter piece to match buttonholes.

3 For ruffle, cut 4½-inch strips, pieced to equal 112 inches. Fold strips in half, wrong sides together, and press. Gather strip to fit pillow front, placing cording between the front and the ruffle. Stitch to pillow front.

4 Right sides together, stitch pillow front to pillow back. Turn to right side through button opening.

NAME FAME

MATERIALS

⅛ yard fabric for border strips (same fabric as background for blocks)

½ yard fabric for backing

⅛ yard fabric for binding

16×28-inch piece of batting

Finished size:
16×28 inches

Block patterns:
12 Pennant blocks L3, page 254
6 alphabet blocks from 127–152, pages 207–219

CONSTRUCTION

1 Join alphabet blocks in a row. Join 2 rows of multicolor pennant blocks. Join these rows to the alphabet blocks.

2 Cut 2—2½×12½-inch border strips and stitch to each end of the assembled unit. Cut 2—2½×28½-inch border strips; join to top and bottom of the unit.

3 Layer backing, batting, and pieced top. Pin or baste. Machine-quilt in-the-ditch around each block.

4 Cut 2½-inch binding strips, piecing as necessary to equal 94 inches. Fold strip in half, wrong sides together. Stitch binding to the front of the quilt, mitering corners. Trim backing and batting. Turn binding to the back and hand-stitch in place.

Pennants proclaim this is a name to know. This wall hanging size easily adjusts to any name length.

Hat and handbag blocks decorate a frilly drawstring bag that could serve as a purse or a place to stash "girl stuff." Border print fabric simplifies construction while spotlighting the appliqué blocks on the bag.

GIRL STUFF

MATERIALS

⅓ yard fabric for lining and ruffle; ¼ yard border fabric
⅛ yard fabric for sashing and bottom; 1 yard of ½-inch-wide satin ribbon; 2 beads; 4½-inch square of cardboard

Finished size:
9¾ high×4½ inches square

Block patterns:
2 handbag blocks K21–K22 and 2 hat blocks K23–K24, pages 251–252

CONSTRUCTION

1 Cut 4 sashing strips 1×4½ inches. Join the 4 blocks with these strips.

2 Cut a 2½×18½-inch strip of border fabric. Join strip to the bottom of the block unit.

3 Cut a 3½×18½-inch strip of border fabric. Join this strip to the top of block unit. Join side seams to make a loop.

4 Cut a 5-inch square for the purse bottom. Matching corners to centers of sashing strips, join the bottom of the bag to the bottom border.

5 Make a vertical ½-inch buttonhole at the center of each side of the top border of bag at the top-edge, seam allowance.

6 Cut a 2×37-inch strip of fabric for ruffle. Fold strip in half lengthwise, wrong sides together. Gather strip to fit and sew to the top of the bag.

7 Make lining for bag by cutting 1—9½×18½-inch rectangle. Join the short ends of this strip, leaving the center of the seam open for turning. Cut a 4½-inch square for the bottom of the bag and join to the bag lining.

8 Right sides together, join top of lining to top of bag (ruffle tucked inside). Turn to right side through the lining opening. Hand-stitch the opening closed.

9 Topstitch bag ½-inch below ruffle to make casing. Thread 18-inch lengths of ribbon through buttonholes across front and back. Ribbon ends together, thread a bead on each side; knot ends. Insert cardboard for stability.

Patriotism is a work of art in this wall hanging that is suited to a variety of styles.

MATERIALS
¾ *yard fabric for backing*
¼ *yard fabric for binding*
26×34-inch piece of batting

Finished size:
24×32 inches

Block patterns:
39 pieced Rocket blocks J19, page 239
9 star blocks J20, page 239

CONSTRUCTION
1 Assemble 3 rows of 3 star blocks; join the rows in a square.
2 Assemble 3 rows of 5 cream and red patchwork blocks. Join the rows. Join to the right side of the star blocks.
3 Assemble 3 rows of 8 cream and red patchwork blocks. Join the rows. Join to the lower edge of the banner.
4 Layer backing, batting, and pieced top. Pin or baste.
5 Using matching thread, machine-quilt a wavy pattern across each stripe.
6 Cut 2-inch binding strips. Piece to make a strip 120 inches long. Fold strip in half lengthwise, wrong sides together. Press. Stitch raw edges to front of banner, mitering corners. Trim backing and batting. Turn binding to the back and hand-stitch in place.

PARTIAL ASSEMBLY DIAGRAM

ALL-AMERICAN TABLE

Patchwork and patriotism are a natural combination. Piece red, white and blue blocks for summer table linens and make every day the 4th of July!

MATERIALS

½ yard blue print fabric ; ½ yard red print fabric
½ yard backing fabric; 16×22-inch piece of batting

Finished size:
Place mat: 15×21 inches; Napkin: 16-inch square

Block patterns:
7 red, white, and blue blocks J5, page 232; J14, page 236; M9, page 263; M17, page 267; N9, page 272; N37, page 286; N55, page 295

CONSTRUCTION

Place mat:

1 Join pieced blocks in 2 strips of 3 blocks each. Cut a 10½×12½-inch piece of blue fabric for place mat center. Sew a strip of 3 blocks to each end of center.

2 From red fabric cut 1-inch strips for inner borders. Join 1×18-inch strips to the top and bottom of the place mat. Join 1×13½-inch strips to each end.

3 From blue cut 1½-inch strips for outer borders. Join 1½×19½-inch strips to the top and bottom; join 1½×15½-inch strips to each end.

4 Layer and baste backing, batting, and pieced top. Machine-quilt 2-inch squares in the center of the place mat, quilt around each pieced block, and in-the-ditch along the borders.

5 Cut 2¾-inch strips of blue fabric for binding and join to equal 75 inches length. Fold strips in half, wrong sides together. Stitch raw edges of binding to front of place mat, mitering corners. Trim backing and batting. Turn binding to back; hand-stitch in place.

Napkin:

1 From blue print fabric, cut 2 A pieces and 1 B piece (short edges on straight grain of fabric), using the patterns, *right*. Join A pieces to each side of block J5. Join B piece to bottom of block.

2 From red print, cut a 16½-inch square. Cut a 16½-inch square of backing fabric.

3 Replace one corner of the red square by sewing on pieced block corner.

4 Layer backing square and napkin front. Cut 2¾-inch binding strips from blue fabric to equal 68 inches. Fold strips in half, wrong sides together. Stitch raw edges of the binding to front of napkin, mitering corners. Turn binding to the back and hand-stitch in place.

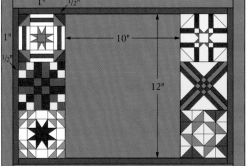

PLACE MAT (*ABOVE*) AND NAPKIN (*RIGHT*) DIAGRAMS

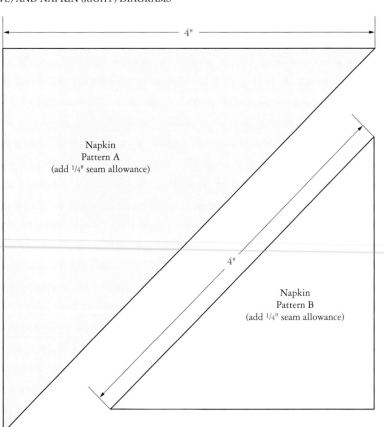

Napkin
Pattern A
(add ¼" seam allowance)

Napkin
Pattern B
(add ¼" seam allowance)

WELL-DRESSED CHAIR

Dress up the entire breakfast nook with your quilting or give a little bedroom chair a complete makeover. This soft touch enhances almost any style wood chair.

MATERIALS

2 yards fabric for each chair back and seat
3½ yards covered cording for each set
13×23-inch piece of batting
12×15-inch piece of foam for chair seat (or to fit chair seat)
Embroidery floss or pearl cotton to tie seat.

Finished size:
Chair back shown: 11×10½ inches;
Seat shown: 12×14 inches (without ruffle)

Block patterns for each chair back:
2 flower blocks from F21–F24, pages 122–123; 2 leaf and stem blocks from F29–F32, pages 126–127

CONSTRUCTION

Chair back:

1 For each back, join each flower block to a stem and leaf block. Cut 3 strips of fabric 1½×8½ inches. Join the 2 flower block units with one strip, then join a strip to each side. Cut 1 strip 1½×11½ inches; join strip to the bottom.

2 Cut a piece of fabric 11½×12 inches; join to top of block unit. Stitch cording around the outer edge. For ties cut 4 strips 1½×10 inches. Fold each strip in half lengthwise, wrong sides together; turn in raw edges and top-stitch. Stitch a tie to each corner of the chair back stitching over cording at corners.

3 Cut backing 13×24 inches. Layer backing and front, right sides together. Pin batting to wrong side of front. Stitch along the top, using cording stitching line as a guide. Leave an opening for turning. Trim backing and batting even with top. Turn to right side and hand-stitch opening closed. Machine-quilt in-the-ditch around the flower block units.

Chair cushion:

1 Make a paper pattern to fit chair seat. Use this pattern to cut foam and fabric for the top of the cushion. Cut pattern in half along the center and add seam allowances to the outer edge. Cut 2 pieces for the cushion backing.

2 For ruffle, cut a 5½-inch strip of fabric 2 times the length of the front and sides of the seat. Fold strip in half lengthwise, wrong sides together. Gather raw edges to fit the front and sides of the cushion.

3 Stitch cording around edge of cushion top. Stitch ruffle to sides and front edge.

4 Join 2 pieces for seat back, leaving center of the seam open. Right sides together with ruffle and cording tucked inside, stitch seat back to seat front. Turn through opening in seat back piece. Insert foam piece and hand-stitch the opening closed. Use floss or pearl cotton to tie seat through all layers.

5 Make 2 ties 1½×16 inches. Fold lengthwise, top-stitch, and sew center of each tie to seat back corners.

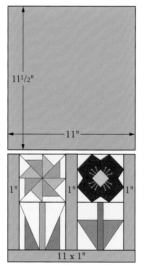

ASSEMBLY DIAGRAM

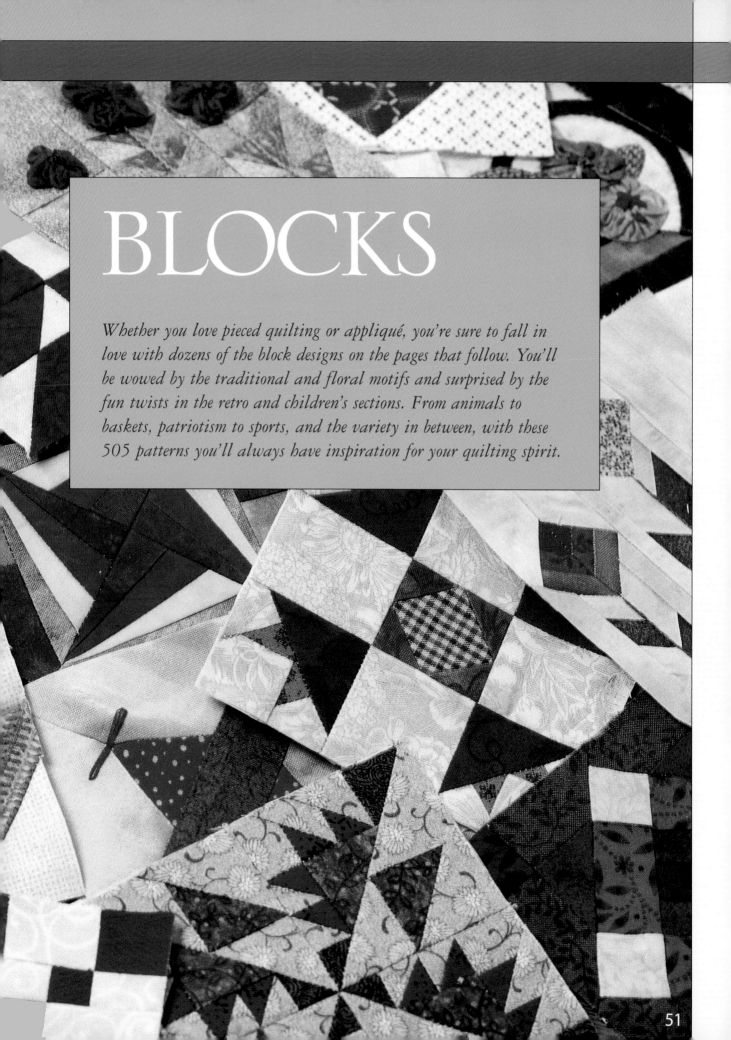

BLOCKS

Whether you love pieced quilting or appliqué, you're sure to fall in love with dozens of the block designs on the pages that follow. You'll be wowed by the traditional and floral motifs and surprised by the fun twists in the retro and children's sections. From animals to baskets, patriotism to sports, and the variety in between, with these 505 patterns you'll always have inspiration for your quilting spirit.

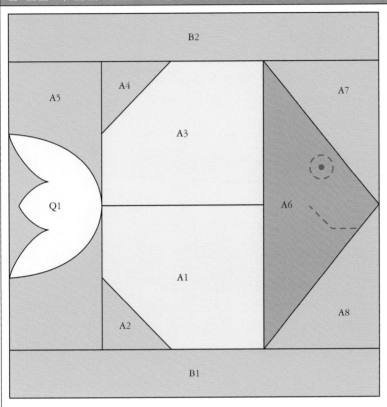

BRIGHT FISH

A1 Make A section by joining pieces in numerical order. Sew B1 and B2 pieces to the top and bottom of the A section. Appliqué Q1 to make fish tail. Embroider mouth and eye on fish using stem stitch and satin stitch.

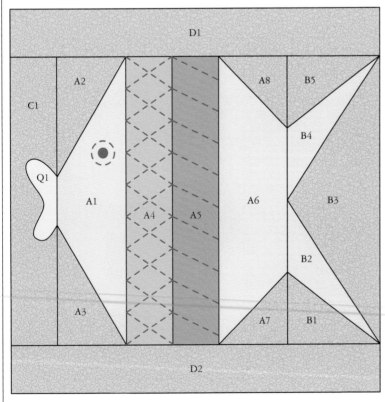

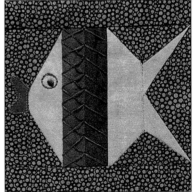

STRIPED FISH

A2 Make A section by joining pieces in numerical order. Piece B section and join to A section. Sew C1 to A-B unit. Sew D1 and D2 pieces to the top and bottom of the A-B-C unit. Appliqué Q1 to make fish lips. Embroider eye using stem stitch and satin stitch. Add straight stitches to fish body, making Xs if desired.

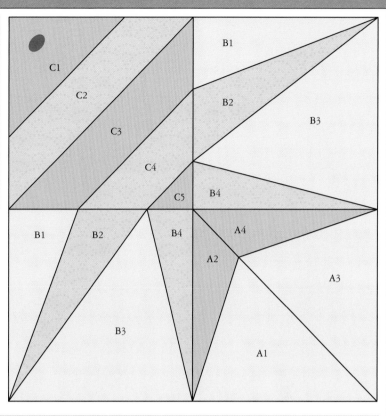

A3 Make A section by joining pieces in numerical order. Make 2 B sections, sew 1 B section to the A section. Make C section, sew to the remaining B section. Join the A-B and B-C units. Embroider eye on the fish using satin stitch.

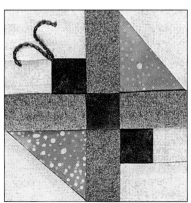

Look Again

(Below) Rotate and combine four Moth blocks to see a large grid pattern appear. With the antennae toward the center, the moths appear in a huddle. Omit the antennae for a graphic look.

MOTH

A4 Make A section by joining pieces in numerical order. Make B section and sew to A section. Make C section and sew to the A-B unit. Embroider antennae using stem stitch.

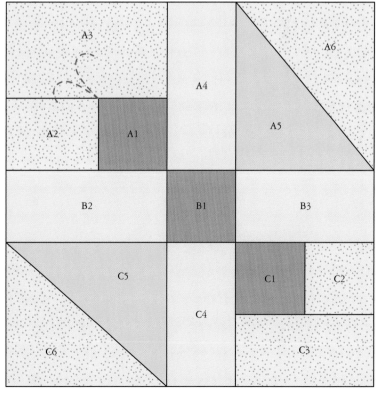

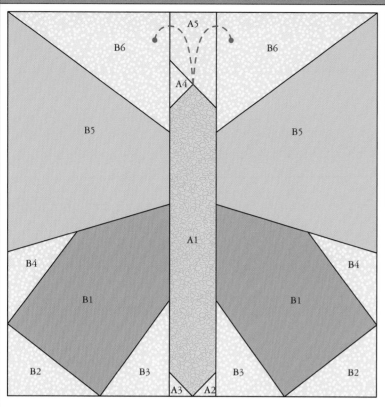

ORANGE BUTTERFLY

A5 Make A section by joining pieces in numerical order. Make 2 B sections and sew to each side of the A section. Embroider antennae using stem stitch with a French knot at each end.

Look Again

(Below) Geometric patterns take flight when Yellow Butterfly blocks are rotated facing outward. If desired, omit the antennae for a purely shape-oriented design.

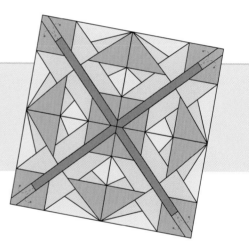

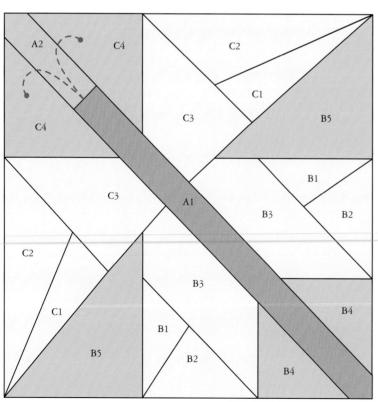

YELLOW BUTTERFLY

A6 Join 2 A pieces. Make 2 B sections by joining pieces in numerical order. Make 2 C sections and sew each to a B section. Join B-C units to opposite sides of the A section. Embroider antennae using stem stitch with a French knot at each end.

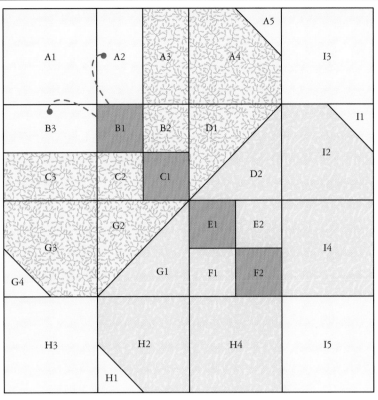

PIECED BUTTERFLY

A7 Make A section by joining pieces in numerical order. Make the B and C sections and join. Make the D section and join it to the B-C unit. Join the B-C-D unit to the A section. Make the E and F sections and join. Make the G section and join to the E-F unit. Join the E-F-G unit to the A-B-C-D unit. Make the H section and join to A-B-C-D-E-F-G. Make I section and join to complete the block. Embroider antennae using stem stitch with a French knot at each end.

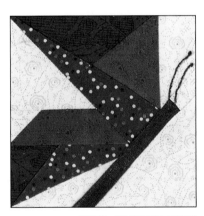

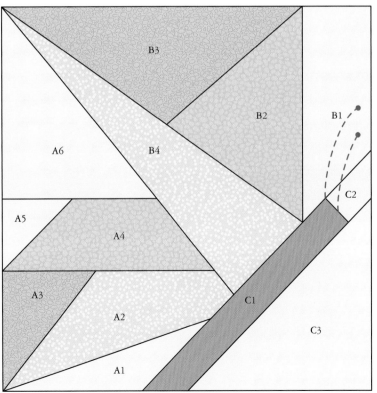

RED BUTTERFLY

A8 Make A section by joining pieces in numerical order. Make B section and sew to A section. Make C section and sew to A-B unit. Embroider antennae using stem stitch with a French knot at each end.

55

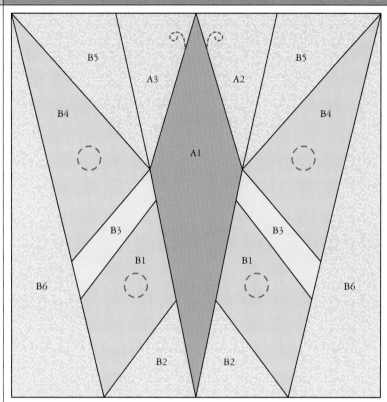

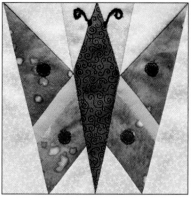

BRIGHT BUTTERFLY

A9 Make A section by joining pieces in numerical order. Make 2 B sections and sew to each side of the A section. Embroider circles on the wings using satin stitch outlined with stem stitch. Use stem stitch for antennae.

Look Again

(Above) Create a field of diamonds by combining pairs of Bright Butterfly blocks. Joining blocks mirror fashion often creates interesting repetitive shapes.

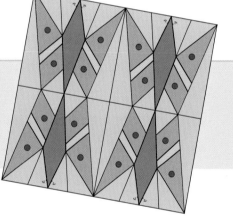

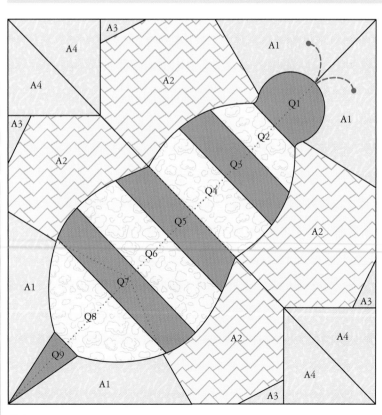

HONEYBEE

A10 Piece the bee body by joining the Q pieces. (The bee will be appliquéd.) Make 4 A sections by joining the A pieces in numerical order. Join the A sections into 2 A-A units. Join the 2 units. Appliqué the bee body to the pieced background. Use stem stitch to embroider the bee's antennae, using French knots at the ends.

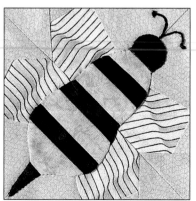

LADYBUG

A11 Make A section by joining pieces in numerical order. Join B1 and B2 pieces to each side of the A section. Join C1 and C2 pieces to sides of the A-B unit. Make D section and join to the A-B-C unit. Sew buttons on the ladybug wings. Use stem stitch to embroider legs.

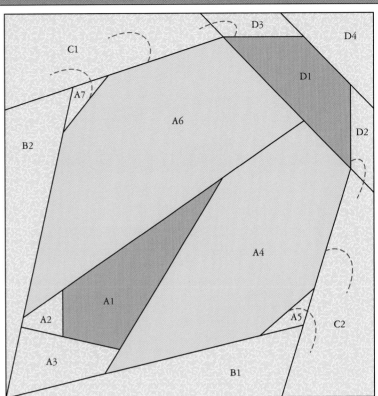

APPLIQUÉ LADYBUG

A12 Appliqué the Q pieces in numerical order to the background block.

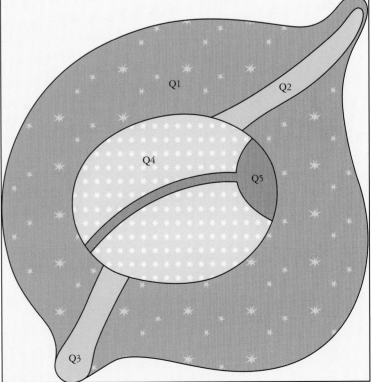

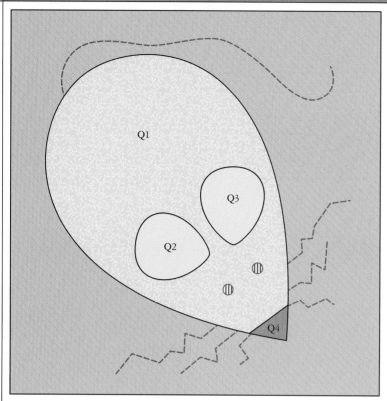

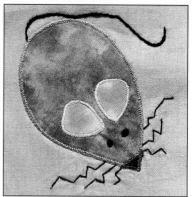

MOUSE

A13 Appliqué the Q1 piece to the background block. Appliqué Q2, Q3 and Q4 pieces in place. Use stem stitch to embroider the tail and whiskers on the mouse. Use satin stitch for the eyes.

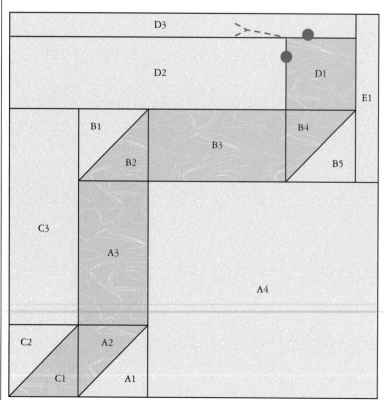

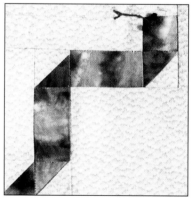

SNAKE

A14 Make A section by joining pieces in numerical order. Make B section and join to the A section. Make the C section and join to the A-B unit. Make the D section and join to the A-B-C unit. Inset the E1 piece. Embroider snake's tongue using stem stitch; use satin stitch to make the eyes.

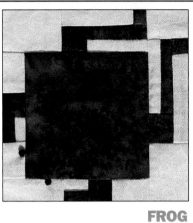

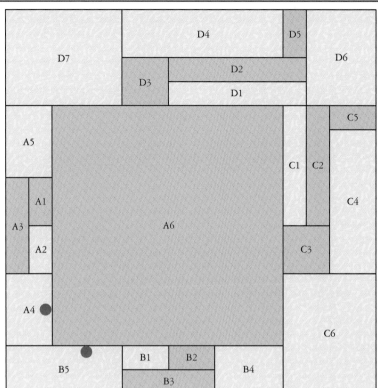

FROG

A15 Make A section by joining pieces in numerical order. Make B section and join to A section. Make C section and join to A-B unit. Made D section and join to A-B-C unit. Embroider eyes using satin stitch.

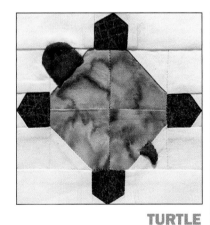

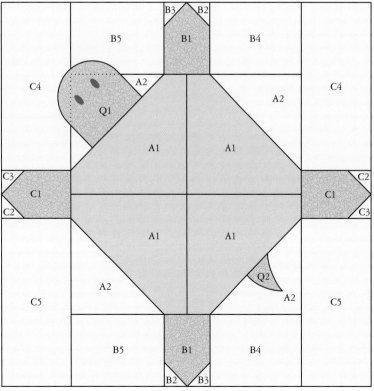

TURTLE

A16 Make 4 A sections by joining A1 and A2 pieces. Join the 4 sections. Make 2 B sections and sew to the top and bottom of the A section. Make 2 C sections and sew to the sides of the A-B unit. Appliqué Q1 and Q2 pieces. Embroider eyes using satin stitch.

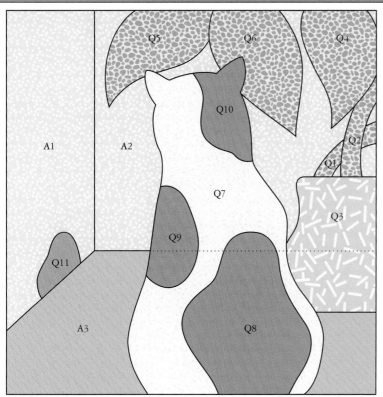

CAT AND MOUSE

A17 Make the background block by joining the A pieces. Appliqué the Q pieces in numerical order. Use stem stitch to embroider over the seam line between the A1 and A2 pieces.

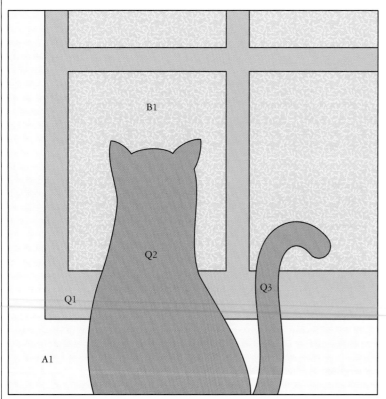

SNOWY DAY

A18 Cut a 4$^{1}/_{2}$" square for A1 piece. Fuse B1 piece for window background. Appliqué Q1 for window frame. Appliqué Q2 and Q3 pieces to make cat.

KITTY WITH PATCHES

A19 Center Q1 on A1 background piece. Fuse and machine appliqué or hand appliqué Q1. Fuse Q2 and then Q3. Use embroidery floss to make straight stitches.

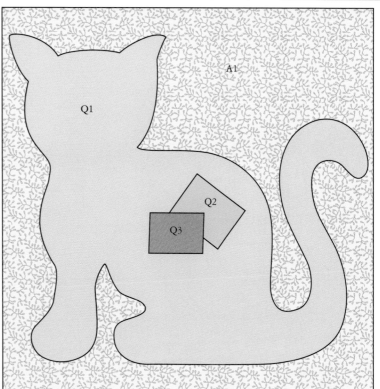

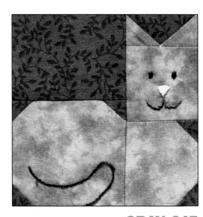

GRAY CAT

A20 Make A section by joining pieces in numerical order. Make B section and join to A section. Make the C section and join to the A-B unit. Embroider cat's tail and mouth using stem stitch; use satin stitch for eyes and nose.

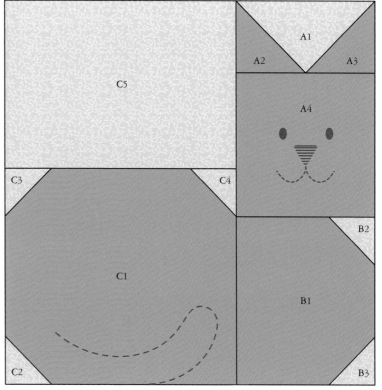

APPLIQUÉ KITTY

A21 Appliqué Q1 piece to background block. Appliqué Q2 and then Q3 pieces. Embroider kitty ears, tail, legs, mouth, and outline eyes using stem stitch. Use satin stitch for eyes, nose, and tongue.

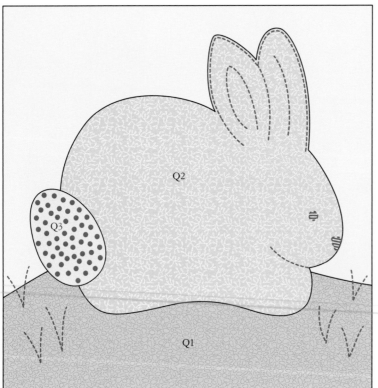

APPLIQUÉ BUNNY

A22 Appliqué Q1 piece to background block. Appliqué Q2 then Q3 pieces. Embroider grass, ear outlines, and neck on bunny using stem stitch. Use satin stitch for nose and eye. Fill in the tail with French knots.

APPLIQUÉ LAMB

A23 Appliqué Q1 piece to background block. Appliqué Q2, Q3 and Q4 in place, then appliqué Q5 piece. Embroider details on lamb's face using stem stitch. Use satin stitch for nose, tongue, tail, and eye. Make a French knot on the mouth. Outline tail with stem stitch. Embroider flowers using stem stitch for stems, lazy daisy stitch for leaves, and French knots for blossoms.

APPLIQUÉ PONY

A24 Appliqué Q1 piece to background block. Appliqué Q2 then Q3 pieces. Embroider grass, ears, mouth, and other details on pony using stem stitch. Use satin stitch for eye. Make the pony's tail by anchoring strands of floss at the dot. Separate strands to fluff the tail.

APPLIQUÉ BABY CHICKEN

A25 Appliqué Q1 piece to background block. Appliqué Q2 then Q3. Embroider chick's feet and grass using stem stitch. Use satin stitch to embroider beak and eye.

APPLIQUÉ BABY DUCK

A26 Appliqué Q1 piece to background block. Appliqué Q2 and Q3, then Q4 pieces. Appliqué Q5 last. Embroider duck's bill using satin stitch; outline with stem stitch. Use satin stitch for the eye. Make raindrops using lazy daisy stitch.

HORSE

A27 Make the A section by joining the A pieces in numerical order. Make the B section and join to the A section. Join the C1 piece to the A-B unit. Make the D section and join to the A-B-C unit. Use stem stitch to embroider the eye on the horse.

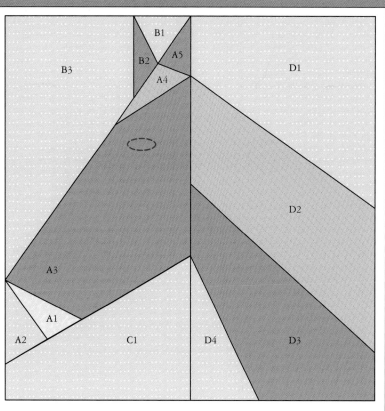

DUCK

A28 Make A section by joining pieces in numerical order. Make B section, inseting B4 and join to A section. Embroider duck wing using stem stitch; use satin stitch for eye.

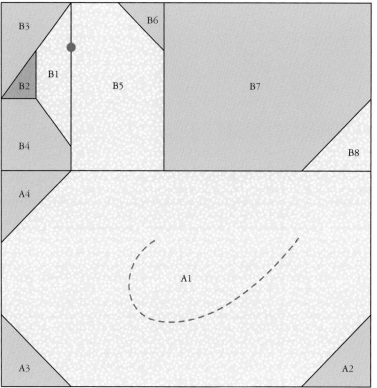

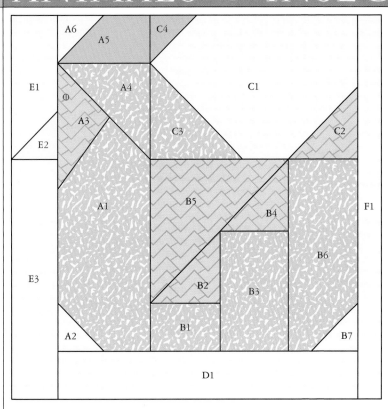

FARM CHICKEN

A29 Make A section by joining pieces in numerical order. Make B and C sections and join to make B-C unit. Join B-C unit to A section. Join D1 to A-B-C unit. Make E section and join to A-B-C-D unit. Join F1 piece to complete the block. Use satin stitch to make the eye and outline with stem stitch.

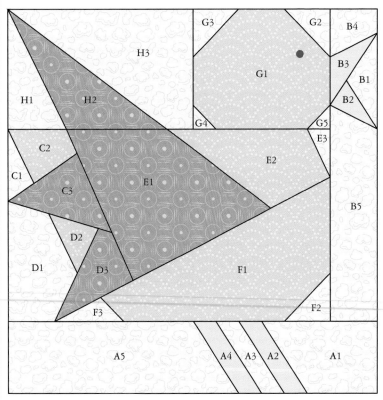

BLUEBIRD

A30 Make the A section by joining the A pieces in numerical order. Make the B section. Make the C and D sections and join. Make the E section and join to the C-D unit. Make the F section and join to the C-D-E unit. Make the G and H units and join, then join to the C-D-E-F unit. Join the B section to the C-D-E-F-G-H unit. Join the A section to the bottom. Group three French knots to make the eye.

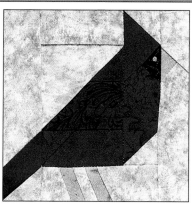

CARDINAL

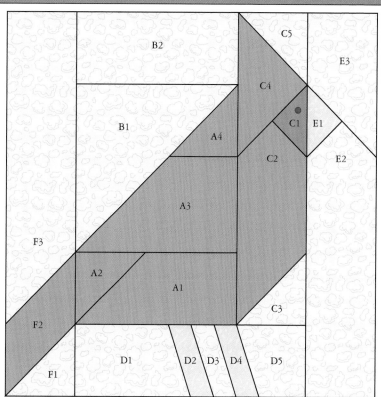

A31 Make the A section by joining the A pieces in numerical order. Make the B section and join to the A section. Make the C section and join to the A-B unit. Make the D section and join to the A-B-C unit. Make the E and F sections and join to opposite sides of the A-B-C-D unit. Use a French knot to make the cardinal's eye.

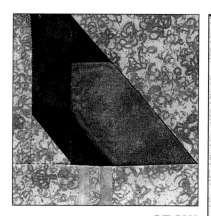

CROW

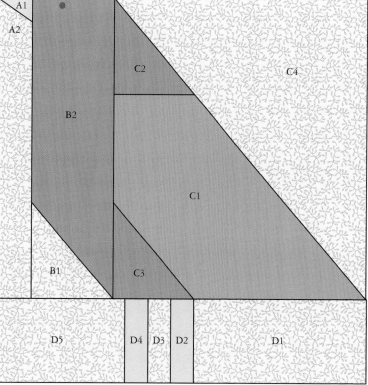

A32 Make the A section by joining the A pieces. Make the B section and join to the A section. Make the C section and join to the A-B unit. Make the D section and join to the A-B-C unit. Use a French knot to make the crow's eye.

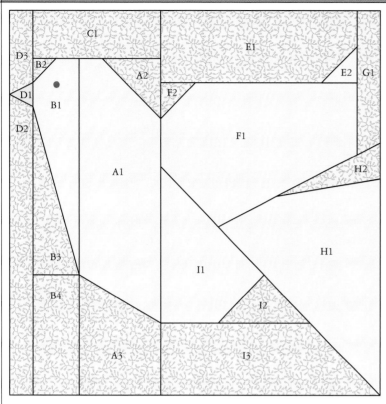

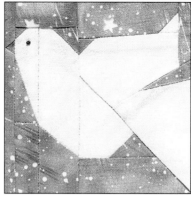

DOVE

A33 Make the A section by joining the A pieces in numerical order. Make the B section and join to the A section. Join the C1 piece to the A-B unit. Make the D section and join to the A-B-C unit. Make the E and F sections and join. Join the G1 piece to the E-F unit. Make the H section and join to the E-F-G unit. Make the I section and join to the E-F-G-H unit. Join the E-F-G-H-I unit to the A-B-C-D unit. Use a French knot to make the dove's eye.

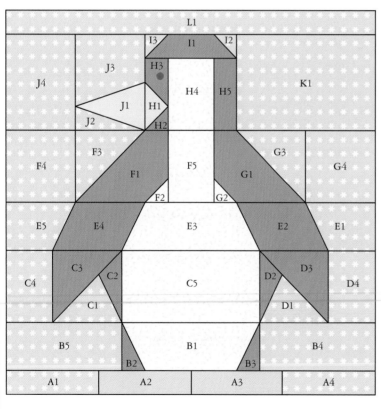

PENGUIN

A34 Make the A section by joining the A pieces. Make the B section and join to the A section. Make the C and D sections and join. Join the C-D unit to the A-B unit. Make the E section and join to the A-B-C-D unit. Make the F and G sections and join, then join to the unit. Make the H and I sections and join. Make the J section and join to the H-I unit. Join the K1 piece to the H-I-J unit then join the H-I-J-K unit to the previously completed unit. Join the L1 piece to the top of the block. Use a French knot to make the penguin's eye.

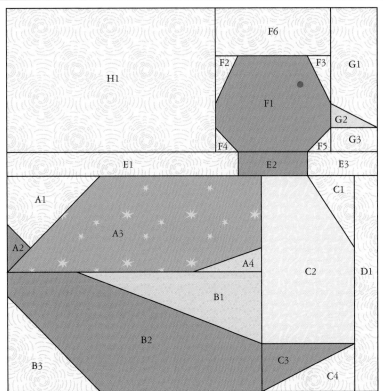

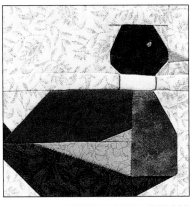

MALLARD DUCK

A35 Make the A section by joining the A pieces in numerical order. Make the B section and join to the A section. Make the C section and join to the A-B unit. Join the D1 piece to the A-B-C unit. Make the E section and join to the A-B-C-D unit. Make the F and G sections and join. Join the H1 piece to the F-G unit. Join the F-G-H unit to the A-B-C-D-E unit.

Look Again

(Below) Rotate four Swallow blocks facing outward to create a large star block with movement. When more blocks are added, the wings create the look of a circular linked chain in the background.

SWALLOW

A36 Make the A section by joining the A pieces in numerical order. Make the B, C, and D sections and join. Join the B-C-D unit to the A section.

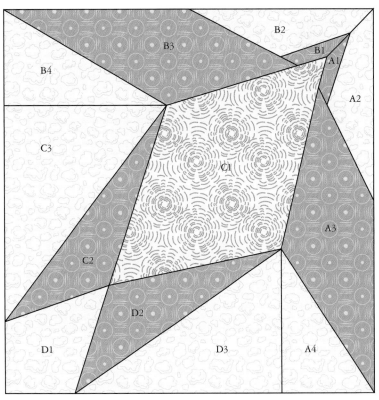

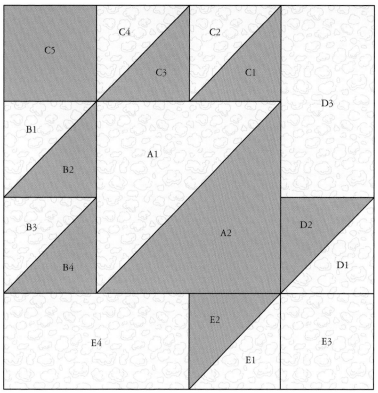

SIMPLE BASKET

B1 Make the A section by joining the
2 A pieces. Make the B section and join to
the A section. Make the C section and join to
the A-B unit. Make the D section and join to
the A-B-C unit. Make the E section and join
to the A-B-C-D unit.

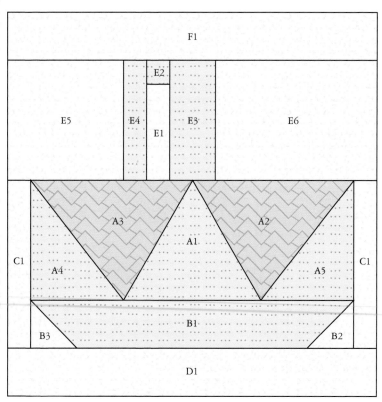

BASKET WITH NAPKINS

B2 Make the A section by joining A pieces in
numerical order. Make the B section and join to
the A section. Join C1 pieces to each side of the
A-B unit. Join D1 piece to the bottom. Make the
E section and join F1 piece to the top. Join the
A-B-C-D unit and the E-F unit to complete
the block.

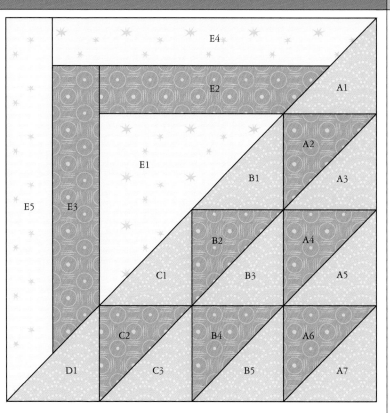

PRAIRIE POINT BASKET

B3 Make the A section by joining the A pieces in numerical order. Make the B and C sections. Join the A, B, and C sections. Join the D1 piece. Join prairie points. (For prairie point instructions, see page 313.) Make the E section. Join the E section to the A-B-C-D unit.

Look Again

(Below) Rotate four Rope Basket blocks to create a geometric diamond with scalloped edges. As more blocks are added, the bands become more prominent, appearing as a disjointed grid.

ROPE BASKET

B4 Make the A section by joining the A pieces in numerical order. Appliqué the Q1 piece to the B1 piece. Join the A and B sections. Join C1 pieces to the A-B unit. Make the D section and join to the A-B-C unit. Join the E1 piece to the A-B-C-D unit.

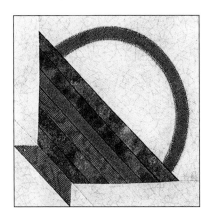

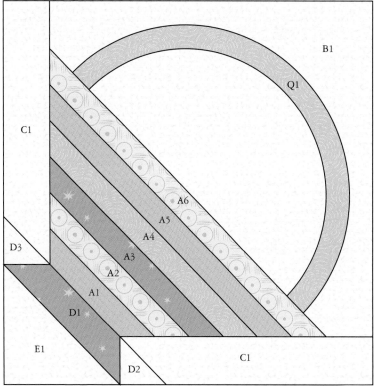

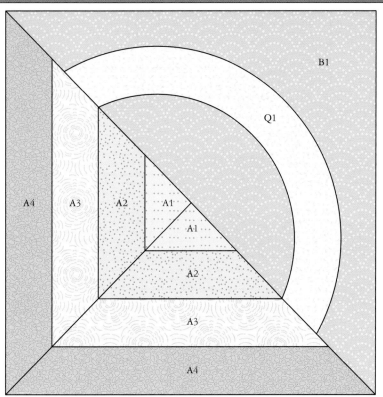

SPRING BASKET

B5 Make 2 A sections by joining the A pieces in numerical order. Join the A sections. Appliqué the Q1 piece to the B1 piece. Join the B section to the A-A unit. Use blanket stitch to embellish the basket.

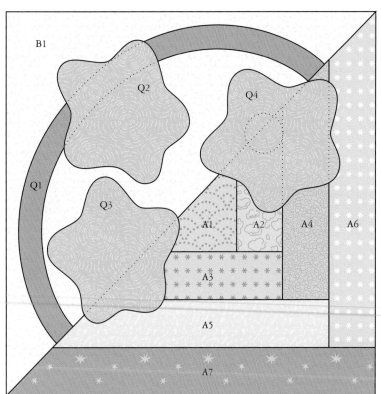

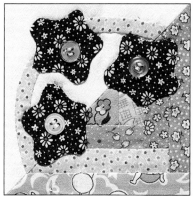

POSY BASKET

B6 Make the A section by joining the A pieces in numerical order. Appliqué the Q1 piece to the B1 piece, then join the A and B sections. Appliqué the flowers (Q2, Q3, and Q4) in place. Sew a small button to the center of each flower.

YO-YO PIECED BASKET

B7 Make the A section by joining the A pieces in numerical order. Make 2 B sections and join to the A section. Join the C1 piece to the A-B unit. Appliqué the Q1 piece to the D1 piece. Join the D1 piece to the A-B-C unit. Appliqué the 3 leaves in place. Make 3 yo-yos from 2¼-inch circles of fabric. (For yo-yo instructions, see page 313.) Stitch yo-yos in place. Use French knots to embroider centers on yo-yo flowers.

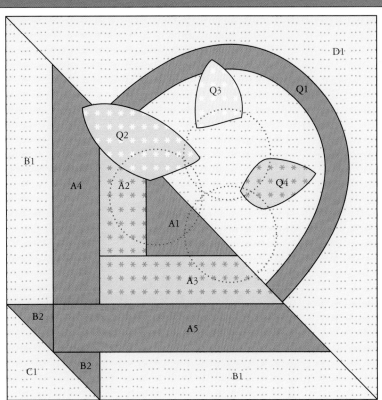

BUTTON BASKET

B8 Make the A section by joining the A pieces in numerical order. Make the B, C, and D sections. Join the B section to the A section, the C section to the A-B unit, and the D section to the A-B-C unit. Make 2 E sections and join to the sides of the A-B-C-D unit. Make the F section and join to the A-B-C-D-E unit. Make 2 G sections. Make the H section. Join the G sections to each side of the H section. Join the G-H unit to the A-B-C-D-E-F unit. Sew 10 buttons to the basket.

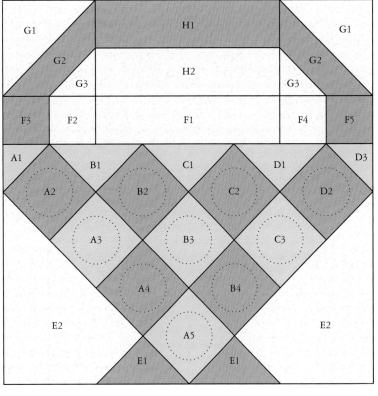

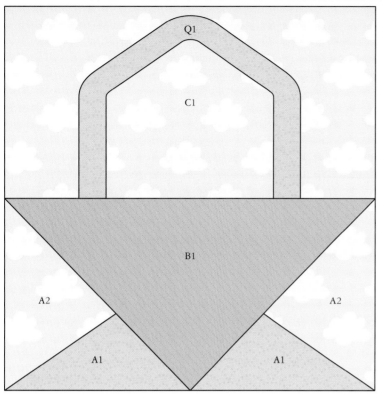

HANDLE BASKET

B9 Make 2 A sections by joining A1 and A2 pieces. Join A sections to B1 piece. Appliqué Q1 piece to C1 piece. Join the C section to the A-B unit.

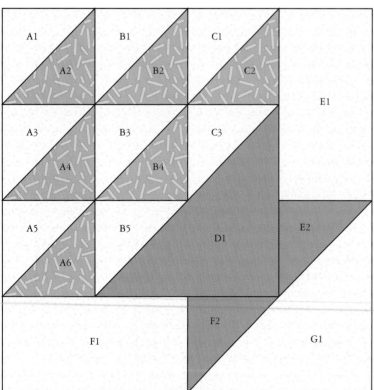

GARDEN BASKET

B10 Make the A section by joining the A pieces in numerical order. Make the B section and join to the A section. Make the C section and join to the A-B unit. Join the D1 piece to the A-B-C unit. Make the E and F sections and join to the A-B-C-D unit. Join the G1 piece to complete the block.

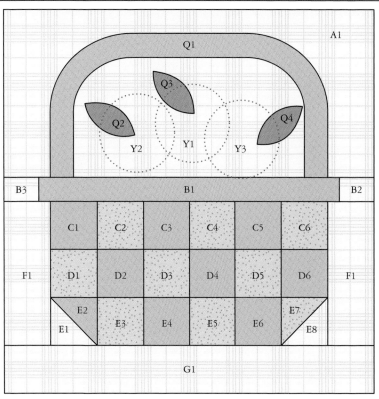

APPLE BASKET

B11 Appliqué Q1 piece on A1. Make B section and join to the A piece. Make the C, D, and E sections and join. Join the F1 pieces to each side of the C-D-E unit. Join the G1 piece to the C-D-E-F unit. Join the A-B unit to the C-D-E-F-G unit. Make 3 apple yo-yos from 2-inch circles of fabric. (For yo-yo instructions, see page 313.) Stitch yo-yos in place as shown. Appliqué leaves in place. Use stem stitch to embroider stems on each apple.

WISH BASKET

B12 Make the A section by joining the A pieces in numerical order. Make the B section and join to the A section. Make 2 C sections and 2 D sections and join as shown. Join the C-D-C-D unit to the A-B unit. Make 2 E sections and join to each side of the A-B-C-D unit. Appliqué Q pieces in numerical order. Use stem stitch and French knots to embellish the flower.

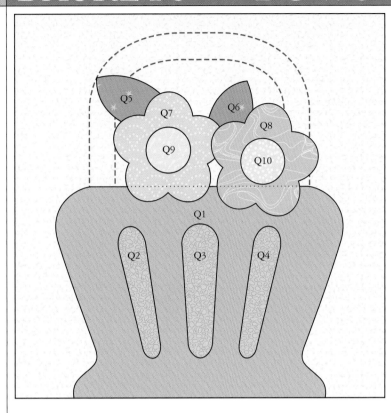

BRAIDED HANDLE BASKET

B13 Make the basket handle by braiding narrow strips of fabric. Sew handle in place on the background block, then appliqué the Q1 piece in place. Appliqué pieces in numerical order to complete the block.

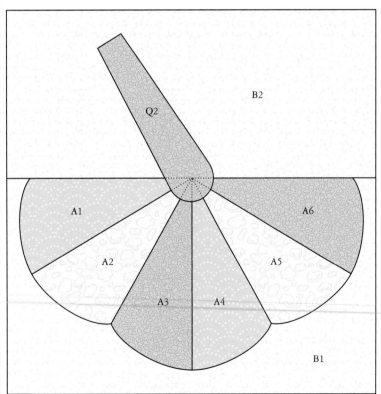

DRESDEN BASKET

B14 Make the A section by joining the A pieces in numerical order. Appliqué the A section to the B1 piece, clipping inside corners. Join the B pieces. Appliqué the Q2 piece in place for the handle.

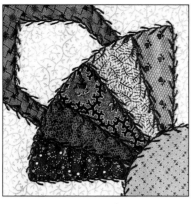

FAN BASKET

B15 Make the A section by joining the A pieces in numerical order. Appliqué the Q1 piece to the background block, then appliqué the A section. Appliqué the Q2 piece. Use a feather stitch to embroider over all edges.

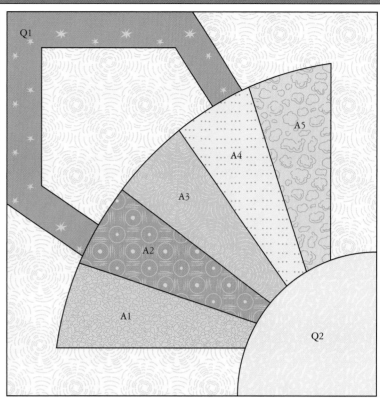

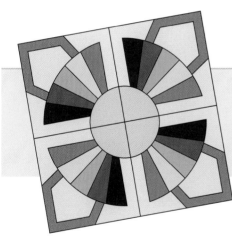

Look Again

(Above) Rotate and combine four Fan Basket blocks to make colorful circular patterns. The rounded basket base joins to make a perfect central circle. The handles, facing outward, resemble the blades on a windmill.

YO-YO BASKET

B16 Join the A2 pieces to each side of A1. Join the B1 pieces to the top and bottom of the A section. Make 3 yo-yos by cutting 2—$2^1/_4$-inch circles and 1—$1^3/_4$-inch circle. (For yo-yo instructions, see page 313.) Appliqué the Q1 piece. Stitch yo-yo (Y1) in place. Appliqué Q2 and Q3 pieces. Stitch Y2 and Y3 in place.

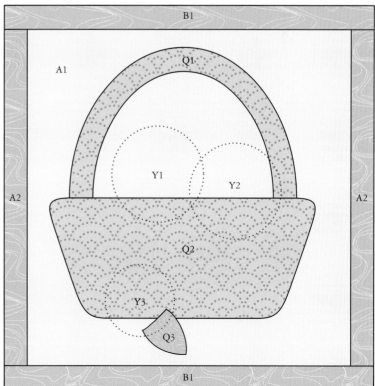

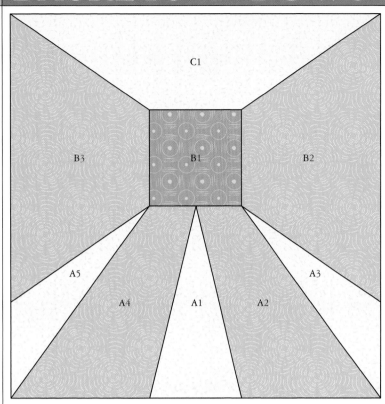

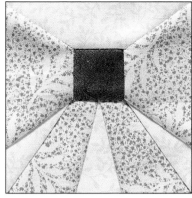

PASTEL BOW

B17 Make the A section by joining the A pieces in numerical order. Make the B section and join to the A section. Join C1 piece to the top of the A-B unit.

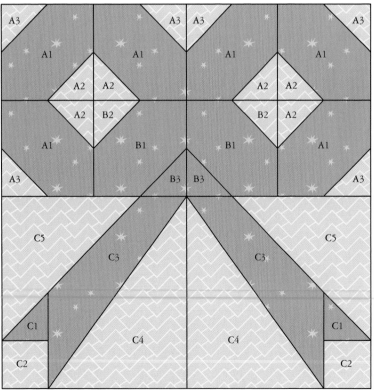

KEYHOLE BOW

B18 Make 6 A sections and 2 B sections. Using pattern as a guide, join the squares in 1 row of 4 A sections and 1 row of A-B-B-A. Join the 2 rows. Make 2 C sections and join. Join the A-B unit to the C-C unit.

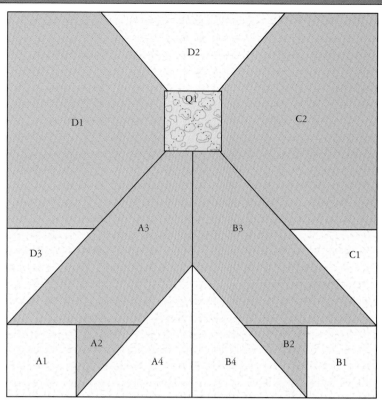

PRETTY BOW

B19 Make the A section by joining the A pieces in numerical order. Make the B section and join to the A section. Make the C section and join to the A-B unit. Make the D section and join to the A-B-C unit. Appliqué the Q1 piece in place.

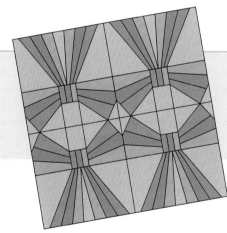

Look Again

(Below) Create two pairs of side-by-side Bow blocks and combine in an arrangement for this stunning pattern. When placed in this mirrorlike arrangement, the pieced bow centers and ends appear as tightly cinched fabric pieces.

BOW

B20 Make the A section by joining the A pieces in numerical order. Make the B and C sections and join to the sides of the A section. Make the D section and join to the A-B-C unit.

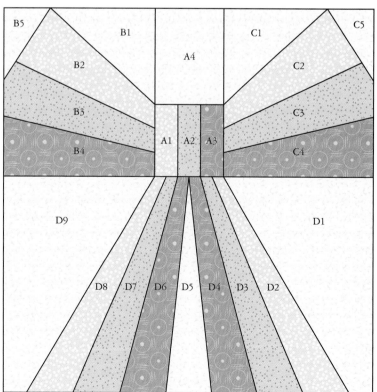

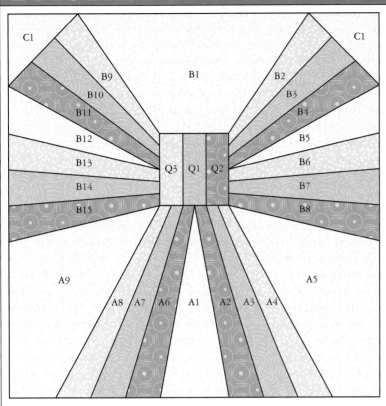

DOUBLE BOW

B21 Make the A section by joining the A pieces in numerical order. Make the B section. Join the C1 pieces to the B section. Join the A section to the B-C unit. Join the Q pieces. Appliqué the Q section to the center of the A-B-C unit.

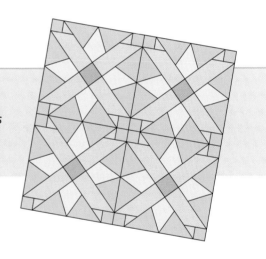

Look Again

(Below) When Ribbon Ties blocks are joined, a trellis pattern emerges. Keep this in mind when choosing fabric colors: you can make the pattern more or less prominent depending on your color choices.

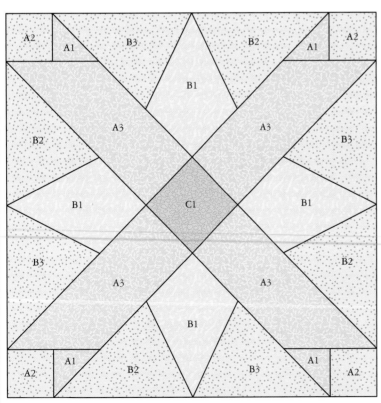

RIBBON TIES

B22 Make 4 A sections by joining the A pieces in numerical order. Join 2 of the A sections with the C1 piece. Make 4 B sections. Join B sections to opposite sides of the remaining A sections. Join the B-A-B units to opposite sides of the A-C-A unit.

COVERED BRIDGE

C1 Working in sections, appliqué the Q1 piece to the Q2 piece. Appliqué the top of the Q3 piece in place. Join pieces to make the A, B and C sections. Appliqué the pieced Q4, Q5, and Q 6 pieces to complete the front of the bridge. Appliqué the Q7 piece to the background block. Position the bridge front and appliqué it and the Q8 and Q9 pieces in place. Appliqué the Q10 piece to complete the block.

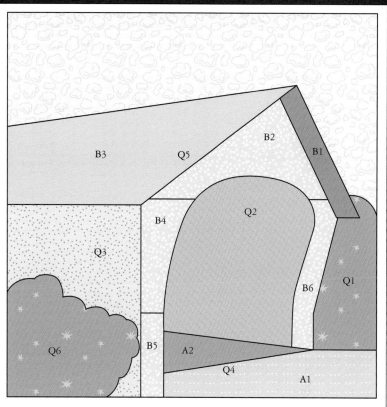

BRICK HOUSE

C2 Make A section by joining pieces in numerical order. Make B and C sections and join. Make D section and join to B-C unit. Make E section and join to B-C-D unit. Join F1 piece to B-C-D-E unit. Make G section and join to B-C-D-E-F unit. Join A section to the top of the block.

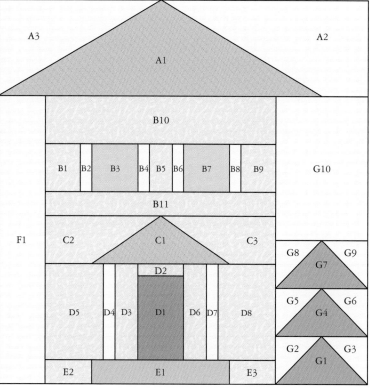

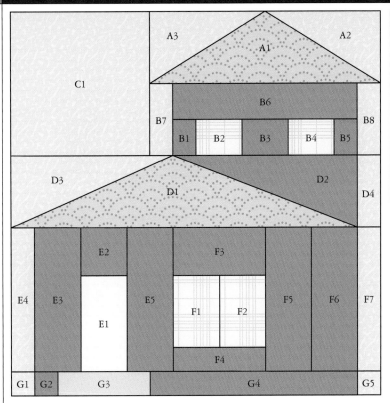

TWO-STORY HOUSE

C3 Make A section by joining pieces in numerical order. Make B section and join to A section. Join C1 piece to A-B unit. Make D section and join to A-B-C unit. Make E and F sections and join. Join E-F unit to A-B-C-D unit. Make G section and join to A-B-C-D-E-F unit.

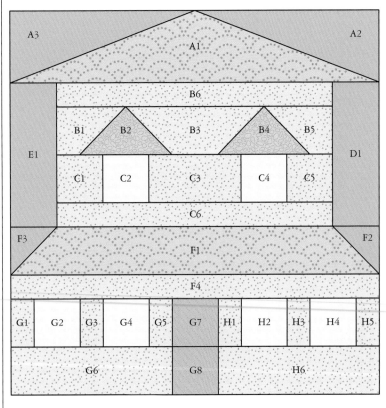

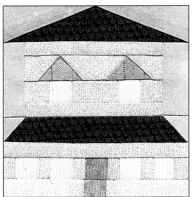

YELLOW HOUSE

C4 Make A section by joining pieces in numerical order. Make B and C sections and join to make B-C unit. Join D1 and E1 pieces to opposite sides of B-C unit. Join B-C-D-E unit to A section. Make F section and join to A-B-C-D-E unit. Make G and H sections and join. Join G-H unit to the bottom of the block.

COUNTRY HOUSE

C5 Make A section by joining pieces in numerical order. Make B and C sections and join to make B-C unit. Make D section and join to B-C unit. Join E1 piece to B-C-D unit. Make F and G sections and join. Make H section and join to F-G unit. Join F-G-H unit to the B-C-D-E unit. Join A section to the top of the block.

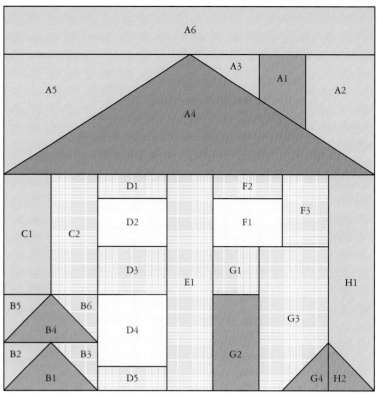

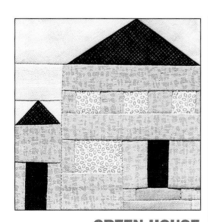

GREEN HOUSE

C6 Make A section by joining pieces in numerical order. Make B section. Make C, D, and E sections and join. Make F section and join to C-D-E unit. Join C-D-E-F unit to B section. Make G and H sections and join. Join G-H unit to B-C-D-E-F unit. Join A section to the top of the block.

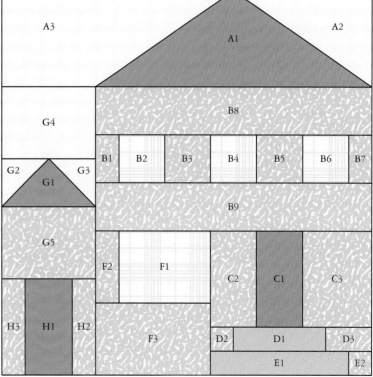

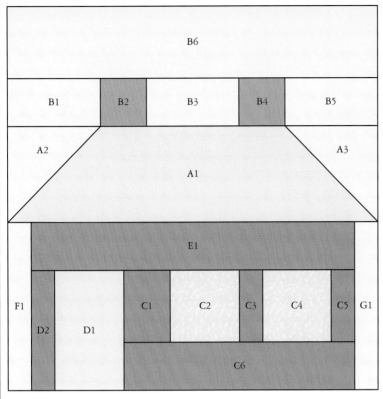

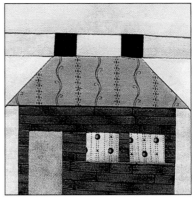

CABIN

C7 Make A section by joining pieces in numerical order. Make B section and join to A section. Make C section. Make D section and join to C section. Join E1 piece to C-D unit. Join F1 and G1 pieces to each side of the C-D-E unit. Join C-D-E-F-G unit to the A-B unit.

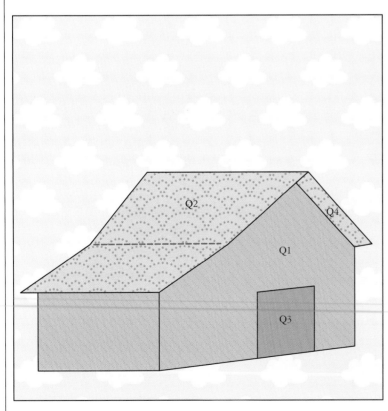

BARN

C8 Appliqué the Q1 piece in place on a background block of landscape fabric. Appliqué the Q2, Q3, and Q4 pieces in place. Use stem stitch to embroider line on the barn roof.

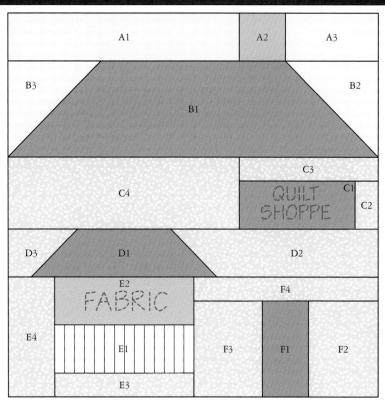

QUILT SHOPPE

C9 Make A section by joining pieces in numerical order. Make B, C, and D sections and join to A section. Piece fabrics to make E1 piece. Join other E pieces to make E section. Make F section and join to E section. Join the E-F unit to the A-B-C-D unit. Embroider "Quilt Shoppe" and "Fabric" using stem stitch.

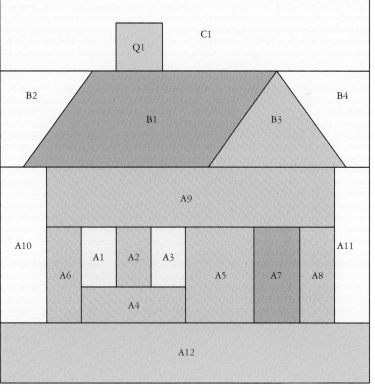

SCHOOLHOUSE

C10 Make A section by joining pieces in numerical order. Make B section and join to A section. Appliqué Q1 piece to C1 to make chimney. Join C1 piece to A-B unit.

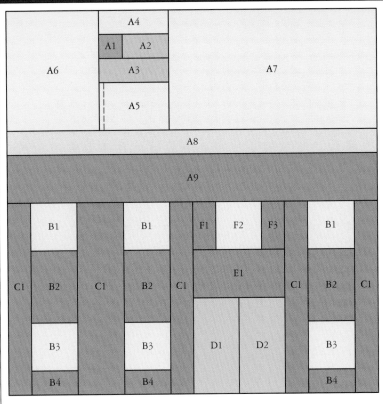

SCHOOL

C11 Using red stripe fabric for A2 and A3 pieces, make A section by joining pieces in numerical order (or use a small flag print for section). Make B sections and join to C sections. Make D section; join to E. Make F section; join to D-E unit. Join a C-B-C-B-C unit to the D-E-F unit; join to the C-B-C unit. Join the two units. Embroider flagpole using stem stitch if desired.

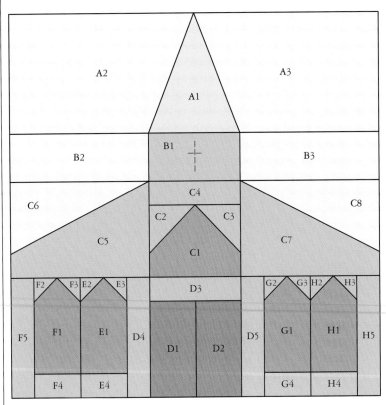

CHURCH

C12 Make A section by joining pieces in numerical order. Make B section and join to A section. Make C section and join to A-B unit. Make D, E, F, G, and H sections and join. Join the D-E-F-G-H unit to the A-B-C unit. Embroider the cross using stem stitch.

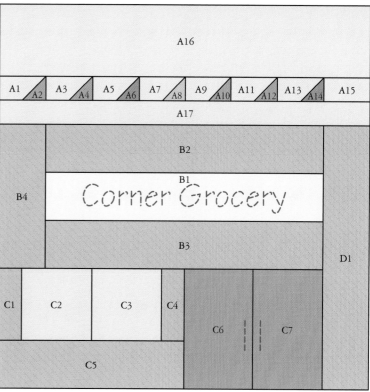

CORNER GROCERY

C13 Make A section by joining pieces in numerical order. Make B and C sections and join. Join D1 piece to B-C unit. Join A section to B-C-D unit. Embroider "Corner Grocery" and door handles using stem stitch.

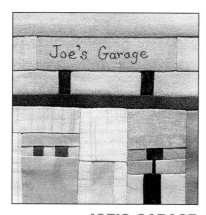

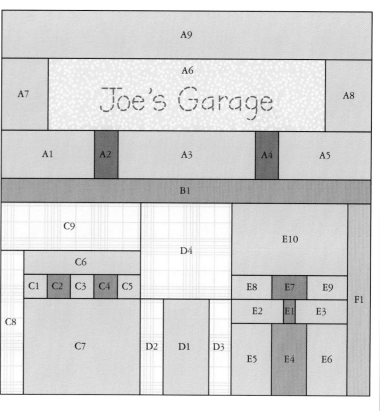

JOE'S GARAGE

C14 Make A section by joining pieces in numerical order. Join B1 piece to A section. Make C, D, and E sections and join to make C-D-E unit. Join F1 piece to the unit. Join C-D-E-F unit to the A-B unit. Embroider "Joe's Garage" using stem stitch.

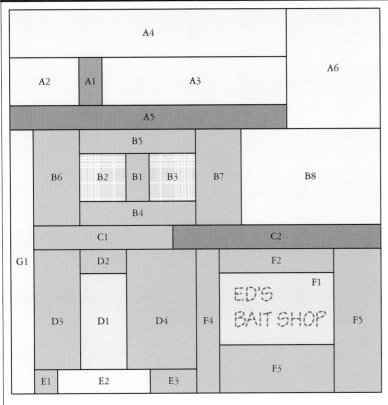

ED'S BAIT SHOP

C15 Make the A section by joining pieces in numerical order. Make B and C sections and join. Make D and E sections and join. Make F section and join to D-E unit. Join D-E-F unit to B-C unit. Join G1 piece to B-C-D-E-F unit. Join A section to the B-C-D-E-F-G unit. Embroider "Ed's Bait Shop" using stem stitch.

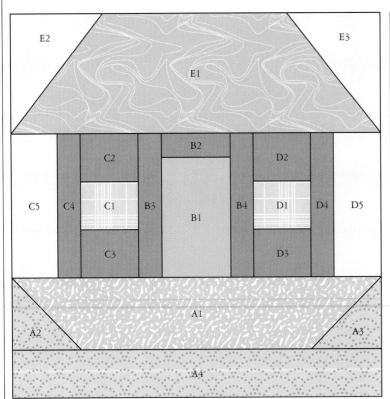

HOUSEBOAT

C16 Make A section by joining pieces in numerical order. Make B, C, and D sections and join. Join B-C-D unit to A section. Make E section and join to the top of the block.

CRUISE SHIP

C17 Make A section by joining pieces in numerical order. Make B section and join to A section. Join C1 piece to A-B unit. Make the D and E sections and join, then join the F1 piece. Join the D-E-F unit to A-B-C unit. Embroider smoke and birds using stem stitch. Embroider portholes using chain stitch.

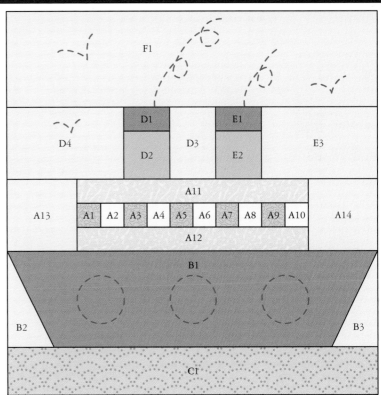

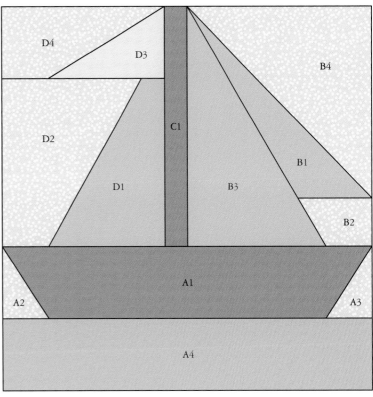

Look Again

(Below) Sets of facing Sailboat blocks create a pattern-behind-bars design. As more blocks are added, the water fabrics connect to make bold stripes.

SAILBOAT

C18 Make A section by joining pieces in numerical order. Make B section and join C1 piece. Make D section and join to B-C unit. Join the B-C-D unit to the A section.

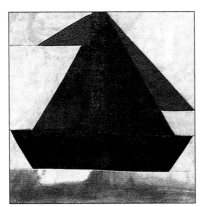

BRIGHT SAILBOAT

C19 Piece 1-inch strips of fabric for the Q3 and Q4 pieces, then cut out appliqué pieces. (Stripe fabric can be used, if desired.) Appliqué the Q pieces in numerical order to the background block.

LIGHTHOUSE

C20 Piece 1-inch strips of fabric for the Q2 piece, then cut out appliqué piece. (Stripe fabric can be used, if desired.) Appliqué the Q pieces in numerical order to the background block.

PULL TOY

D1 Tack on twisted cord to make handle. Appliqué pieces in numerical order on background block. Use stem stitch to embroider eye.

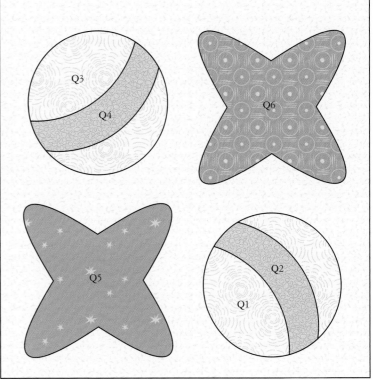

BALLS AND JACKS

D2 Appliqué Q2 piece onto Q1 piece, then appliqué in place on background block. Appliqué Q4 onto Q3, then appliqué to block. Appliqué Q5 and Q6 pieces in place.

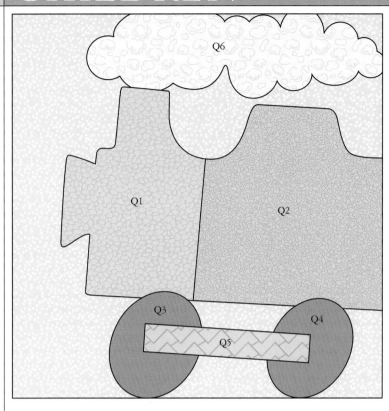

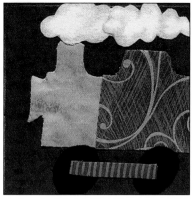

TOY TRAIN

D3 Appliqué the Q1 and Q2 pieces in place on the background block. Appliqué pieces in numerical order to complete the block.

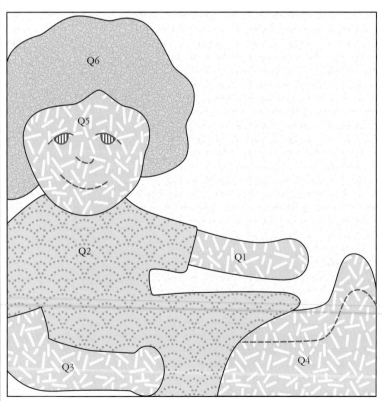

DOLL

D4 Appliqué the pieces in numerical order on the background block. Use a running stitch to define the doll's legs. Use satin stitch to embroider the eyes; use stem stitch to embroider the eyelids, nose, and mouth.

PULL TOY

D1 Tack on twisted cord to make handle. Appliqué pieces in numerical order on background block. Use stem stitch to embroider eye.

BALLS AND JACKS

D2 Appliqué Q2 piece onto Q1 piece, then appliqué in place on background block. Appliqué Q4 onto Q3, then appliqué to block. Appliqué Q5 and Q6 pieces in place.

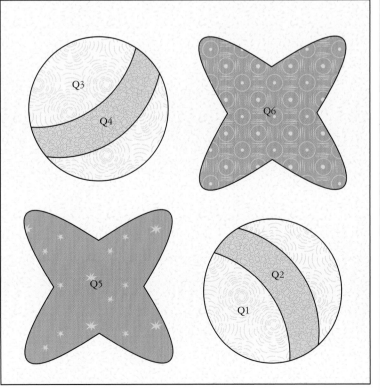

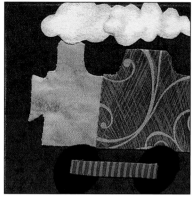

TOY TRAIN

D3 Appliqué the Q1 and Q2 pieces in place on the background block. Appliqué pieces in numerical order to complete the block.

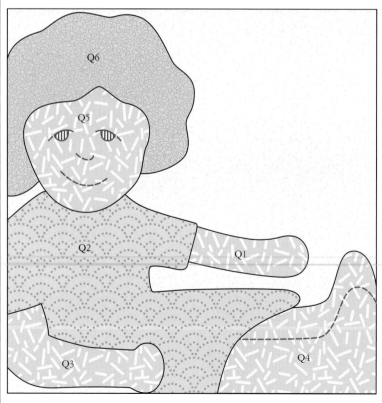

DOLL

D4 Appliqué the pieces in numerical order on the background block. Use a running stitch to define the doll's legs. Use satin stitch to embroider the eyes; use stem stitch to embroider the eyelids, nose, and mouth.

SAND AND BUCKET

D5 Make the A section by joining pieces in numerical order. Join the B1 piece to the bottom and the C1 piece to the top. Appliqué Q1 and Q2 pieces in place. Satin-stitch handle on the bucket.

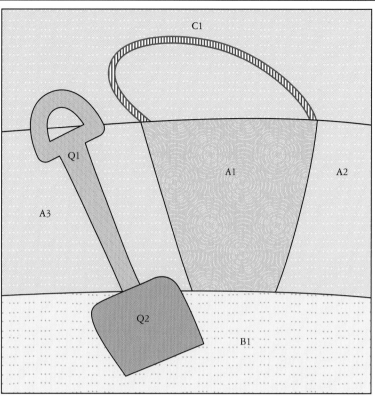

BOOK WORM

D6 The Q1 piece can be cut as one piece or as 3 pieces as desired. Appliqué the Q pieces in numerical order to the background block. Use stem stitch to define the corners of the pages. Use a French knot for the worm's eye.

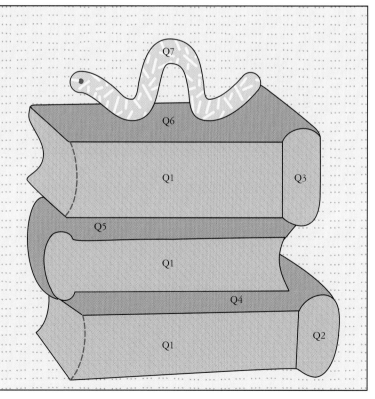

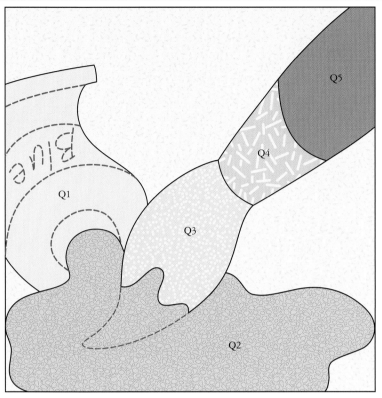

PAINTING

D7 Appliqué the Q pieces in numerical order to the background block. Use stem stitch or running stitch to define the tip of the brush and to embroider detail on the tube of paint.

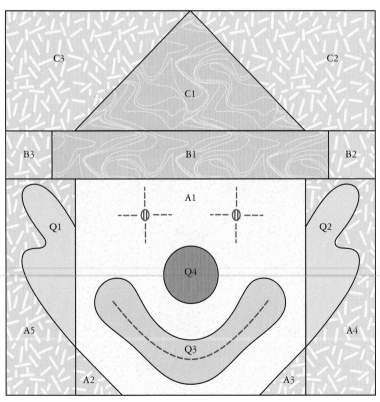

CLOWN

D8 Make the A section by joining pieces in numerical order. Make the B section and join to the A section. Make the C section and join to the A-B unit. Appliqué Q1, Q2, Q3, and Q4 pieces in place. Use stem stitch to embroider mouth. Use satin stitch and running stitch to embroider the eyes.

SAND AND BUCKET

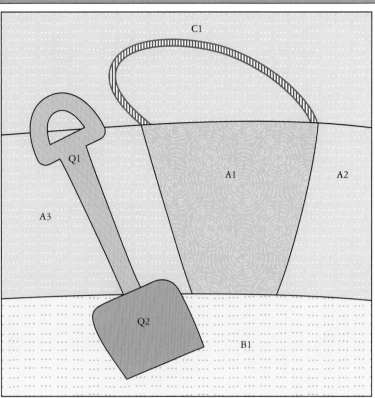

D5 Make the A section by joining pieces in numerical order. Join the B1 piece to the bottom and the C1 piece to the top. Appliqué Q1 and Q2 pieces in place. Satin-stitch handle on the bucket.

BOOK WORM

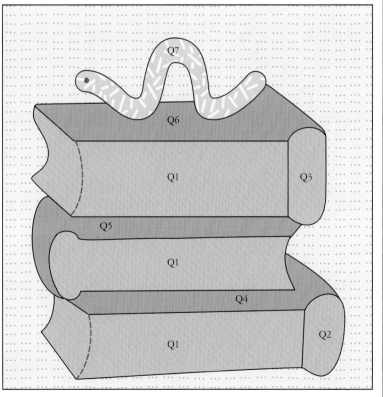

D6 The Q1 piece can be cut as one piece or as 3 pieces as desired. Appliqué the Q pieces in numerical order to the background block. Use stem stitch to define the corners of the pages. Use a French knot for the worm's eye.

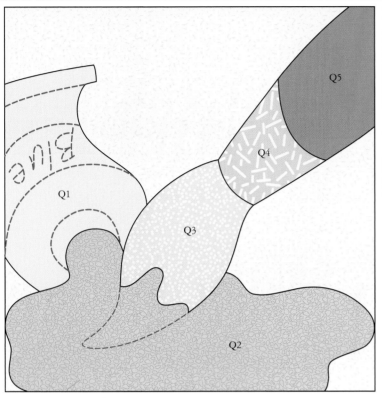

PAINTING

D7 Appliqué the Q pieces in numerical order to the background block. Use stem stitch or running stitch to define the tip of the brush and to embroider detail on the tube of paint.

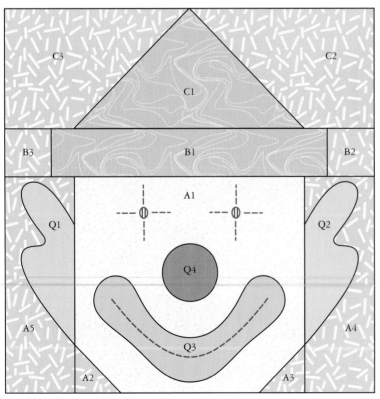

CLOWN

D8 Make the A section by joining pieces in numerical order. Make the B section and join to the A section. Make the C section and join to the A-B unit. Appliqué Q1, Q2, Q3, and Q4 pieces in place. Use stem stitch to embroider mouth. Use satin stitch and running stitch to embroider the eyes.

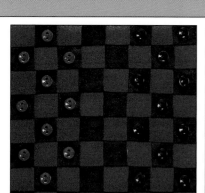

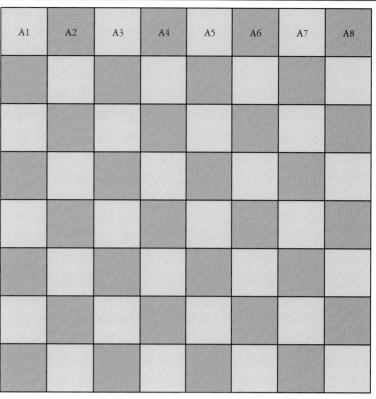

CHECKERBOARD

D9 Cut 1-inch strips of black and red fabric. Alternating colors, join 8 strips (A1–A8). Cut the stitched fabric into 1-inch segments. Join the segments to form the checkerboard pattern. Sew 12 small red buttons to black squares and 12 small black buttons to black squares.

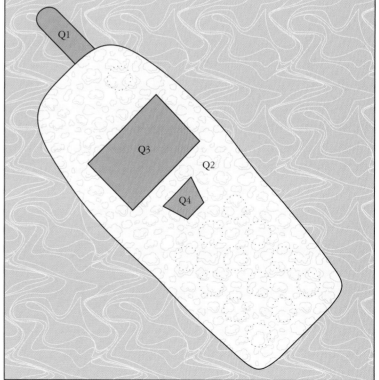

CELL PHONE

D10 Appliqué the Q pieces in numerical order to the background block. Sew ¼-inch buttons in place to represent the buttons on the phone.

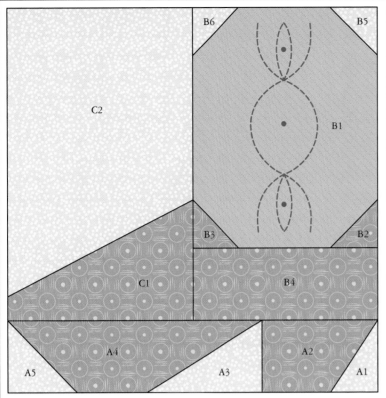

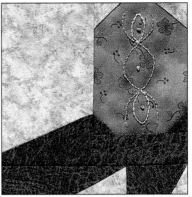

COWBOY BOOT

D11 Make the A section by joining the A pieces in numerical order. Make the B and C sections and join. Join the B-C unit to the A section. Use stem stitch to embroider the design on the boot. Use French knots for accents.

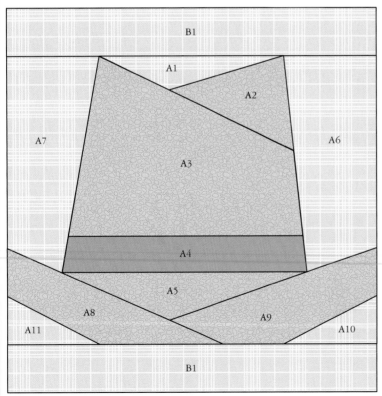

COWBOY HAT

D12 Make the A section by joining the A pieces in numerical order. Join the B1 pieces to the top and bottom of the block.

PAPER DOLLS

D13 Appliqué Q1 piece on background block. Use satin stitch to embroider hearts.

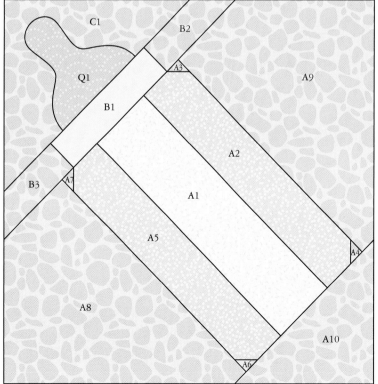

BABY BOTTLE

D14 Make the A section by joining the A pieces in numerical order. Make the B section and join to the A section. Appliqué the Q1 piece to the C1 piece, then join the C section to the A-B unit.

CAT AND FIDDLE

D15 Appliqué Q1 piece in place on background block. Appliqué Q2–Q7 pieces in numerical order. Use stem stitch to embroider strings on the fiddle, cat's mouth and whiskers. Use satin stitch for cat's nose and eyes.

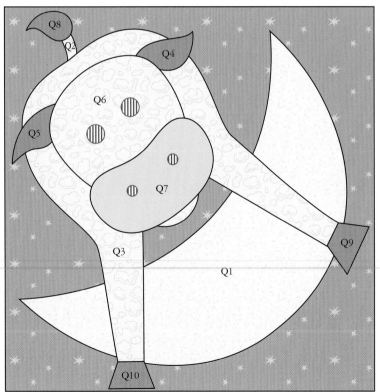

COW JUMPED OVER THE MOON

D16 Appliqué the Q1 piece on the background block. Appliqué remaining pieces in numerical order. Use satin stitch to embroider eyes and nostrils on the cow.

LITTLE DOG LAUGHED

D17 Appliqué the Q1 and Q2 pieces in place on the background block. Appliqué Q3 piece. Use stem stitch to embroider mouth, ear, and eye on the dog.

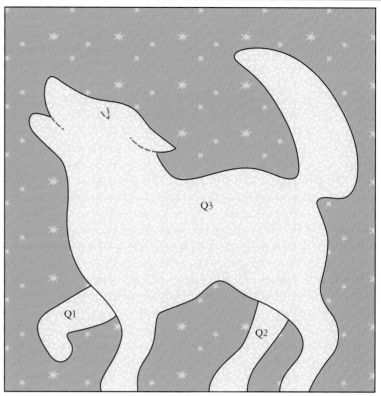

DISH AND SPOON

D18 Appliqué Q pieces in numerical order on background block. Use stem stitch to embroider arms, legs, and mouths. Use satin stitch to embroider eyes.

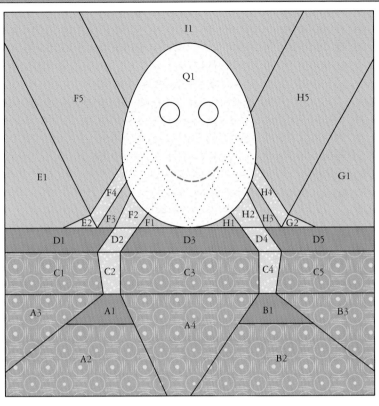

HUMPTY DUMPTY

D19 Make the A section by joining the A pieces in numerical order. Make the B section and join to the A section. Make the C and D sections and join. Join the C-D unit to the A-B unit. Make the E and F sections and join. Make the G and H sections and join, then join the I1 piece. Join the G-H-I unit to the E-F unit, then join to the A-B-C-D unit. Appliqué the Q1 piece in place. Sew buttons in place for the eyes. Use stem stitch to embroider the mouth.

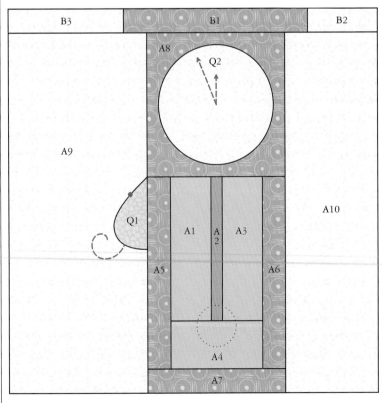

HICKORY DICKORY

D20 Appliqué the Q1 piece to the A9 piece. Make the A section by joining the A pieces in numerical order. Make the B section and join to the A section. Draw the face and hands of the clock on the Q2 piece with fabric pens, then appliqué the Q2 piece in place. Use stem stitch and a French knot to embroider the mouse's tail and eye. Sew a button in place for the pendulum.

GIRL

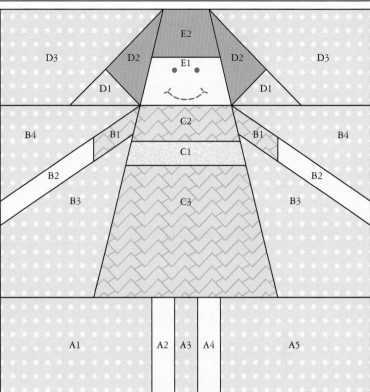

D21 Make the A section by joining pieces in numerical order. Make 2 B sections. Make the C section and join a B section to each side. Join the A section to the B-C-B unit. Make 2 D sections and 1 E section. Join as shown. Join the D-E-D unit to the A-B-C unit. Use stem stitch to embroider the mouth. Make French knots for the eyes.

BOY

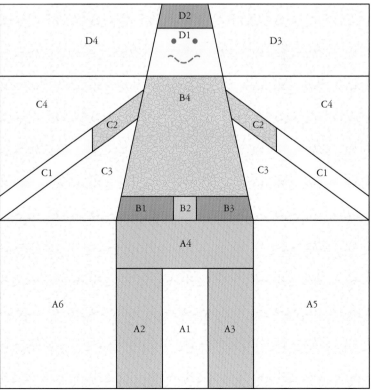

D22 Make the A section by joining pieces in numerical order. Make the B section, then make 2 C sections. Join a C section to each side of the B section. Join the A section to the bottom of the C-B-C unit. Make the D section and join to the top of the A-B-C unit. Use stem stitch to embroider the mouth and satin stitch for the eyes.

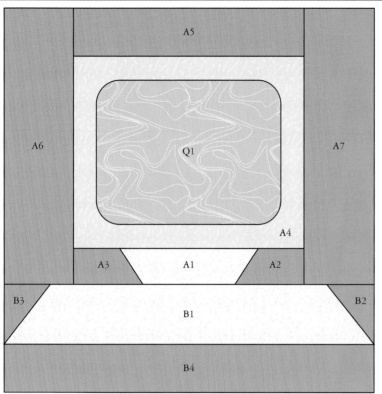

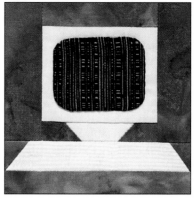

COMPUTER MONITOR

D23 Make the A section by joining the A pieces in numerical order. Make the B section and join to the A section. Appliqué the Q1 piece to make the screen on the monitor.

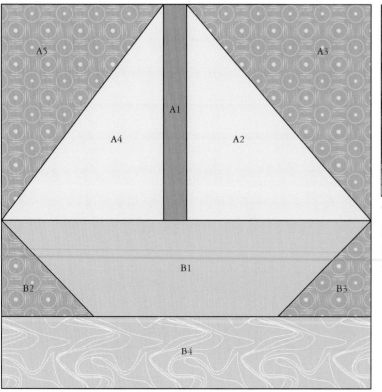

TOY BOAT

D24 Make the A section by joining the A pieces in numerical order. Make the B section and join to the A section.

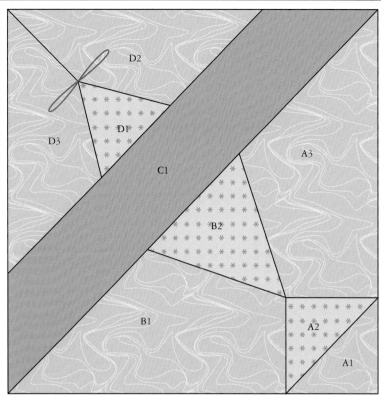

HAPPY PLANE

D25 Make the A section by joining pieces in numerical order. Make the B section and join to the A section. Join the C1 piece to the A-B unit. Make the D section and join to the A-B-C unit. Use a lazy daisy stitch to embroider a propeller on the plane.

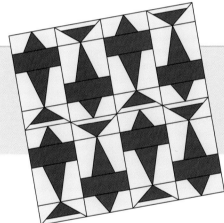

Look Again

(Below) Place Two Planes blocks as shown, left, to create rows of planes heading in opposite directions.

TWO PLANES

D26 Make 2 A sections by joining the A pieces in numerical order. Make 2 B sections and 2 C sections. Join the sections into 2 A-B-C units, then join the units.

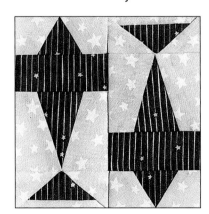

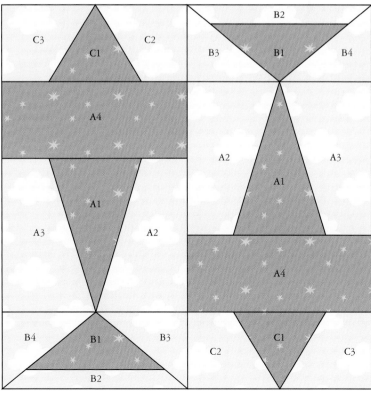

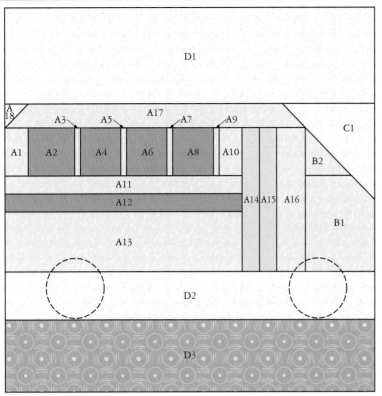

SCHOOL BUS

D27 Make the A section by joining the A pieces in numerical order. Make the B section and join to the A section. Join the C1 piece to the A-B unit. Join the D pieces to the A-B-C unit. Sew buttons in place for the bus wheels.

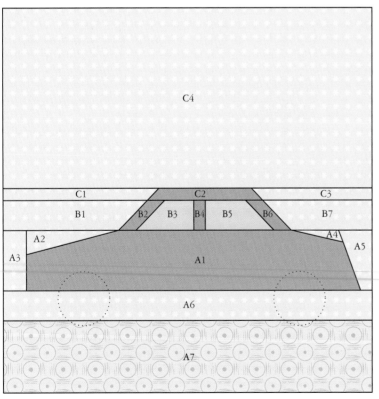

RED CAR

D28 Make the A section by joining the A pieces in numerical order. Make the B section and join to the A section. Make the C section and join to the A-B unit. Sew buttons in place for the car wheels.

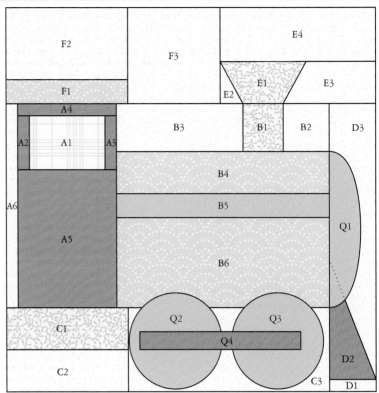

ENGINE

D29 Make the A section by joining the A pieces in numerical order. Make the B section and join to the A section. Make the C section and join to the A-B unit. Make the D section and join to the A-B-C unit. Make the E and F sections and join. Join the E-F unit to the A-B-C-D unit. Appliqué the Q pieces in place in numerical order.

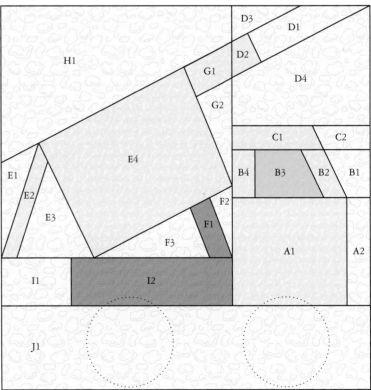

DUMP TRUCK

D30 Make the A section by joining the 2 A pieces. Make the B section and join to the A section. Make the C and D sections and join. Join the C-D unit to the A-B unit. Make the E, F, and G sections and join, then join the H1 piece. Join the I pieces, then join to the E-F-G-H unit. Join the E-F-G-H unit to the A-B-C-D unit. Join the J1 piece. Sew buttons in place for the truck wheels.

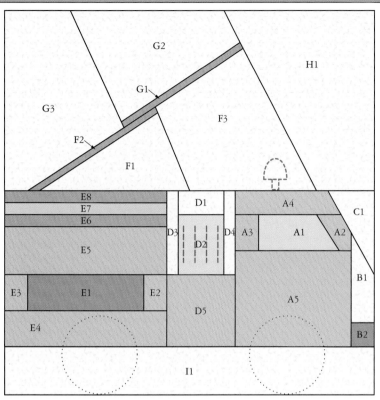

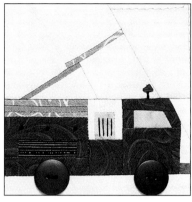

FIRE TRUCK

D31 Make the A section by joining the A pieces in numerical order. Make the B section and join to the A section, then join the C1 piece. Make the D and E sections and join, then join the D-E unit to the A-B-C unit. Make the F and G sections and join, then join the H1 piece. Join the F-G-H unit to the A-B-C-D-E unit, then join the I1 piece to the bottom. Use stem stitch and satin stitch to embroider bell and hose on the truck.
Sew buttons in place for the truck wheels.

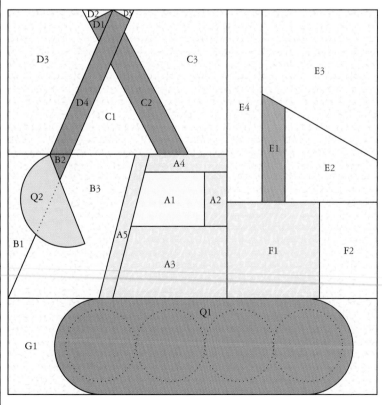

BACKHOE

D32 Make the A section by joining the A pieces in numerical order. Make the B section and join to the A section. Make the C and D sections and join. Join the C-D unit to the A-B unit. Make the E and F sections and join. Join the E-F unit to the A-B-C-D unit. Appliqué the Q1 piece to the G1 piece and then join to the A-B-C-D-E-F unit. Appliqué the Q2 piece in place. Sew 4 buttons to the Q1 piece.

TEAKETTLE

E1 Appliqué the Q pieces in numerical order to the background block. Use satin stitch to embroider handles, adding lazy daisy and stem stitches to the top handle. Use satin stitch to embroider knob, top of spout, and heart. Outline the heart with stem stitch. Use lazy daisy stitches and French knots for embellishment below the heart.

BOILING POT

E2 Appliqué Q1 and Q2 pieces on background block, then appliqué Q3 piece. Use satin stitch to make diamond pattern across the pot. Use stem stitch to outline each diamond and embroider lines above and below the row of diamonds. Use satin stitch to embroider knob on the lid. Use stem stitch to outline the knob, make lines of steam, and to detail the handle.

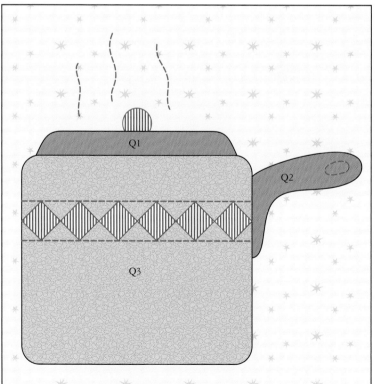

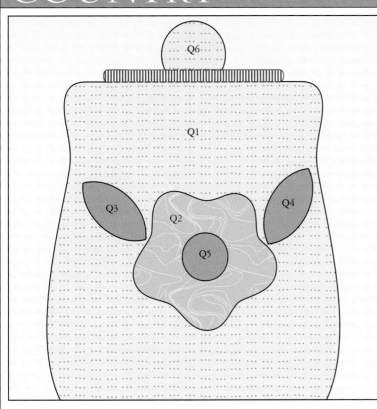

COOKIE JAR

E3 Appliqué Q1 piece to background block. Use stem stitch to embroider lines to define lid on the jar; satin stitch the lid. Appliqué flower, leaves, and handle in numerical order. Use blanket stitch to outline the flowers and leaves.

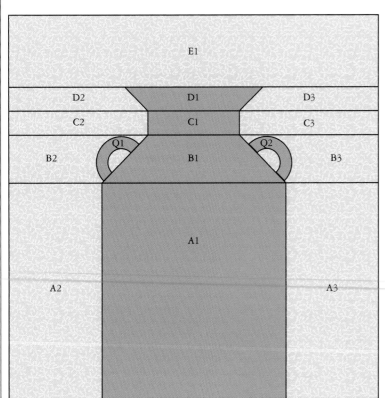

MILK CAN

E4 Make the A section by joining the A pieces in numerical order. Appliqué the Q1 and Q2 pieces to the B2 and B3 pieces. Join B1 to B2 and B3, then join the B section to the A section. Make the C and D sections and join to the A-B unit. Join the E1 piece to the top of the block.

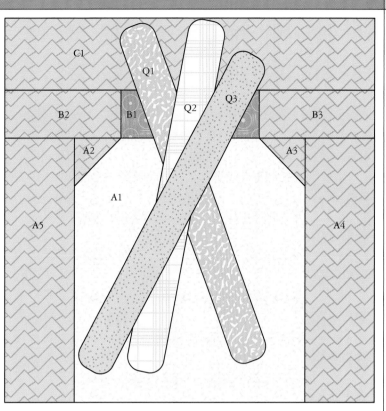

CANDY STICKS

E5 Make the A section by joining the A pieces in numerical order. Make the B section and join to the A section. Join the C1 piece to the A-B unit. Appliqué the candy sticks, Q1, Q2, and Q3, in numerical order to complete the block.

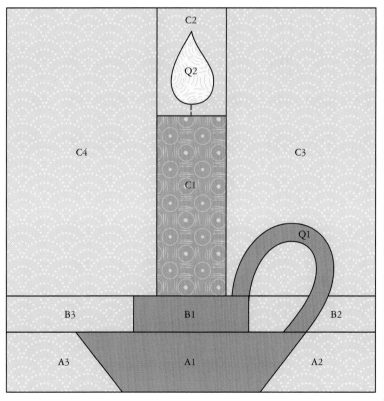

CANDLE

E6 Make the A section by joining the A pieces in numerical order. Make the B section and join to the A section. Make the C section and join to the A-B unit. Appliqué Q1 and Q2 pieces in place. Use stem stitch to embroider candle wick.

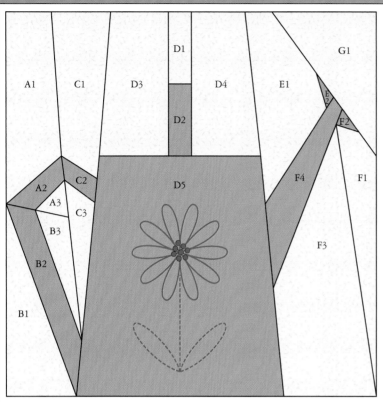

WATERING CAN

E7 Make the A section by joining the A pieces in numerical order. Make the B section and join to the A section. Make the C and D sections and join. Join the C-D unit to the A-B unit. Make the E and F sections and join. Join the G1 piece to the E-F unit. Join the E-F-G unit to the A-B-C-D unit. Use lazy daisy stitches to embroider a flower on the watering can. Use stem stitch for the leaves and the stem and French knots for the flower center.

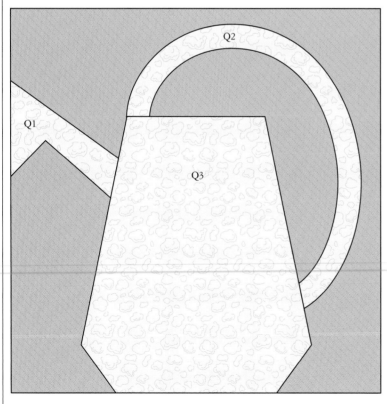

WATERING CAN

E8 Appliqué Q pieces in numerical order on the background block.

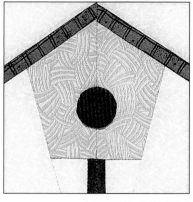

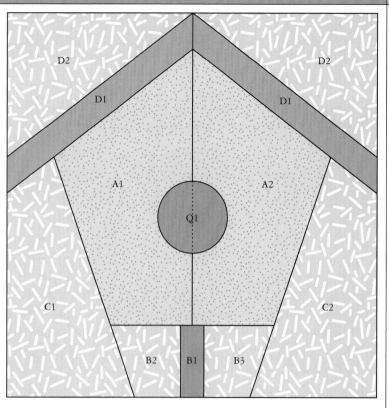

WREN HOUSE

E9 Join the A1 and A2 pieces to make the A section. Make the B section and join to the A section. Join the C1 and C2 pieces to the sides of the A-B unit. Make 2 D sections and join to the A-B-C unit. Appliqué the Q1 piece to complete the block.

Look Again

(Below) When Country Pinwheel blocks are combined, the borders connect to create a pattern of their own. As more blocks are added, you'll see rows of diamonds appear.

COUNTRY PINWHEEL

E10 Join A1, A2, A3, and A4. Repeat to make a second A section. Join the 2 A sections. Join a B piece to each side of the A section. Join a C piece to each side of the A-B unit.

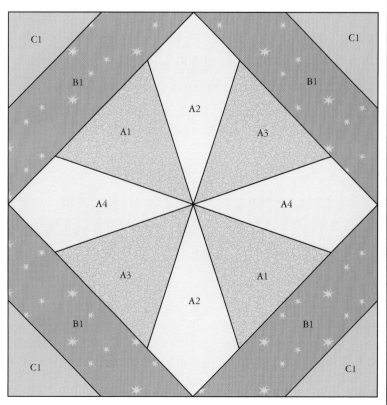

FLORAL

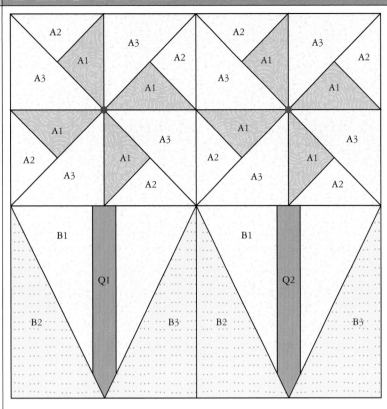

PINWHEEL GARDEN

F1 Make 8 A1-2-3 sections. Join as shown to make top half of the block. Make 2 B sections; join B sections. Appliqué Q1 and Q2 pieces to make flower stems. Join B unit to A unit. Embroider a French knot in the center of each pinwheel flower.

Look Again

(Above) Rotate and combine four Pinwheel Garden blocks to create a larger, more intricate pinwheel. To make this pattern stand out as much as possible, choose vivid and contrasting colors.

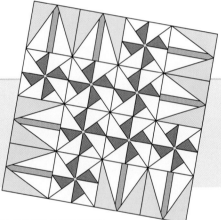

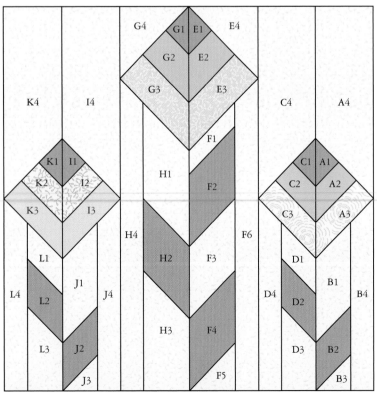

SPRING FLOWERS

F2 Make A section by joining pieces in numerical order. Make B section and join to A section. Make C and D sections and join. Join C-D unit to A-B unit. Make the E and F sections and join. Make the G and H sections and join. Join the E-F and G-H units then join to the A-B-C-D unit. Continue with the I-J-K-L sections to complete the block. Use stem stitch to embroider stem along seam line of each flower.

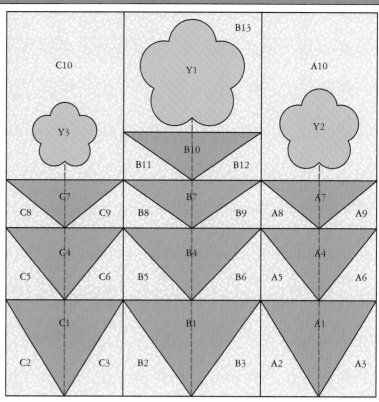

DAHLIA

F3 Join A2 and A3 pieces to A1; join A5 and A6 pieces to A4. Join A1-2-3 section to A4-5-6 section. Complete the A section. Make B and C sections and join sections into the A-B-C unit. Make 3 yo-yos by cutting a 3-inch circle for Y1, a 2^1/$_2$-inch circle for Y2, and a 2-inch circle for Y3. (For yo-yo instructions, see page 313.) When sewing yo-yos on the block, take one long stitch from the inside, up and around the outside edge of the yo-yo and back under to the center to form flower petals. Make French knots in the center of each yo-yo. Use stem stitch to embroider the flower stems.

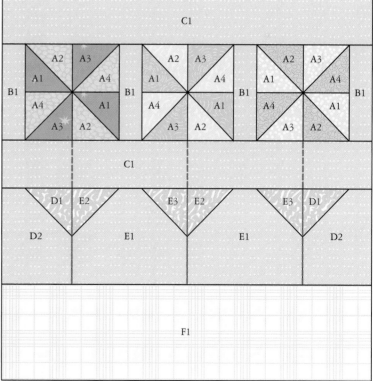

WINDOW BOX

F4 Make 6 A sections by joining the A pieces in numerical order. Join the A sections into 3 A-A units, then join together with the 4 B1 pieces. Join C1 pieces to the top and bottom of the B-A-B-A-B-A-B unit. Make 2 D sections and 2 E sections and join into the D-E-E-D unit. Join the F1 piece to the bottom. Join the 2 completed units. Use French knots to embroider flower centers and stem stitch to make flower stems.

113

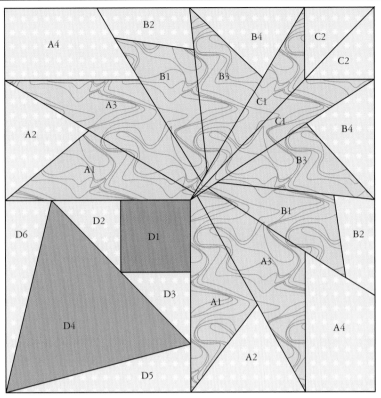

CHRYSANTHEMUM

F5 Make 2 A sections by joining the A pieces in numerical order. Make 2 B secions and add to A units. Make 2 C sections. Join to AB sections. Join the 2 units. Make the D section and inset the section in the ABCABC unit.

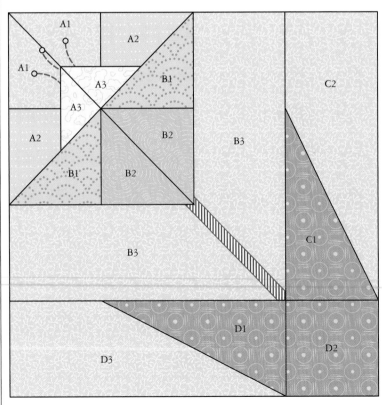

PINK FLOWER

F6 Make 2 A sections by joining the A pieces in numerical order. Make 2 B sections. Join each B section to an A section. Join the 2 A-B units. Make the C section and join to the AB-AB unit. Make the D section and join to the bottom of the block. Use satin stitch to embroider the flower stem. Use stem stitch to outline the stem and to embroider flower stamens. Use French knots at the end of each stamen.

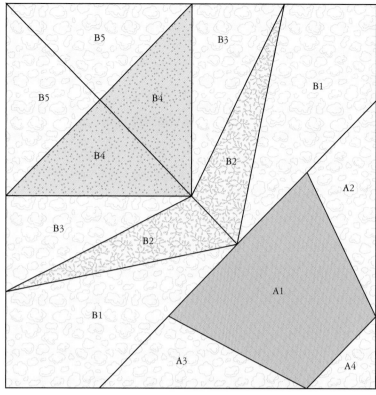

GARDEN OF FRIENDSHIP

F7 Make the A section by joining the A pieces in numerical order. Make 2 B sections and join. Join the B-B unit to the A section.

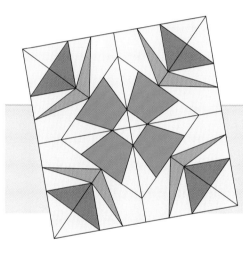

Look Again

(Above) Rotate and combine four Garden of Friendship blocks, keeping the flower pots in the center, for a pretty symmetrical design. When carefully stitched, the leaf and flower tips touch to continue the pattern.

FLOWER VASE

F8 Make the A section by joining the A pieces in numerical order. Make the B and C sections and join. Join the B-C unit to the A section. Make the D and E sections and join. Join the D-E unit to the A-B-C unit. Make the F section and join to the A-B-C-D-E unit.

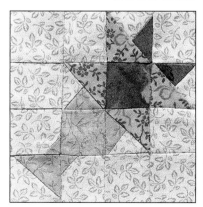

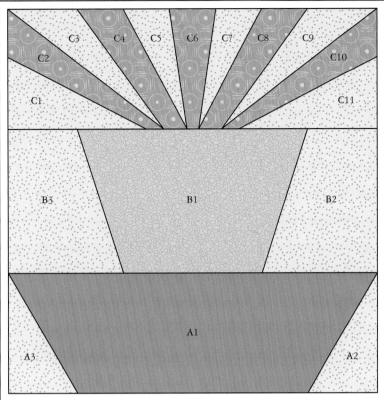

CACTUS FLOWER

F9 Make the A section by joining the A pieces in numerical order. Make the B section and join to the A section. Make the C section and join to the A-B unit.

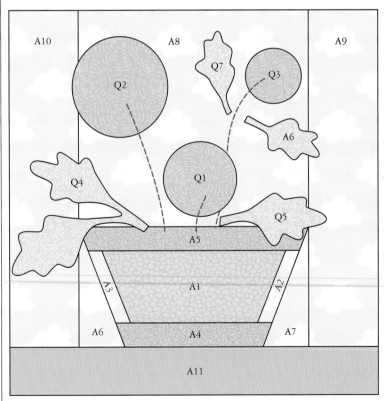

POTTED DAISIES

F10 Make the block by joining the A pieces in numerical order. Appliqué the Q pieces in place. Use stem stitch to embroider flower stems and veins on the leaves.

POTTED CACTUS

F11 Make A section by joining pieces in numerical order. Make B section and join to A section. Make C section and join to the A-B unit. Add D pieces to each side of the A-B-C unit. Add E1 piece to the bottom of the block.

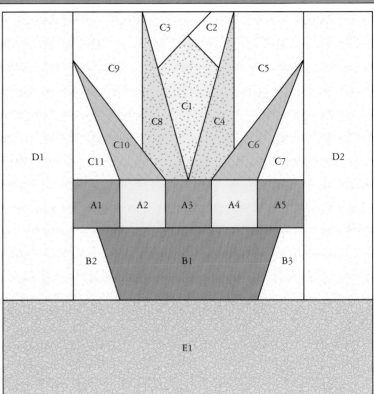

POTTED POSY

F12 Make A section by joining pieces in numerical order. Join B1 and B2 pieces to each side of the A section. Join C1 piece to A-B unit. Appliqué Q1 and Q2 pieces, then add Q3 piece. If desired, embroider French knots on each flower; add lazy daisy stitches for leaves.

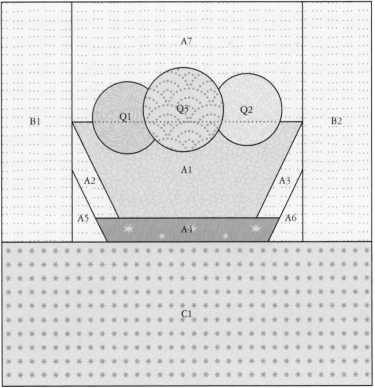

117

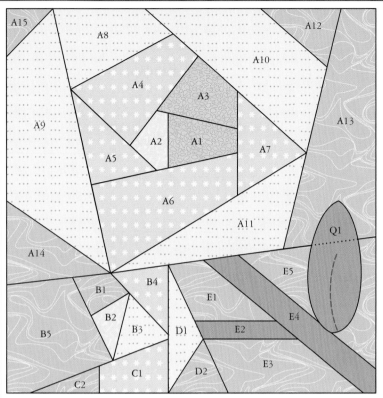

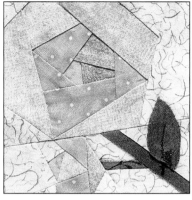

ROSE

F13 Make the A section by joining the A pieces in numerical order. Make the B and C sections and join. Make the D section and join to the B-C unit. Make the E section and join to the B-C-D unit. Join the A section to the B-C-D-E unit. Appliqué the Q1 piece in place. Use stem stitch to embroider a vein on the leaf.

Look Again

(Below) Create a central star motif by rotating and joining four Cabin Bud blocks. The leaves form the star while the flowers are colorful bursts emerging from the center.

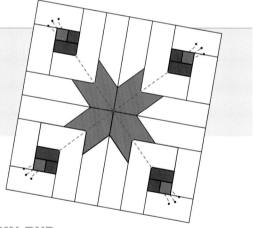

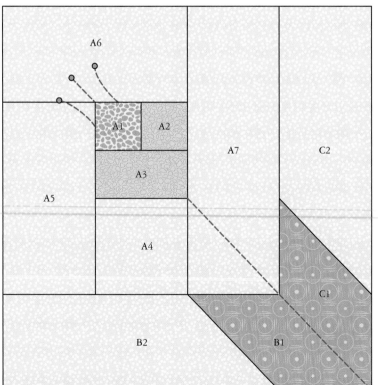

CABIN BUD

F14 Make the A section by joining the A pieces in numerical order. Make the B section and join to the A section. Make the C section and inset into the A-B unit. Use stem stitches for the stem and stamen. Add French knots at the stamen ends.

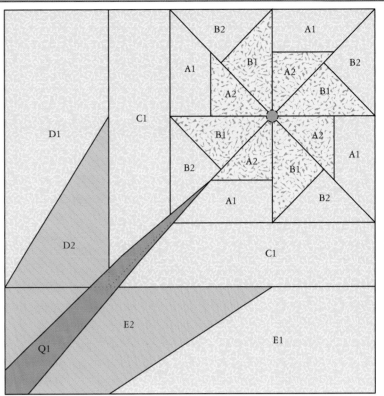

WINDMILL FLOWER

F15 Make 4 A sections by joining the A1 and A2 pieces. Make 4 B sections. Join the A and B sections to make 2 triangle A-B-A-B units. Join a C1 piece to each unit. Join the 2 A-B-A-B-C units. Make the D section and join to the left side of the unit. Make the E section and join to the bottom of the unit. Appliqué the Q1 piece to make the stem. Use satin stitch to embroider the flower center.

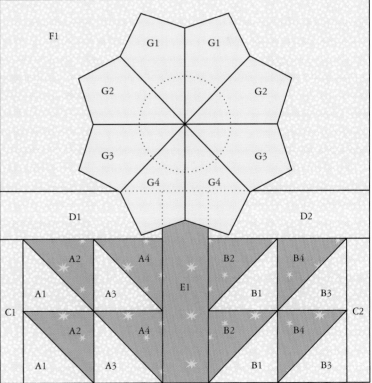

DAFFODIL

F16 Make 2 G sections by joining the G pieces in numerical order. Join the 2 sections. Set aside to appliqué this unit later. Make 2 A sections and join, then join the C1 piece. Make 2 B sections and join, then join the C2 piece. Join the D pieces to the top of the C-A-A and the B-B-C units. Join these units with the E1 piece. Join the F1 piece to the A-B-C-D-E unit. Appliqué the G-G unit in place. Cut a 2$\frac{1}{4}$-inch circle for a yo-yo. Make yo-yo (see instructions, page 313) and attach to the center of the G-G unit.

119

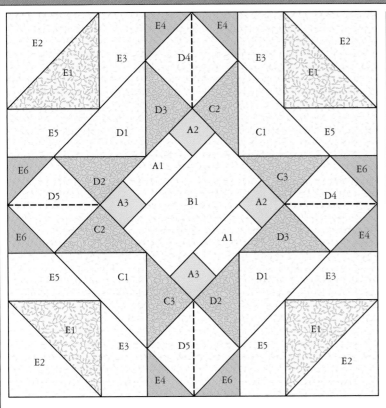

FORGET ME NOT

F17 Make 2 A sections by joining the 3 A pieces. Join A sections to opposite sides of the B1 piece. Make 2 C sections and join to the A-B unit. Make 2 D sections and join to the A-B-C unit. Make 4 E sections and join to the 4 sides of the A-B-C-D unit. Use stem stitch to embroider the flower stems.

Look Again

(Above) When Forget Me Not blocks are combined, an intricate grid pattern appears. Look closely and you'll also see additional diamond and star patterns take shape.

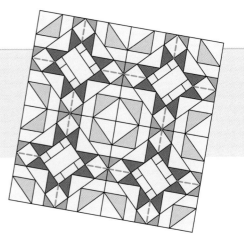

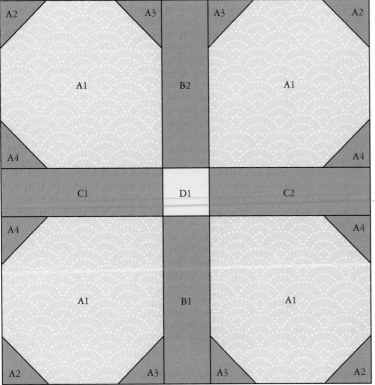

SQUARE FLOWER

F18 Join A pieces in numerical order to make 4 A sections as shown. Join 2 A sections with B1 piece. Join 2 A sections with B2 piece. Make C unit. Join A-B units with C unit to complete the block.

SUNSHINE TULIP

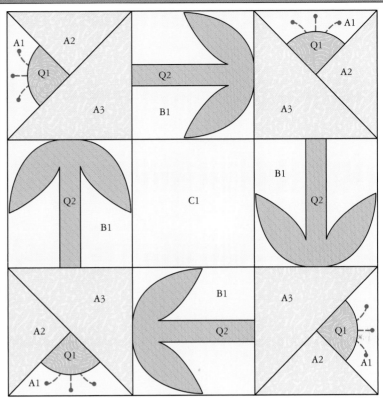

F19 Appliqué the Q1 pieces to the 4 A1 pieces. Join the appliquéd A1 pieces to A2 and A3 to make 4 A sections. Appliqué the Q2 pieces to the four B1 pieces. Join 2 A sections to opposite sides of a B section to make 2 A-B-A units. Join B sections to opposite sides of the C1 piece to make a B-C-B unit. Join the three units to complete the block. Use stem stitch and French knots to embellish the Q1 pieces.

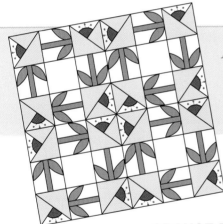

Look Again

(Above) Combine Sunshine Tulip blocks to make origami-looking patterns where the blossoms meet. The way the stems and leaves flip-flop adds movement.

ORANGE POPPY

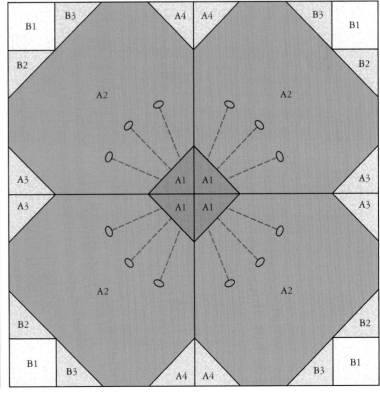

F20 Make 4 A sections by joining the A pieces in numerical order. Join 2 A sections twice. Join the A-A units. Make 4 B sections and join to the corners of the A units. Use stem stitch to embroider stamens, making a French knot at the end of each stamen.

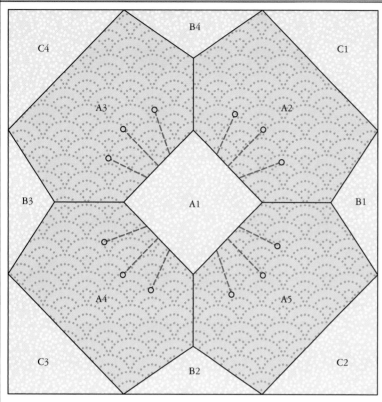

GARDEN FLOWER

F21 Make the A section by joining the A pieces in numerical order. Inset the B pieces in the A units. Join the C pieces to the corners of the block. Use stem stitch to embroider stamens on the flower, using a French knot at the end of each stamen.

Look Again

(Below) The petals of Prairie Flower blocks join to make a continuous grid pattern, made interesting by the circle designs and squares formed in the center of a 4-block unit.

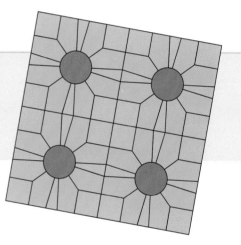

PRAIRIE FLOWER

F22 Make 2 A sections by joining the A pieces in numerical order. Make 2 B sections. Join the A and B sections as shown. Cut a 3-inch fabric circle to make the center yo-yo (see instructions, page 313). Join yo-yo to block; use satin stitch to fill center.

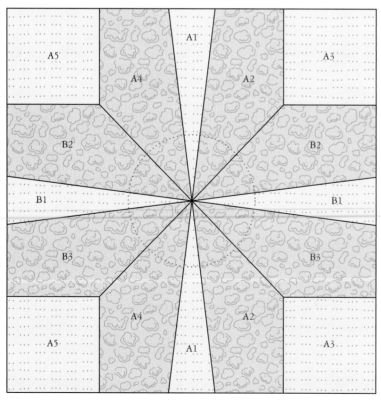

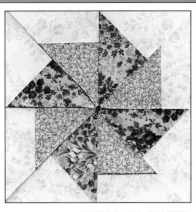

FIELD FLOWER

F23 Make 4 A sections by joining the 2 A pieces. Make 4 B sections. Join the sections into 4 A-B units. Join the units to complete the block. Make a French knot in the center of the flower.

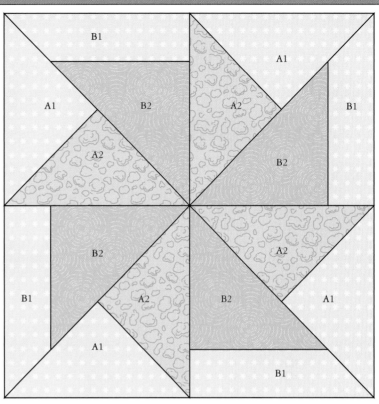

WILDFLOWER

F24 Make the A section by joining the A pieces in numerical order. Make 2 B sections and join to opposite sides of the A sections. Use stem stitch with a French knot to embroider each stamen around the flower center.

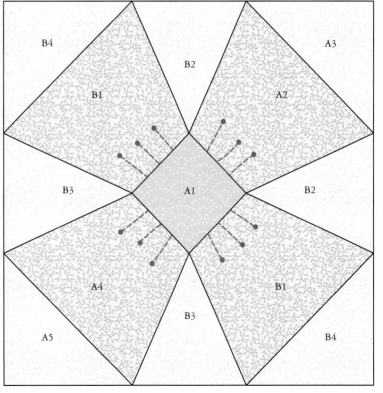

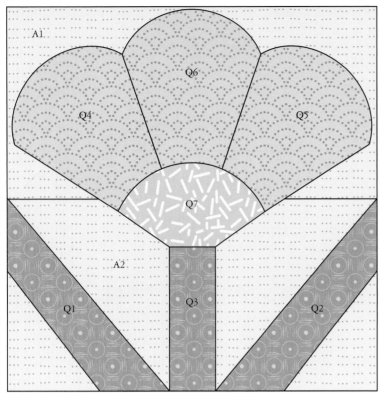

DRESDEN FLOWER

F25 Make background block by joining A1 and A2. Appliqué Q1 and Q2 for leaves, then appliqué Q3. Appliqué flower pieces in numerical order. Embellish flower pieces with buttonhole stitch.

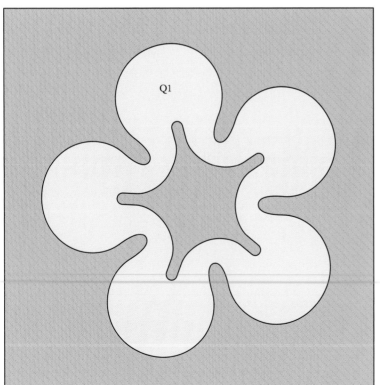

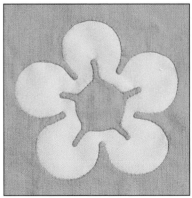

PRETTY REVERSE FLOWER

F26 Hand-appliqué Q1 piece on background block.

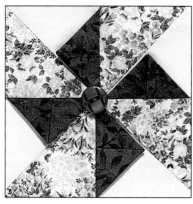

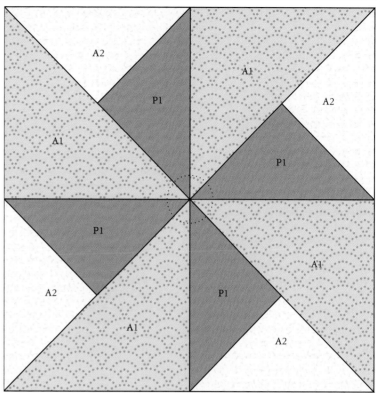

PRAIRIE POINT FLOWER

F27 Cut four 2¹/₂-inch squares and fold into 4 prairie points (P1 pieces). (For prairie point instructions, see page 313.) Sew P to A2 to make AP unit. (Note: A1 and A2 are the same size.) Make 4 A-P units. Join the units to complete the block, stitching the long edge of each prairie point into the seam of the A1 and A2 pieces to make a triangle. Sew a button to the center.

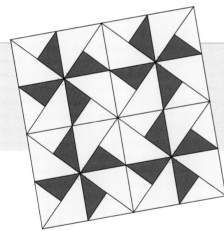

Look Again

(Above) When four Prairie Point Flowers are joined together in a block, the center becomes another flower with the colors rotated.

TULIP

F28 Make the A section by joining the A pieces in numerical order. Make 2 B sections and join to opposite sides of the A section. Make 2 C sections and join with the D1 piece. Join the C-D-C unit to the B-A-B unit.

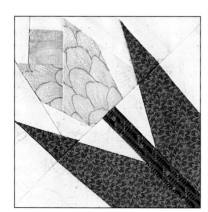

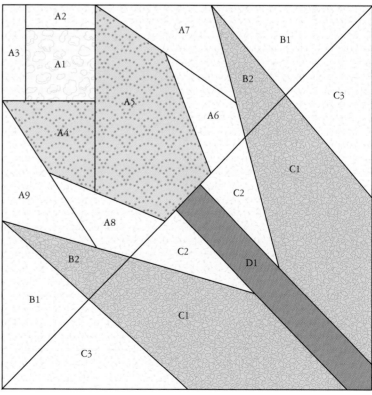

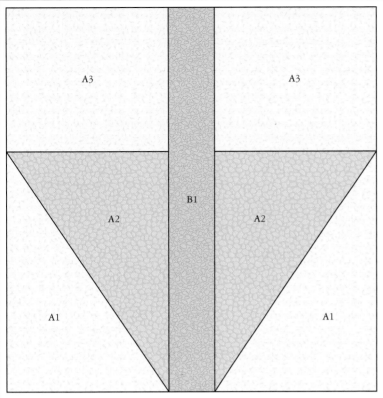

PRAIRIE FLOWER STEM

F29 Make 2 A sections by joining the A pieces in numerical order. Join the A sections to opposite sides of the B1 piece.

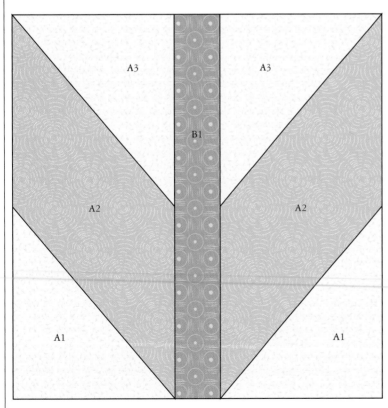

FIELD FLOWER STEM

F30 Make 2 A sections by joining the A pieces in numerical order. Join the A sections to opposite sides of the B1 piece.

WILDFLOWER STEM

F31 Make 2 A sections by joining the A pieces in numerical order. Join the A sections to opposite sides of the B1 piece.

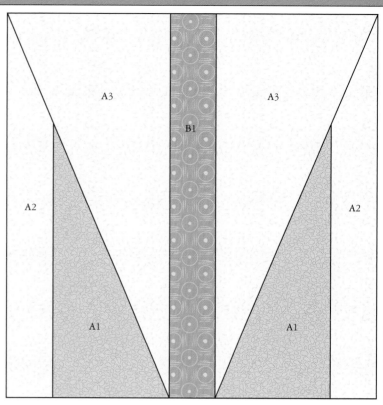

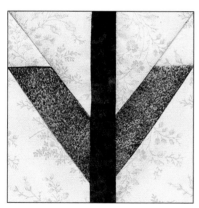

GARDEN FLOWER STEM

F32 Make 2 A sections by joining the A pieces in numerical order. Join the A sections to opposite sides of the B1 piece.

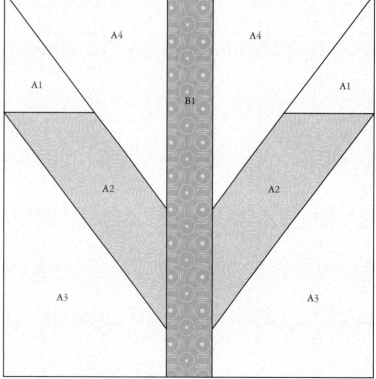

ALABAMA—CAMELLIA

F33 Use lightweight fusible webbing to fuse pieces in numerical order. Machine-appliqué edges and follow pattern lines to add stitching to Q4 piece. Use stem stitch to embroider veins in leaves and the word "Camellia." Fill in the center with French knots stemming from straight stitches. Use a French knot for the dot in the word.

ALASKA—FORGET-ME-NOT

F34 Use lightweight fusible webbing to fuse flower petals in place in numerical order. Machine-appliqué over raw edges. Fuse flower center in place and machine appliqué. Fuse leaf pieces in place and machine-appliqué. Use stem stitch to embroider flower stem and words.

ARIZONA—CACTUS FLOWER

F35 Use lightweight fusible webbing to appliqué pieces in numerical order. Machine-appliqué over edges of all pieces, extending stitching to make flower petals. Use stem stitch to embroider the words.

ARKANSAS—APPLE BLOSSOM

F36 Use lightweight fusible webbing to fuse pieces in numerical order. Machine-appliqué all raw edges. Use stem stitch to embroider flower center, making a French knot at the end of each stamen. Use stem stitch to embroider words.

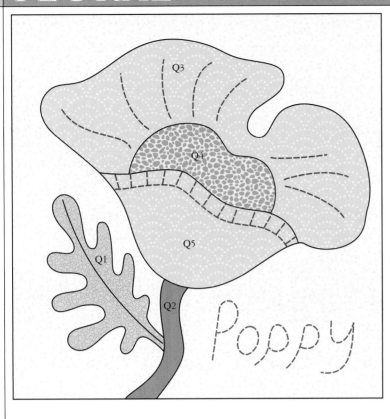

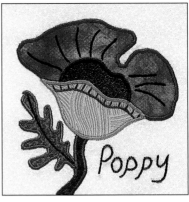

CALIFORNIA—POPPY

F37 Use lightweight fusible webbing to fuse pieces in place in numerical order on background block. Machine-appliqué over raw edges. Use stem stitch to embroider detail on the flower and the leaf and for "Poppy."

COLORADO—COLUMBINE

F38 Cut leaves (Q1) as 1 piece. Use lightweight fusible webbing to fuse all pieces in place in numerical order on background block. Machine-appliqué over raw edges and extend stitching to define petals. Use stem stitch to embroider details on the flower and leaves and "Columbine." Use French knots to fill the flower center.

CONNECTICUT—MT. LAUREL

F39 Use lightweight fusible webbing to fuse leaves to background fabric. Machine-appliqué around the leaf pieces. Appliqué flowers in place. Satin-stitch berries and flower centers, outlining with stem stitches. Use buttonhole stitch around outer edges of the flowers, add straight stitches to each bloom. Use stem stitch to embroider stems and the words. Make a French knot period.

DELAWARE—PEACH BLOSSOM

F40 Use lightweight fusible webbing to fuse pieces in place in numerical order on background block. Machine-appliqué over raw edges and extend stitching to add detail to the petals. Use stem stitch and a French knot to embroider each stamen around the flower center. Use stem stitch for veins on the leaves and the words.

FLORIDA—ORANGE BLOSSOM

F41 Use lightweight fusible webbing to appliqué pieces in numerical order. Machine-appliqué over edges of all pieces. Make flower stem by machine-or hand-embroidered satin stitch. Use stem stitch to embroider words and veins in petals and leaves.

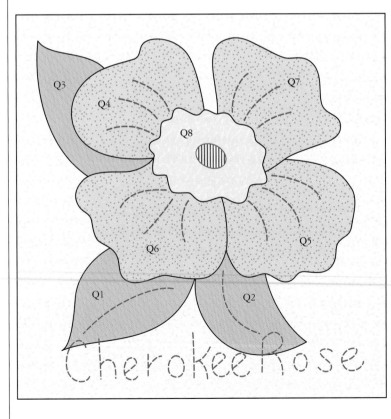

GEORGIA—CHEROKEE ROSE

F42 Use lightweight fusible webbing to appliqué pieces in numerical order. Machine-appliqué over edges of all pieces. Satin-stitch flower center; outline with stem stitch. Use stem stitch to make veins on leaves and petals. Use stem stitch to embroider words.

HAWAII—HIBISCUS

F43 Use lightweight fusible webbing to fuse pieces in numerical order. Machine-appliqué edges of leaves and blossom, making petals of flowers with stitching. Machine-appliqué flower center; satin-stitch stamen. Use stem stitch to outline stamen and to embroider blossom and "Hibiscus." Surround stamen with French knots, and use French knots for the dots in the word.

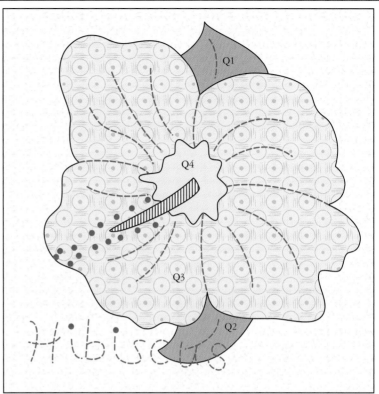

IDAHO—SYRINGA

F44 Use lightweight fusible webbing to appliqué pieces in numerical order. Machine-appliqué over edges of all pieces. Make flower stem by machine- or hand-embroidered satin stitch. Use stem stitch to embroider veins in leaves and petals and flower stamens. Add French knots to each stamen. Use stem stitch to embroider "Syringa, using a French knot to dot the i."

ILLINOIS—VIOLET

F45 Use lightweight fusible webbing to fuse violet and leaves to background block. Machine-appliqué around the edges and machine-satin-stitch a stem. Use stem stitch to embroider leaf stems and leaf veins. Satin-stitch flower center, outlining with stem stitch. Use stem stitch to embroider the word "Violet," dotting the i with a French knot.

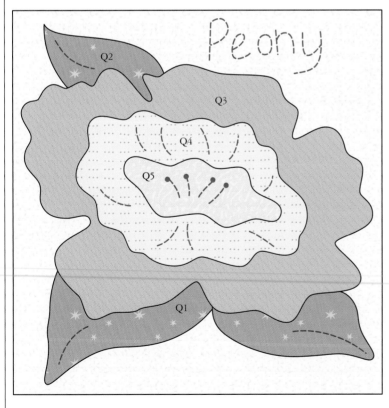

INDIANA—PEONY

F46 Use lightweight fusible webbing to fuse pieces in place in numerical order on background block. Machine-appliqué over raw edges. Use stem stitch to add details on the leaves and petals and for "Peony." Make a French knot at the end of each stamen in the flower center.

IOWA—WILD ROSE

F47 Use lightweight fusible webbing to appliqué pieces in numerical order. Machine-appliqué over edges of all pieces, extending stitching on Q7 piece to define petals. Make flower stem by machine- or hand-embroidered satin stitch. Use stem stitch to embroider veins in leaves and stamens, making a French knot at the end of each stamen. Use stem stitch to embroider words, using a French knot for the dot.

KANSAS—SUNFLOWER

F48 Use lightweight fusible webbing to fuse flower stems and leaves in place. Machine-appliqué over raw edges. Fuse flower bloom and flower center in place and machine-appliqué over edges, extending lines of petals. Use stem stitch to embroider "Sunflower" and veins in leaves. Make French knots around flower center.

KENTUCKY—GOLDENROD

F49 Appliqué the Q pieces in numerical order to the background block. Use stem stitch to embroider a line on the flower stem and for "Goldenrod." Stitch French knots where indicated.

LOUISIANA—MAGNOLIA

F50 Use lightweight fusible webbing to fuse pieces in place in numerical order on background block. Machine-appliqué over raw edges and extend stitching to define flower petals. Use satin stitch to embroider the flower stem, outlining with stem stitch. Use stem stitch to detail the leaves and petals and for "Magnolia."

MAINE—PINECONE TASSEL

F51 Use lightweight fusible webbing to fuse the Q1 piece in place on the background block. Machine-appliqué over raw edges. Use satin stitch to embroider the branch and stem stitch for the pine needles. Use stem stitch for the words with a French knot for the dot.

MARYLAND—BLACK-EYED SUSAN

F52 Use lightweight fusible webbing to fuse pieces in place in numerical order on background block. Machine-appliqué over raw edges. Use stem stitch to embroider the stem and "Black-eyed Susan." Embellish the flower center with straight stitches and French knots.

MASSACHUSETTS—MAYFLOWER

F53 Use lightweight fusible webbing to fuse pieces in place in numerical order on background block. Machine-appliqué over all raw edges. Use satin stitch to make stems and flower centers. Use stem stitch to embroider veins on leaves and petals, to outline flower centers, and for "Mayflower."

MICHIGAN—APPLE BLOSSOM

F54 Use lightweight fusible webbing to fuse pieces in place in numerical order on background block. Machine-appliqué over all raw edges and to define flower petals. Use satin stitch to make stem and base of flower bud. Use stem stitch to embroider a vein on the leaf and stamens around flower center. Make a French knot at the end of each stamen. Use stem stitch to embroider the words.

MINNESOTA—SHOWY LADY SLIPPER

F55 Use lightweight fusible webbing to fuse the Q pieces in numerical order to the background block. Machine-appliqué over raw edges. Use satin stitch to embroider the flower stem. Use stem stitch to embroider veins on the leaves and petals and for the words. Use a French knot to dot the i.

MISSISSIPPI—MAGNOLIA

F56 Use lightweight fusible webbing to fuse pieces in place in numerical order on background block. Machine-appliqué over raw edges and extend stitching to define the petals. Use stem stitch to embroider detail on the petals and leaves and for "Magnolia." Fill the center of the flower with French knots. Use a French knot to dot the i.

MISSOURI—RED HAWTHORN

F57 Appliqué the Q pieces in numerical order to the background block. Use stem stitch to embroider definition lines on the petals and to make veins on the leaves and petals. Make a ring of French knots around each flower center. Use stem stitch to embroider the words.

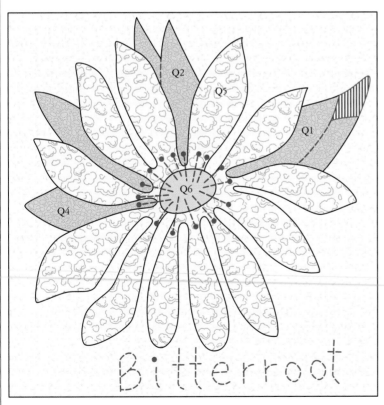

MONTANA—BITTERROOT

F58 Use lightweight fusible webbing to fuse pieces in place in numerical order on background block. Machine-appliqué over raw edges and extend stitching to define leaves. Use satin stitch to make the flower bud. Use stem stitch to embroider the center stamens and "Bitterroot." Make French knots at the end of each stamen. Use a French knot to dot the i.

NEBRASKA—GOLDENROD

F59 Use lightweight fusible webbing to fuse pieces in place in numerical order on background block. Machine-appliqué over all raw edges. Use satin stitch to make flower stem. Use stem stitch to embroider blooms; use French knots along each vein. Use stem stitch to embroider "Goldenrod."

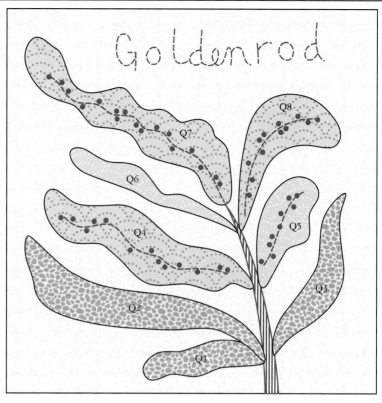

NEVADA—SAGEBRUSH

F60 Use lightweight fusible webbing to fuse the Q1 piece in place on the background block. Machine-appliqué over raw edges. Use stem stitch and lazy daisies to embroider the flowers. Use stem stitch for "Sagebrush."

NEW HAMPSHIRE—LILAC

F61 Use lightweight fusible webbing to fuse pieces in place in numerical order on background block. Machine-appliqué over raw edges. The top 3 blossoms are embroidered using satin stitch outlined with stem stitch. Use stem stitch to embroider stems, the veins on the leaves, the stamens on the top bloom, and "Lilac." Make French knots in the center of each bloom and at the ends of the stamens.

NEW JERSEY—VIOLET

F62 Use lightweight fusible webbing to fuse pieces in place in numerical order on background block. Machine-appliqué over all raw edges. Use satin stitch to make stems. Use stem stitch to embroider veins on leaves and petals and for "Violet." Use French knots to cover the flower center.

NEW MEXICO—YUCCA FLOWER

F63 Use lightweight fusible webbing to fuse pieces in place in numerical order on background block. Machine-appliqué over raw edges and extend stitching to outline flower petals. Use satin stitch to embroider stems on leaves and blossoms. Use stem stitch for the veins in the leaves and "Yucca Flower."

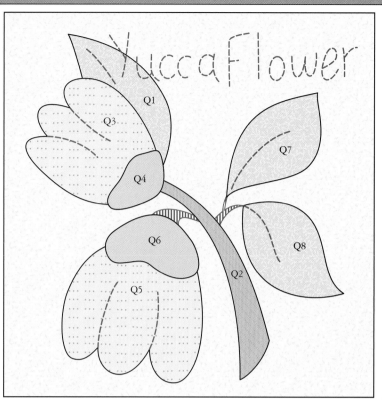

NEW YORK—ROSE

F64 Appliqué the Q pieces in numerical order to the background block. Extend machine-appliqué stitch or use stem stitch to embroider definition lines on the petals. Use satin stitch to stitch flower bud on Q7 and the leaf on Q4. Use stem stitch to embroider veins on the leaves. Use stem stitch with a French knot at each end to add stamens to the buds. Use straight stitches and French knots for the stamens around the flower center. Use stem stitch to embroider "Rose."

143

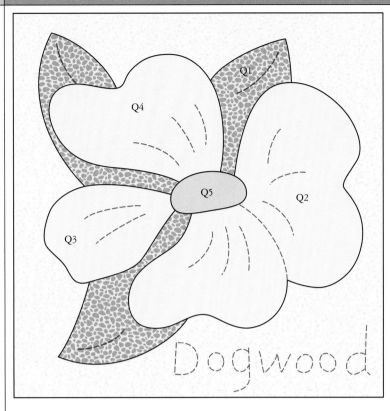

NORTH CAROLINA—DOGWOOD

F65 Use lightweight fusible webbing to fuse pieces in place in numerical order on background block. Machine-appliqué over raw edges and extend stitching to define petals on the Q2 piece. Use stem stitch to embroider detail on the petals and leaves and for "Dogwood."

NORTH DAKOTA—PRAIRIE ROSE

F66 Use lightweight fusible webbing to fuse pieces in place in numerical order on background block. Machine-appliqué over raw edges and extend stitching to define flower petals. Use stem stitch to embroider the stems on the leaves, the veins in the leaves, detail on the petals, and the words, using French knots for the dots.

OHIO—CARNATION

F67 Use lightweight fusible webbing to fuse pieces in place in numerical order on background block. Machine-appliqué over raw edges and extend stitching to detail flower stem and flower bud. Use stem stitch to embroider "Carnation." Use a French knot to dot the i.

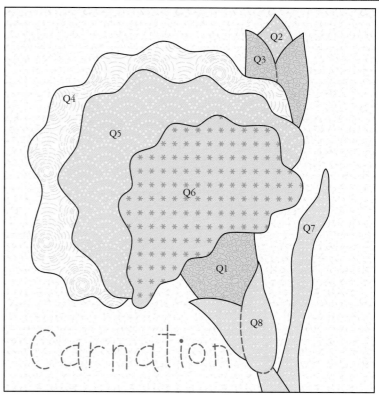

OKLAHOMA—MISTLETOE

F68 Use lightweight fusible webbing to fuse Q1 in place on background block. Machine-appliqué over all raw edges and define leaf as shown. Use satin stitch to make berries. Use stem stitch to outline berries, for stems, veins on leaves, and for "Mistletoe." Use a French knot to dot the i.

OREGON—OREGON GRAPE

F69 Use lightweight fusible webbing to fuse pieces in place in numerical order on background block. Machine-appliqué over all raw edges and as indicated on the center. Use stem stitch to embroider veins on the leaves and the words. Make 5 or 6 French knots within each stitched center outline.

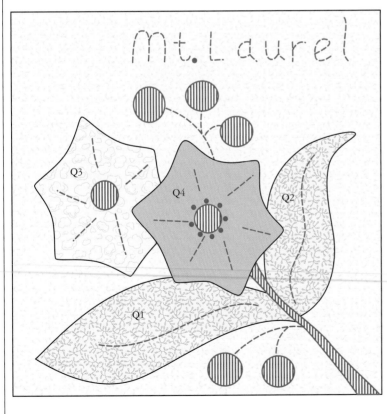

PENNSYLVANIA—MT. LAUREL

F70 Use lightweight fusible webbing to fuse pieces in place in numerical order on background block. Machine-appliqué over all raw edges. Use satin stitch to make flower stem, berries, and flower centers. Outline berries and flower centers with stem stitch. Make French knots in the center of Q4. Use stem stitch to embroider veins on leaves, berry stems, and for the words. Make a French knot period. Use straight stitches on each blossom.

RHODE ISLAND—VIOLET

F71 Use lightweight fusible webbing to fuse pieces in place in numerical order on background block. Machine-appliqué over all raw edges and to define petals. Use satin stitch to make stems and to embroider the flower center. Use stem stitch to embroider outline on the center, veins on leaves and petals, and for "Violet."

SOUTH CAROLINA—JESSAMINE

F72 Use lightweight fusible webbing to fuse pieces in place in numerical order on background block. Machine-appliqué over raw edges. Use stem stitch to embroider detail on the leaves and petals and for "Jessamine."

Pasqueflower

SOUTH DAKOTA—PASQUEFLOWER

F73 Use lightweight fusible webbing to fuse pieces in place in numerical order on background block. Machine-appliqué over raw edges, extending stitching to detail the petals. Use stem stitch to embroider detail on the base of the flower and for the word.

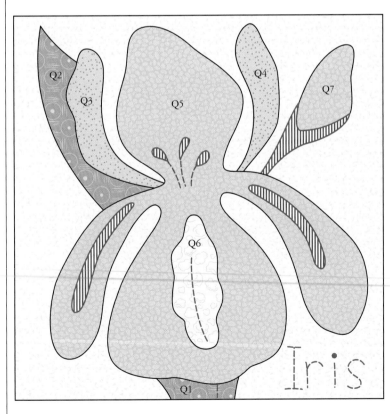

TENNESSEE—IRIS

F74 Use lightweight fusible webbing to fuse pieces in place in numerical order on background block. Machine-appliqué over all raw edges. Use satin stitch to make stem for bud. Use satin stitch to embroider petals, outlining stitching with stem stitch. Use stem stitch to embroider other lines and stamens. Fill in stamens with satin stitch. Use stem stitch to embroider "Iris."

TEXAS—BLUEBONNET

F75 Use lightweight fusible webbing to fuse the Q pieces in place in numerical order on background block. Machine-appliqué over raw edges, extending stitching to detail the petals. Use satin stitch to embroider the flower stem and the top blossoms of the flower. Use stem stitch to embroider "Bluebonnet."

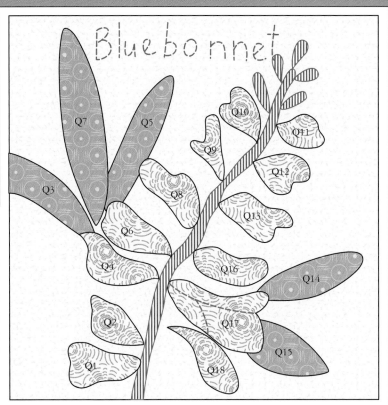

UTAH—SEGO LILY

F76 Use lightweight fusible webbing to fuse pieces in place in numerical order on background block. Machine-appliqué over raw edges and extend stitching to detail the petals. Use stem stitch and satin stitch to embroider stamens on the flower. Use stem stitch for the words.

VERMONT—RED CLOVER

F77 Use lightweight fusible webbing to fuse pieces in place in numerical order on background block. Machine-appliqué over raw edges. Use satin stitch to embroider the stem, then outline with stem stitch. Use stem stitch and straight stitches to embroider details on the leaves. Use stem stitch and French knots to embellish the blossom. Use stem stitch for "Red Clover."

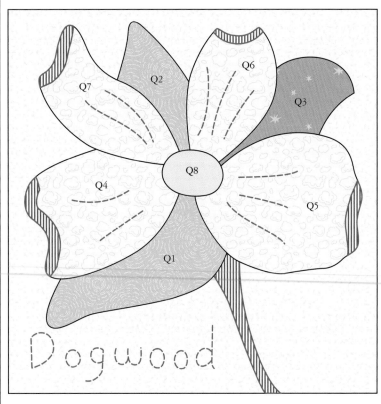

VIRGINIA—DOGWOOD

F78 Use lightweight fusible webbing to fuse pieces in numerical order on background block. Machine-appliqué over all raw edges. Use satin stitch to make flower stem and trim petals. Use stem stitch to embroider the flower petals and "Dogwood."

WASHINGTON—RHODODENDRON

F79 Use lightweight fusible webbing to fuse pieces in place in numerical order on background block. Machine-appliqué over all raw edges and as indicated on the center. Use stem stitch to embroider veins in leaves and petals, stamens in flower center, and "Rhododendron." Make a French knot at the end of each stamen.

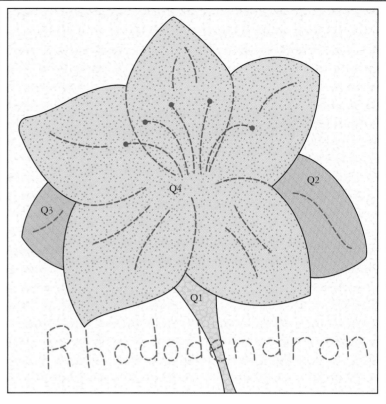

WEST VIRGINIA—RHODODENDRON

F80 Use lightweight fusible webbing to fuse pieces in place in numerical order on background block. Machine-appliqué over all raw edges and as indicated on Q4. Use stem stitch to embroider veins in leaves and petals, stamens in flower center, and "Rhododendron." Make a French knot at the end of each stamen.

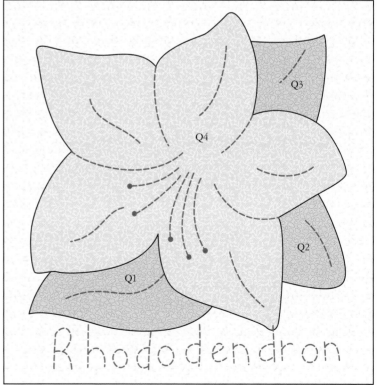

Wood Violet

Wood Violet

WISCONSIN—WOOD VIOLET

F81 Use lightweight fusible webbing to fuse leaf, flower, and bud in place on the background block. Machine-appliqué over raw edges and along each petal. Use satin stitch to make all the stems and to add to flower bud. Use satin stitch to make flower center; outline it with stem stitch. Use stem stitch to embroider veins in leaves and petals and the words.

Indian Paintbrush

Indian Paintbrush

WYOMING—INDIAN PAINTBRUSH

F82 Use lightweight fusible webbing to fuse pieces in place in numerical order on background block. Machine-appliqué over all raw edges. Use stem stitch to embellish bloom and to embroider words.

APPLE

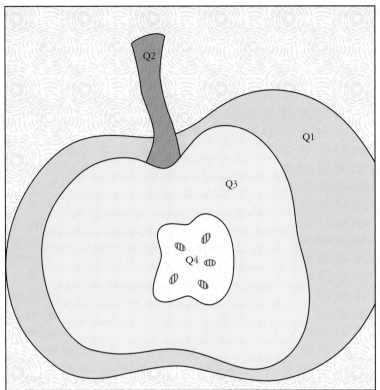

G1 Appliqué the Q pieces in numerical order to the background block. Use satin stitch to embroider the apple seeds.

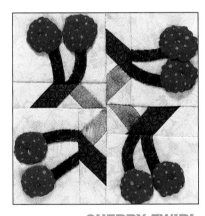

CHERRY TWIRL

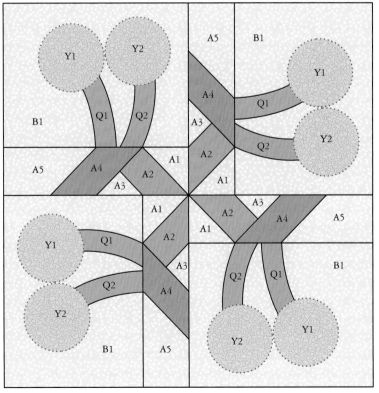

G2 Make 4 A sections by joining the A pieces in numerical order. Appliqué the Q1 and Q2 pieces to the four B1 pieces. Join the 4 A sections to the 4 B sections. Join the 4 A-B units. Make 8 cherries by cutting 1-inch fabric circles. Cut a cardboard circle the size of a penny and gather each fabric circle around the cardboard. Remove the cardboard and insert a small amount of batting. Appliqué the cherries to the block. Add a tiny stitch to each cherry to dimple.

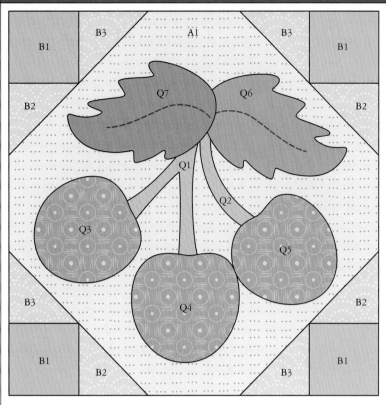

CHERRIES

G3 Center appliqué (Q pieces) on the A1 piece. Appliqué pieces in numerical order. Use stem stitch to embroider veins on the leaves. Make 4 B sections. Join the B sections to the sides of the appliquéd A section.

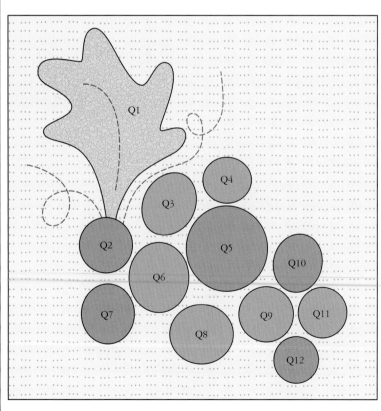

GRAPES

G4 Appliqué the Q pieces in numerical order to the background block. Use stem stitch to embroider the grape vine tendrils and the vein on the leaf.

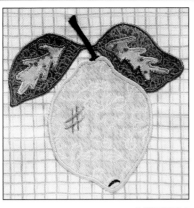

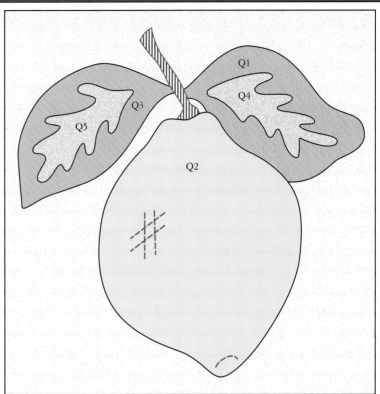

LEMON

G5 Appliqué the Q pieces in numerical order to the background block. Use satin stitch to embroider the stem. Use stem stitch to embellish the lemon.

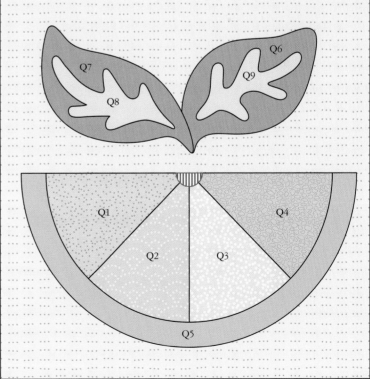

ORANGE SLICE

G6 Appliqué the Q pieces in numerical order to the background block. Use satin stitch for the center of the orange.

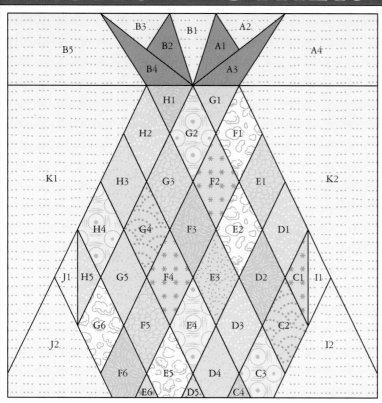

PINEAPPLE

G7 Make the A section by joining the A pieces in numerical order. Make the B section and join to the A section. Make the C, D, E, F, G, and H sections and join to make the C-D-E-F-G-H unit. Join the I and J pieces to each side of the C-D-E-F-G-H unit. Join the K pieces. Join the A-B unit to the top of the block.

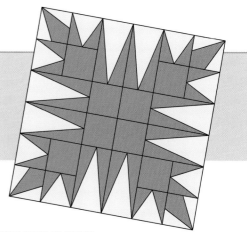

Look Again

(Below) Rotate four Pineapple Top blocks to make the interesting pattern, right. Depending on the fabric colors used, this block can resemble a snowflake, Aztec design, or leaf pattern.

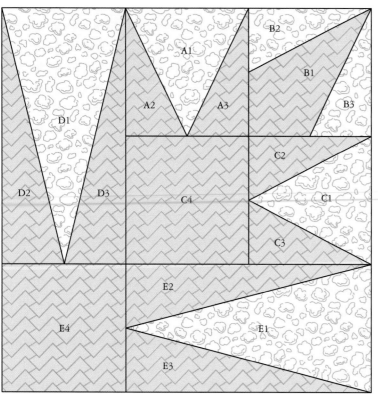

PINEAPPLE TOP

G8 Make the A section by joining the A pieces in numerical order. Make the B section and join to the A section. Make the C section and join to the the A-B unit. Make the D section and join to the A-B-C unit. Make the E section and join to the A-B-C-D unit.

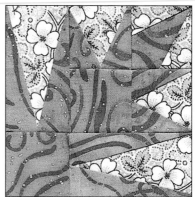

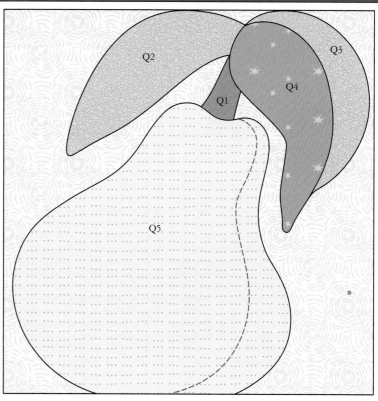

PEAR

G9 Appliqué the Q1 and Q2 pieces in place on the background block. Join the Q3 and Q4 pieces and appliqué as 1 unit. Appliqué the Q5 piece. Use stem stitch to embroider the line on the pear.

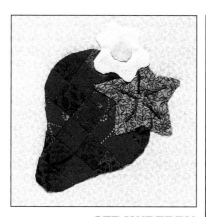

STRAWBERRY

G10 Piece rows of $1/2$-inch squares, making the A, B, C, D, E, and F sections. Join the sections and cut the strawberry shape. Appliqué strawberry to the background block. Appliqué the Q pieces in numerical order. Use stem stitch to embroider veins on the leaves.

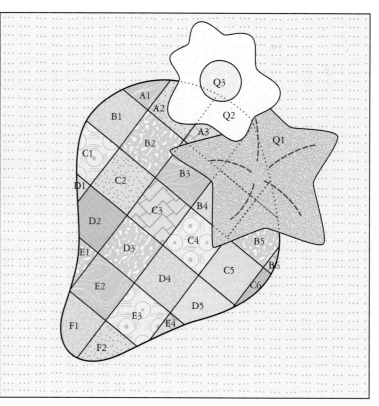

157

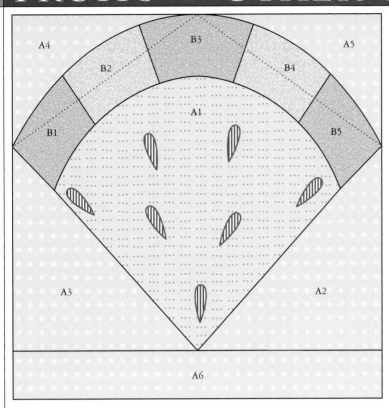

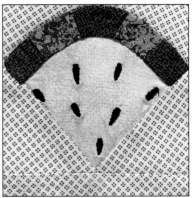

WATERMELON SLICE

G11 Make the A section by joining the A pieces in numerical order. Make the B section by joining the pieces, then appliqué the B section to the A section. Satin-stitch seeds to complete the block.

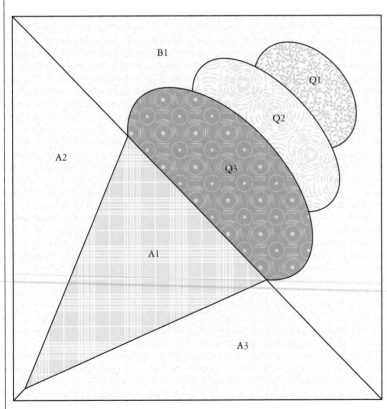

ICE CREAM

G12 Make the A section by joining the A pieces in numerical order. Appliqué the Q pieces in numerical order to the B1 piece. Join the B-Q unit to the A section.

PEAR

G9 Appliqué the Q1 and Q2 pieces in place on the background block. Join the Q3 and Q4 pieces and appliqué as 1 unit. Appliqué the Q5 piece. Use stem stitch to embroider the line on the pear.

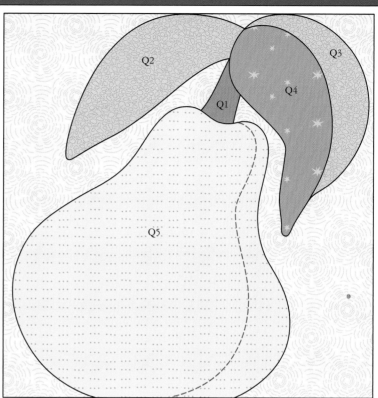

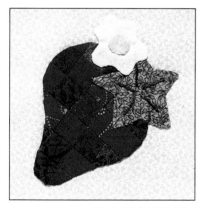

STRAWBERRY

G10 Piece rows of ¹/₂-inch squares, making the A, B, C, D, E, and F sections. Join the sections and cut the strawberry shape. Appliqué strawberry to the background block. Appliqué the Q pieces in numerical order. Use stem stitch to embroider veins on the leaves.

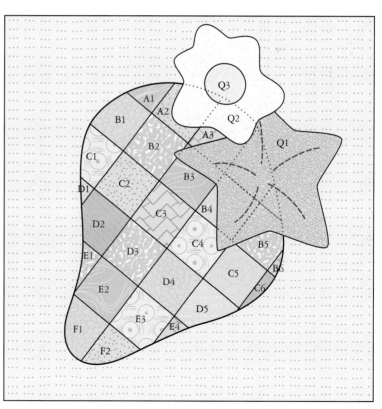

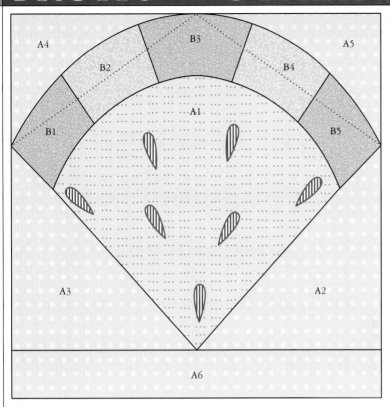

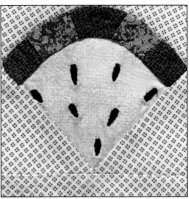

WATERMELON SLICE

G11 Make the A section by joining the A pieces in numerical order. Make the B section by joining the pieces, then appliqué the B section to the A section. Satin-stitch seeds to complete the block.

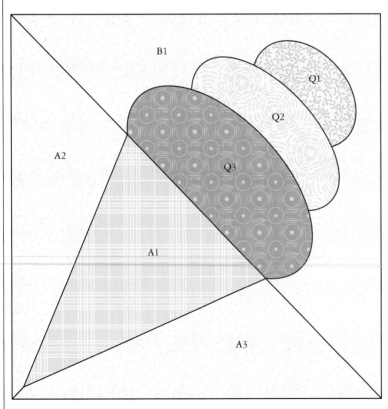

ICE CREAM

G12 Make the A section by joining the A pieces in numerical order. Appliqué the Q pieces in numerical order to the B1 piece. Join the B-Q unit to the A section.

COTTON CANDY

G13 Make the A section by joining the A pieces in numerical order. Appliqué the Q1 piece to the B1 piece. Use machine appliqué stitch or stem stitch to embroider detail on the cotton candy. Join the B-Q section to the A section.

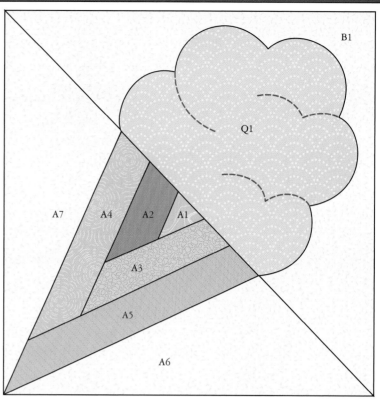

CUPCAKE

G14 Make the A section by joining the A pieces in numerical order. Appliqué the Q1 piece to the B1 piece, then appliqué the Q2 piece. Join the B section to the A section. Join the C1 piece to the A-B unit. Use satin stitch to embroider the flame on the candle. Use stem stitch or machine embroidery to add lines on the cupcake.

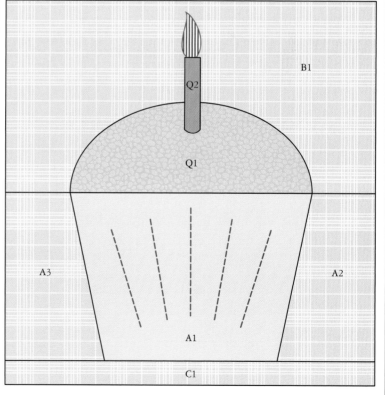

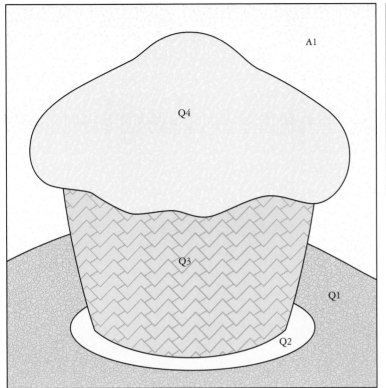

A MUFFIN A DAY

G15 Appliqué the Q1 piece to the background block (A1). Appliqué Q2 piece, then Q3 and Q4.

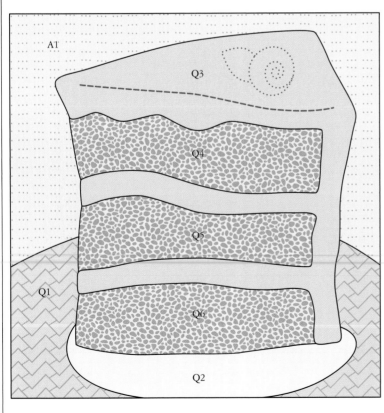

PIECE OF CAKE

G16 Appliqué the Q1 piece to the background block (A1). Appliqué Q2 piece in place. Make the piece of cake by appliquéing Q4, Q5, and Q6 pieces to the Q3 piece, then appliqué the completed unit to the block. Use stem stitch to embroider line in the frosting. Add a ribbon rose to decorate the cake.

PETIT FOUR

G17 Appliqué the Q pieces in numerical order to the background block. Use running stitch to embroider lines on the plate and frosting. If desired, sew ribbon roses on the cake and plate to embellish.

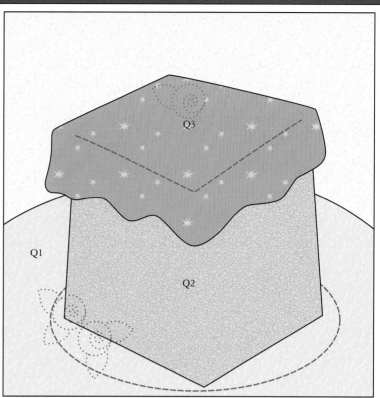

PIECE OF PIE

G18 Appliqué the Q1 piece to the background block, then appliqué Q2 piece. Cut vent holes (Q5, Q6, Q7) in the Q3 piece and reverse-appliqué, using a small piece of the Q4 fabric. Appliqué the Q4 piece to the Q3 piece, then appliqué unit in place. Use stem stitch to embroider lines on the pie crust.

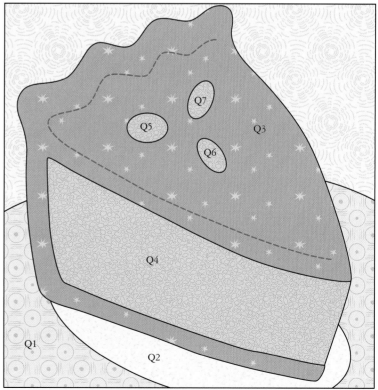

161

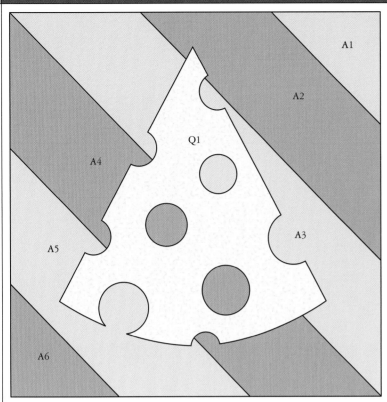

SWISS CHEESE

G19 Make the background block by joining the A pieces in numerical order. Appliqué the Q1 piece to the background block.

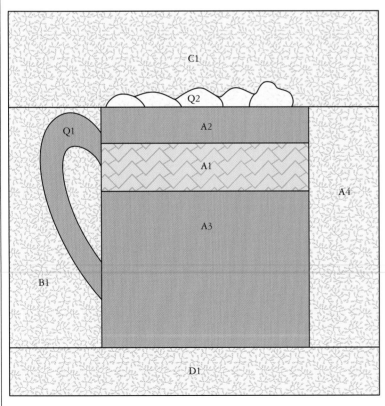

HOT CHOCOLATE

G20 Make the A section by joining the A pieces in numerical order. Appliqué the Q1 piece to the B1 piece, then join to the A section. Appliqué the Q2 piece to the C1 piece, then join to the A-B unit. Join the D1 piece to the A-B-C unit to complete the block.

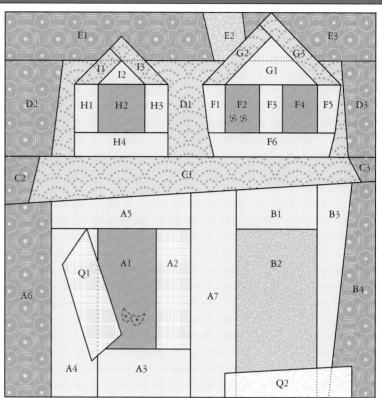

HAUNTED HOUSE

H1 Make the A section by joining the A pieces in numerical order. Make the B section and join to the A section. Make the C section and join to the A-B unit. Make the D and E sections and join. Join the D-E unit to the A-B-C unit. Make the F and G sections and join. Make the H and I sections and join. Appliqué the F-G and H-I units in place on top of D and E sections. Appliqué the Q1 and Q2 pieces in place. Embroider eyes in windows.

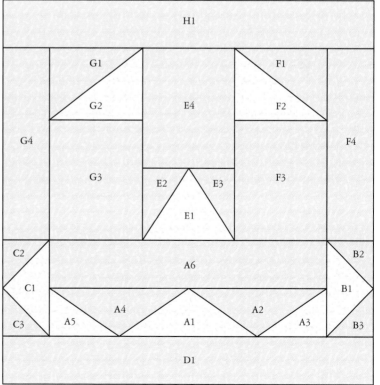

JACK-O'-LANTERN

H2 Make the A section by joining the A pieces in numerical order. Make the B and C sections and join to opposite sides of the A section. Join the D1 piece to the A-B-C unit. Make the E, F, and G sections and join. Join the H1 piece to the E-F-G unit. Join the A-B-C-D unit to the E-F-G-H unit.

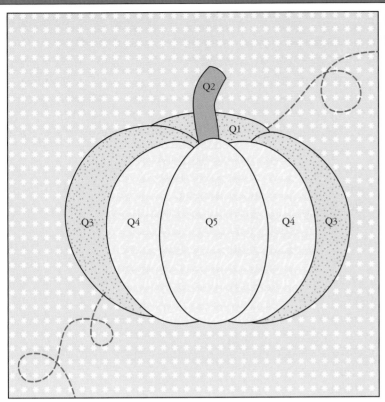

PUMPKIN

H3 Appliqué the Q1 piece on the background block. Make the Q2 piece by enclosing a piece of cording in the fabric and appliqué in place. Appliqué the Q3 piece. Place a small amount of batting under the Q4 piece and appliqué in place. Add batting under the Q5 piece and appliqué. Tack a piece of green cord in place for the vine or use stem stitch to embroider it.

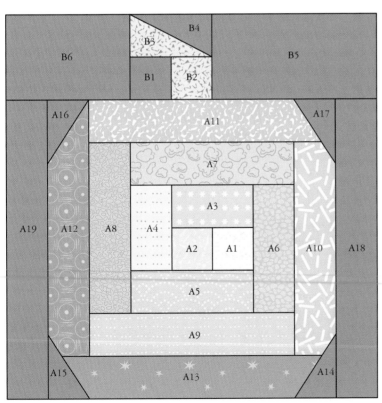

PATCHY PUMPKIN

H4 Make the A section by joining the A pieces in numerical order. Make the B section and join to the A section.

TRICK OR TREAT

H5 Join the pieces of the A section. Appliqué the A section to the background block. Make 3 B sections. Appliqué the 3 B sections in place.

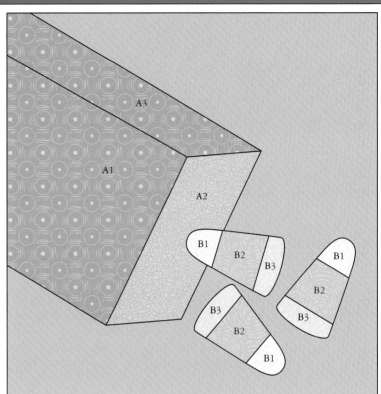

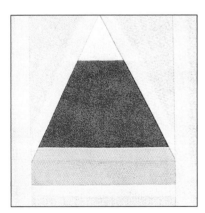

CANDY CORN

H6 Join the A pieces in numerical order to complete the block.

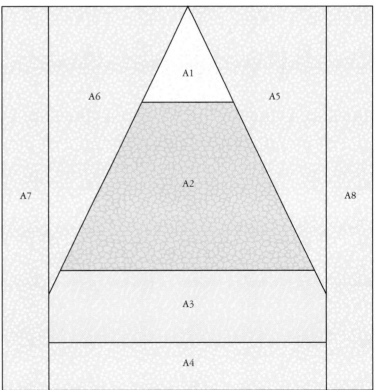

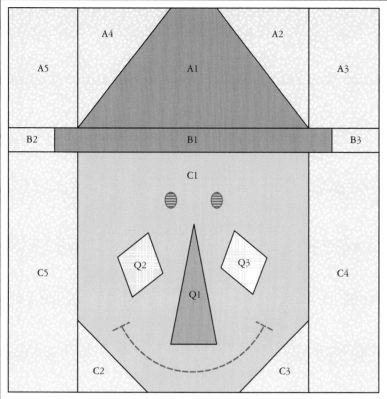

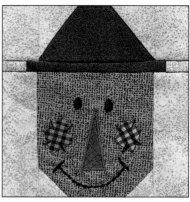

SCARECROW

H7 Make the A section by joining the A pieces in numerical order. Make the B section and join to the A section. Make the C section and join to the A-B unit. Appliqué the Q pieces in place. Use straight stitches around the Q2 and Q3 pieces. Use stem stitch to embroider the mouth. Use satin stitch for the eyes.

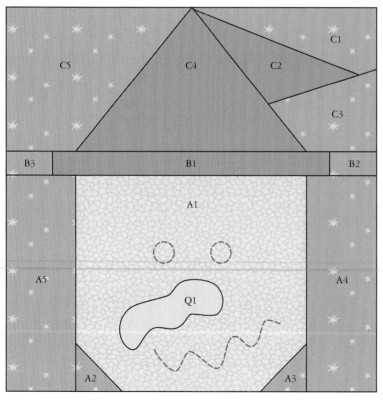

WITCH'S FACE

H8 Make the A section by joining the A pieces in numerical order. Make the B section and join to the A section. Make the C section and join to the A-B unit. Appliqué the Q1 piece for the nose. Machine-zig-zag or hand-embroider buttonhole stitch for the eyes. Machine-appliqué or stem-stitch the mouth.

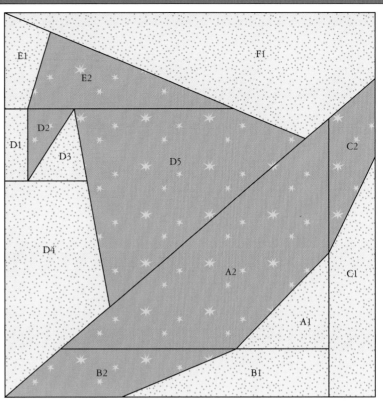

WITCH'S HAT

H9 Make the A section by joining the 2 A pieces. Make the B and C sections and join to the A section to make the A-B-C unit. Make the D and E sections and join. Join the F1 piece to the D-E unit. Join the D-E-F unit to the A-B-C unit. Hand-stitch narrow ribbon to the hat and tie a bow.

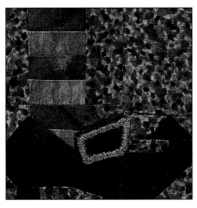

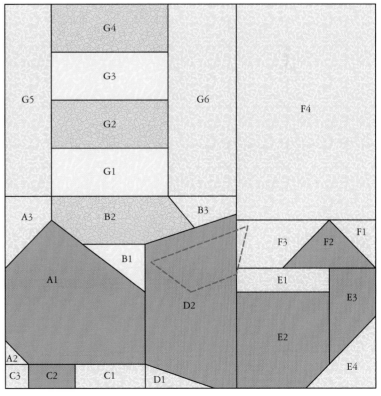

WITCH'S SHOE

H10 Make the A section by joining the A pieces in numerical order. Make the B and C sections and join to the A section. Make the D section and inset into the A-B-C unit. Make the E and F units and join. Make the G unit and join to the A-B-C-D unit. Join the E-F unit to the A-B-C-D-G unit. Use satin stitch to embroider a buckle on the shoe.

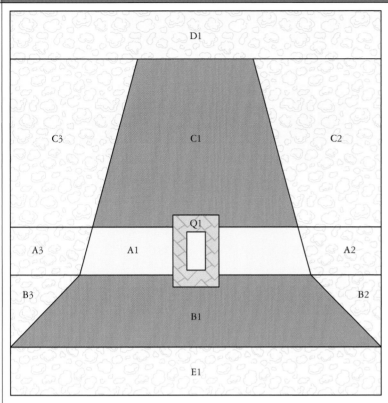

PILGRIM HAT

H11 Make the A section by joining the A pieces in numerical order. Make the B and C sections and join to the A section to make the A-B-C unit. Join the D1 and E1 pieces to the top and bottom of the block. Appliqué the Q1 piece in place to make the buckle on the hat.

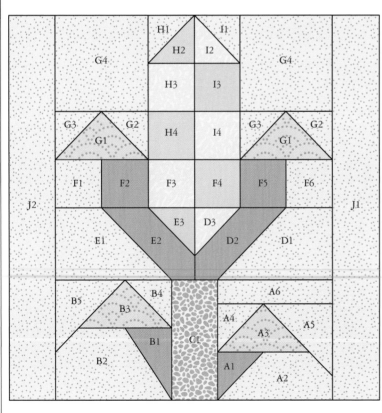

INDIAN CORN

H12 Make the A section by joining the A pieces in numerical order. Make the B section. Join the A and B sections to C1 to make the A-B-C unit. Make the D and E sections and join. Join the D-E unit to the A-B-C unit. Make the F section and join to the completed unit. Make 2 G sections, the H and I sections, and join to make the G-H-I-G unit. Join to the A-B-C-D-E-F unit. Join the J pieces to opposite sides of the completed unit.

GINGERBREAD MAN

H13 Make the A section by joining the A pieces in numerical order. Make the B and C sections. (If desired, rickrack or other trim may be stitched to the B1, C1, B4, and C4 pieces before assembly.) Join the B and C sections and inset the D1 piece. Join the B-C-D unit to the A section. Join the E pieces to opposite sides of the A-B-C-D unit. Use stem stitch to embroider the mouth. Use French knots for eyes. Sew buttons in place.

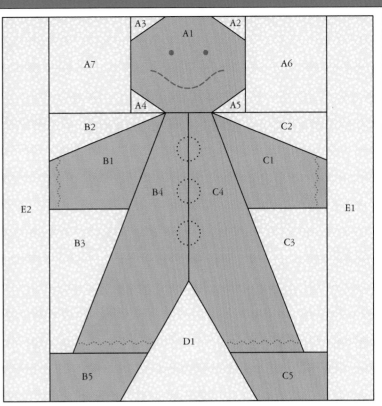

SANTA CLAUS

H14 Appliqué the Q1 piece to the A1 piece. Make the A section by joining the remaining A pieces in numerical order. Make the B section and join to the A section. Make the C section and join to the A-B unit. Machine- or hand-embroider nose and eyes. Sew a button to the tip of the cap.

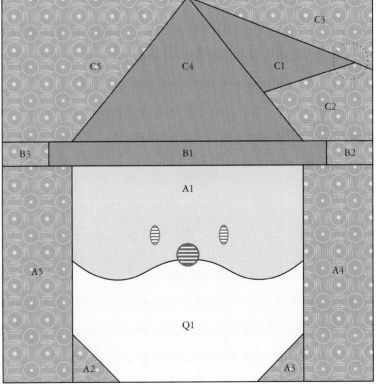

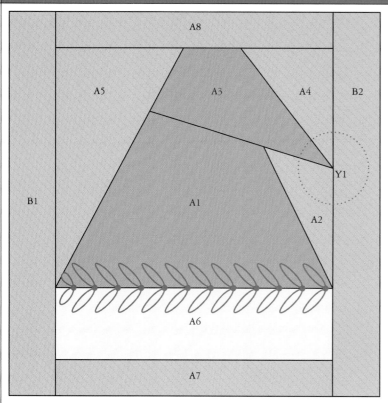

SANTA'S HAT

H15 Make the A section by joining the A pieces in numerical order. Join the B1 and B2 pieces to opposite sides of the A section. Cut a 2-inch circle to make a yo-yo; attach it to the point of the hat. (For yo-yo instructions, see page 313.) Use lazy daisy stitches and French knots to embellish the hat.

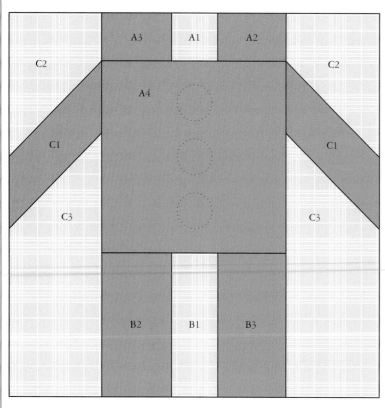

RED LONG JOHNS

H16 Make the A section by joining the A pieces in numerical order. Make the B section and join to the A section. Make 2 C sections and join to opposite sides of the A-B unit. Sew 3 small buttons to the A4 piece.

OH CHRISTMAS TREE

H17 Make the A section by joining the A pieces in numerical order. Make the B, C, and D sections and join to the A section to make the A-B-C-D unit. Make the E section and join to the bottom of the block.

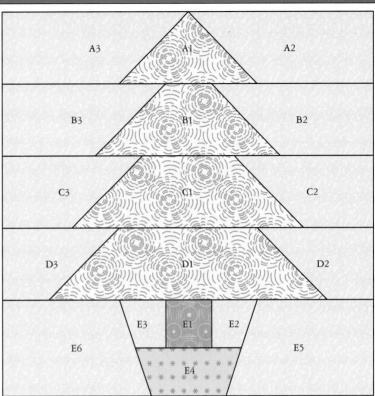

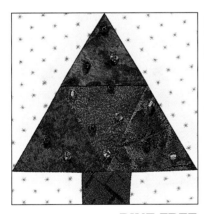

PINE TREE

H18 Make the A section by joining the A pieces in numerical order. Make the B section and join to the A section to complete the block. Embellish the tree with beads or small buttons.

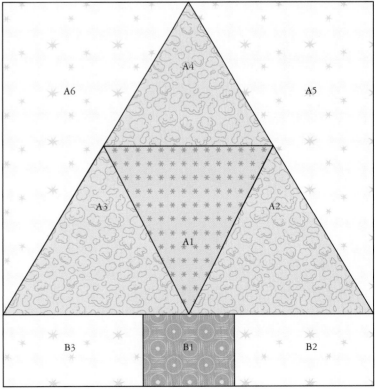

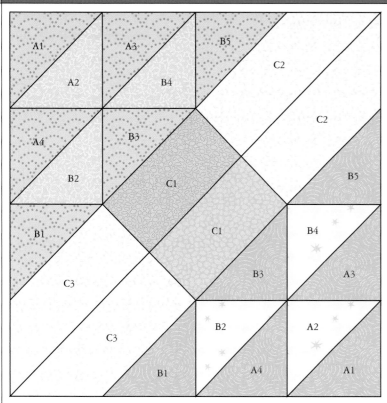

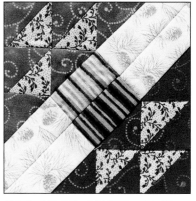

RED TREE–GREEN TREE

H19 Make 2 A sections by joining the A pieces in numerical order. Make 2 B sections and join to the 2 A sections to make 2 A-B units. Make 2 C sections. Join a C section to each A-B unit. Join the 2 A-B-C units.

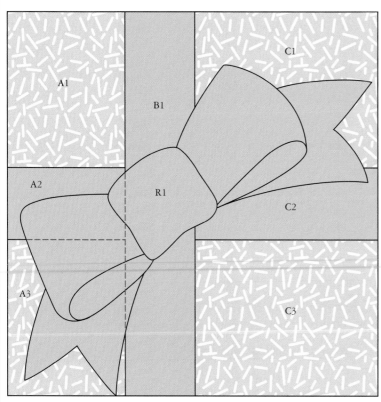

FOR YOU

H20 Make the A section by joining the A pieces. Join the B1 piece to the A section. Make the C section and join to the A-B unit. Tie a ribbon or fabric bow for the R1 piece and sew in place. (The R1 shape can be appliquéd and embroidered.) Make a fabric gift tag and attach with cord, if desired.

CHRISTMAS STOCKING

H21 Piece the stocking by joining the A pieces in numerical order. Appliqué the pieced stocking to the background block. Use decorative embroidery stitches to embellish as desired.

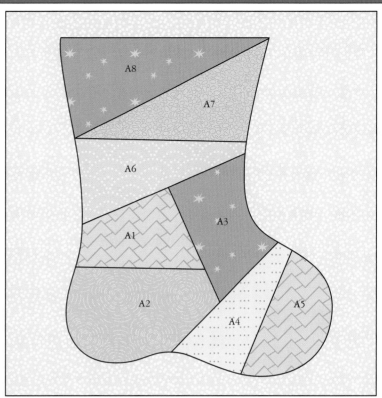

NUTCRACKER

H22 Make A section by joining A pieces in numerical order. Make B section and join to A section. Make C, D, and E sections and join. Join F1 piece to C-D-E unit. Make 2 G sections and join to opposite sides of C-D-E-F unit. Join C-D-E-F-G unit to A-B unit, then join H1 piece. Make I and J sections and join to top of completed unit. Make L and K sections and join. Make M and N sections and join. Join M-N and K-L units to O1 piece. Join P1 piece. Join K-L-M-N-O-P unit to previously completed unit. Use embroidery floss to make a bow on package. Embroider face and buttons and around hands on nutcracker.

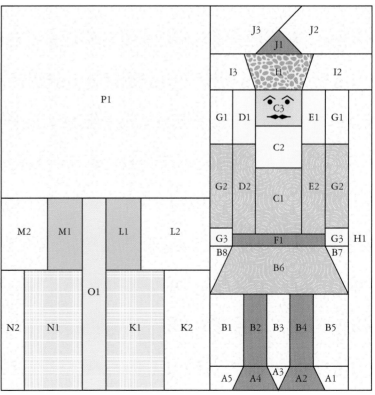

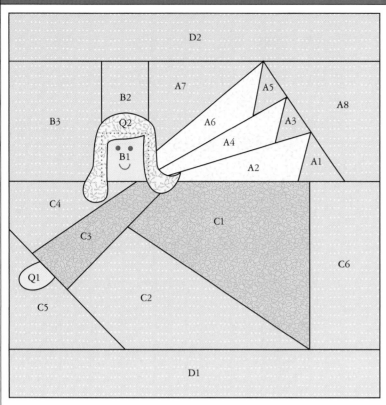

ANGEL

H23 Make the A section by joining the A pieces in numerical order. Make the B section and join to the A section. Appliqué the Q1 piece to the C5 piece, then join the pieces for the C section in numerical order. Join the C section to the A-B unit. Join the D pieces to the top and bottom of the A-B-C unit. Appliqué the Q2 piece for the angel's hair. Use stem stitch to embroider the mouth and French knots for the eyes.

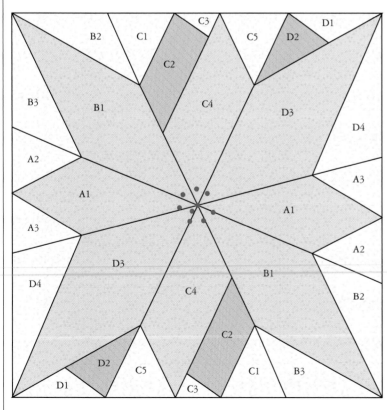

POINSETTIA

H24 Make 2 A sections by joining the A pieces in numerical order. Make 2 B sections and join each to an A section to make 2 A-B units. Make 2 C sections and 2 D sections and join to make 2 C-D units. Join each C-D unit to an A-B unit. Join the 2 A-B-C-D units. Use French knots to make flower center.

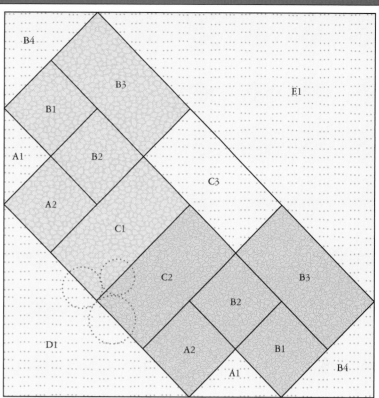

HOLLY

H25 Make 2 A sections by joining the A1 and A2 pieces. Make 2 B sections and join to the A sections to make 2 A-B units. Make the C section and join to the 2 A-B units. Join the D1 and E1 pieces to opposite sides of the AB-C-AB unit. Sew 3 red buttons to the block for the berries.

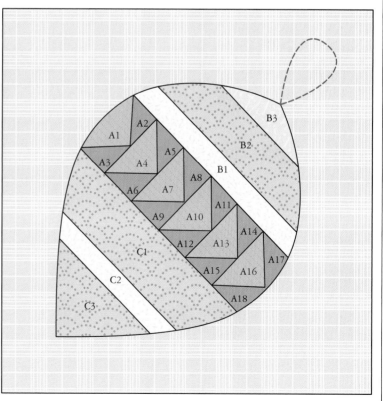

CHRISTMAS ORNAMENT

H26 Make the A section by joining the A pieces in numerical order. Make the B and C sections and join to opposite sides of the A section. Appliqué the pieced A-B-C unit to the background block, inserting cording under the B3 piece.

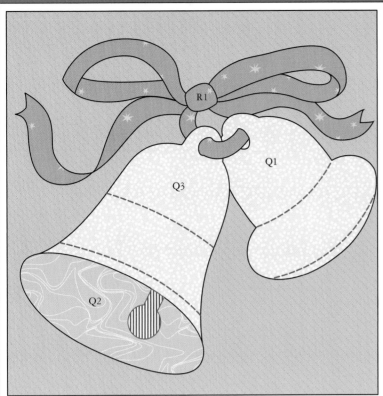

BELLS

H27 Make buttonholes in the Q1 and Q3 pieces and insert ribbon through the openings. Appliqué the Q pieces in numerical order to the background block. Tie ribbon into bow and sew in place, tacking ribbon ends at intervals. Sew decorative trim to the bells. Use satin stitch to embroider clapper in the Q3 bell.

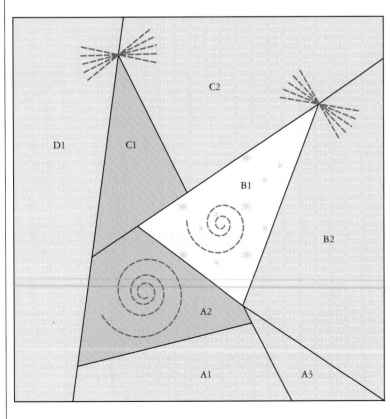

HAPPY NEW YEAR

H28 Make the A section by joining the A pieces in numerical order. Make the B section and join to the A section. Make the C section and join to the A-B unit. Join the D1 piece to the A-B-C unit. Use stem stitch to embroider embellishments on the hats. Use stem stitch and French knots to embellish the background as desired. Cut lengths of floss and tie in the center, then tack to the top of the hats.

STARRY NIGHT

H29 Join the A1 and A2 pieces. Appliqué the Q pieces to make the nose, eyes, and mouth of the snowman. Use Smyrna-cross variation stitches (page 315) to embroider the snowflakes.

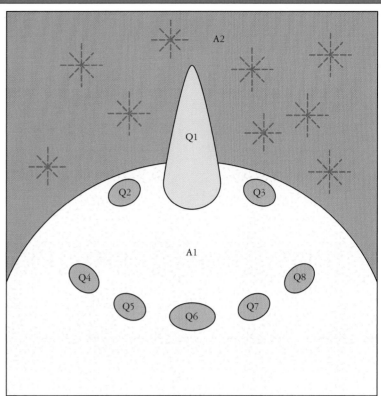

SNOWMAN

H30 Make the A section by joining the A pieces in numerical order. Make the B section and join to the A section. Appliqué the Q pieces to make the snowman's nose and holly leaves for his hat. Use satin stitch to embroider the eyes and mouth. Sew a red button next to the holly leaves.

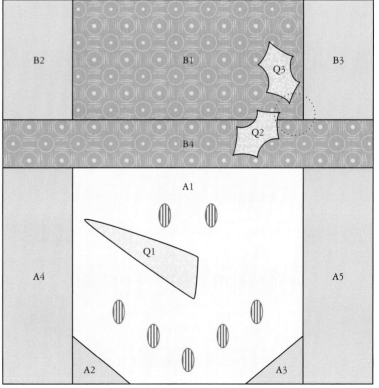

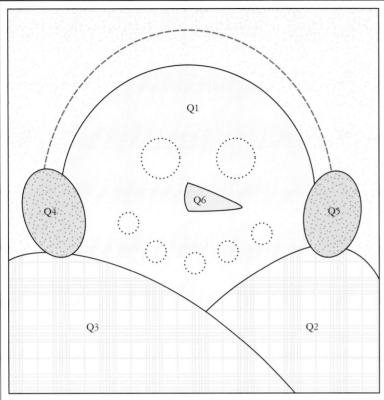

APPLIQUÉ SNOWMAN

H31 Appliqué the Q pieces in numerical order to the background block. Sew buttons in place for eyes and mouth. Use stem stitch to embroider head band for the ear muffs.

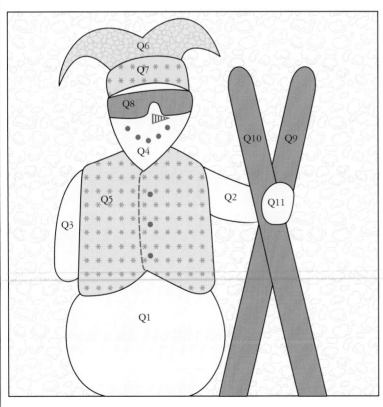

SKIER

H32 Appliqué the Q pieces in numerical order to the background block. Use stem stitch to embroider front of vest, satin stitch for the nose, and French knots for mouth, buttons, and ends of hat.

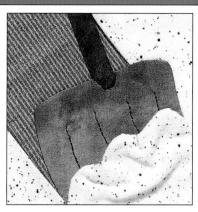

SNOW CHORES

H33 Cut background block and the Q4 piece from "snow" fabric. Appliqué the Q1 piece to the background, then appliqué Q2 and Q3. Appliqué the Q4 piece to complete the block, scrunching a bit for a 3-D effect. Use stem stitch to embroider lines on the shovel and to sew detail in "scoop" of snow.

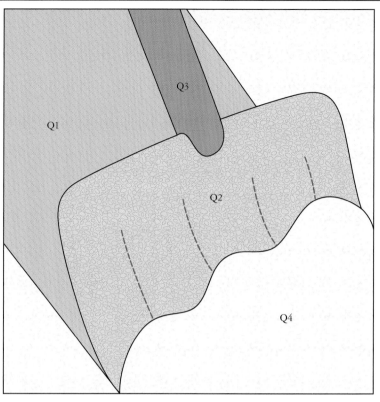

HOT CHOCOLATE

H34 Appliqué the Q1 piece to the background block. Appliqué the Q2 piece. Use stem stitch to embroider the steam lines.

179

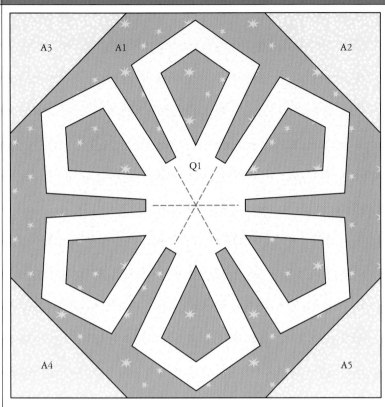

SNOWFLAKE A

H35 Piece the background block by joining the 4 corner pieces to the A1 piece. Appliqué the Q1 piece. Use a running stitch to embroider the center of the snowflake.

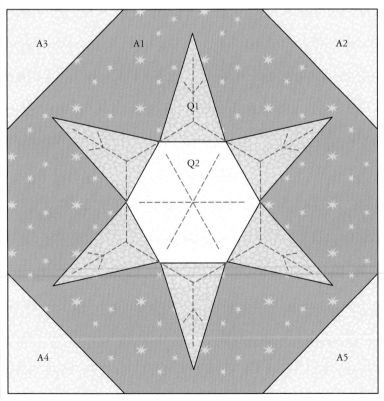

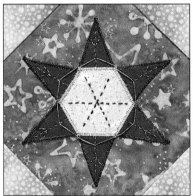

SNOWFLAKE B

H36 Piece the background block by joining the 4 corner pieces to the A1 piece. Appliqué the Q1 piece and then the Q2 piece. Use a running stitch to embroider points on the snowflake and the snowflake center. Use straight stitches around center.

SNOWFLAKE C

H37 Piece the background block by joining the 4 corner pieces to the A1 piece. Appliqué the Q1 piece, then the Q2 piece. Use a running stitch to embroider lines at the center of the snowflake.

Look Again

(Above) Place four blocks together to form a larger block and the corners of this snowflake design create diamond shapes. The background fabrics behind the snowflakes join to make a continuous pattern.

SNOWFLAKE D

H38 Piece the background block by joining the 4 corner pieces to the A1 piece. Appliqué the Q1 star-shape piece, then appliqué the Q2 and Q3 pieces. Use stem stitch to embroider the Q1 piece. Use a running stitch on the Q3 piece.

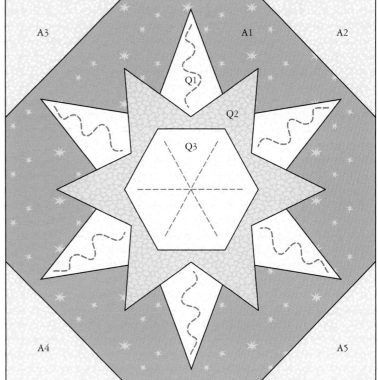

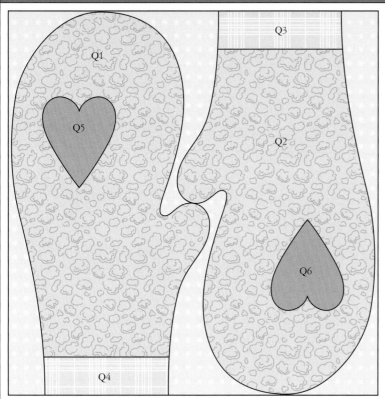

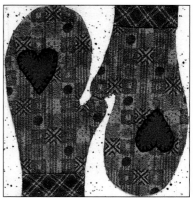

MITTENS

H39 Appliqué the Q pieces in numerical order to the background block. Use a blanket stitch to outline the hearts.

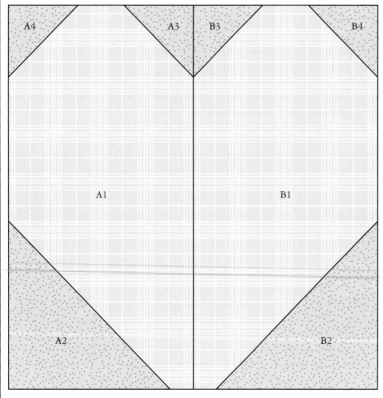

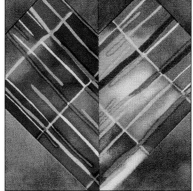

HEART

H40 Make the A section by joining the A pieces in numerical order. Make the B section and join to the A section.

LOG CABIN HEART

H41 Make the block by joining the A pieces in numerical order.

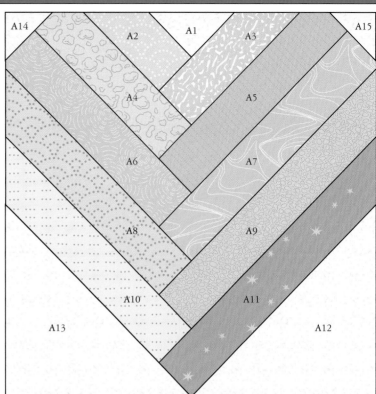

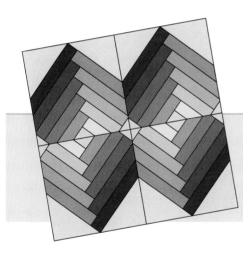

Look Again

(Above) Join Log Cabin Heart blocks as shown, left, to make a dimensional-looking interwoven chain. As more blocks are added, large diamonds separate the chains.

WOVEN HEARTS

H42 Make 2 A sections by joining the A pieces in numerical order. Make 2 B sections. Join the A and B sections to make 2 A-B units. Make 2 C sections by joining the C pieces in numerical order. Join each A-B unit to a C section. Join the 2 A-B-C units to complete the block.

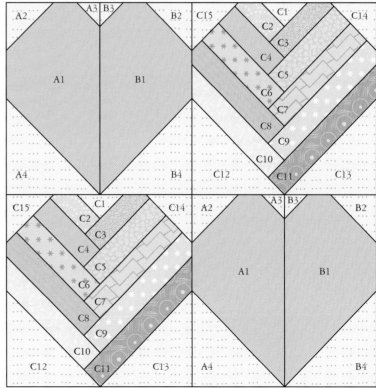

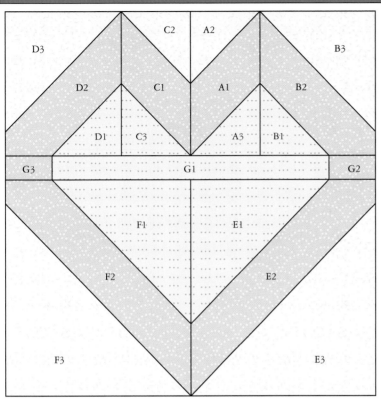

DOUBLE HEART

H43 Make the A section by joining the A pieces in numerical order. Make the B section and join to the A section. Make the C and D sections and join. Join the A-B unit to the C-D unit. Make the E and F sections and join. Make the G section and join to the A-B-C-D unit. Join the E-F unit to the A-B-C-D-G unit.

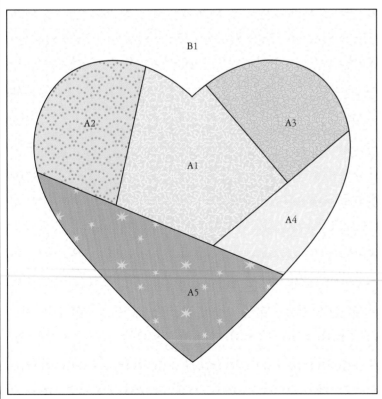

VICTORIAN HEART

H44 Piece the heart by joining the A pieces in numerical order. Appliqué the completed heart to the B1 background piece. Embellish the heart with decorative embroidery.

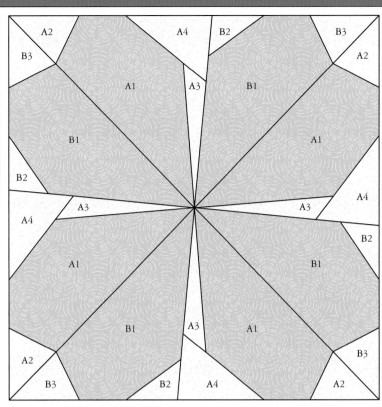

SHAMROCK

H45 Make 4 A sections by joining the A pieces in numerical order. Make 4 B sections. Join A and B sections to make 4 A-B units. Join the 4 units to complete the block.

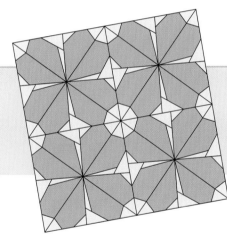

Look Again

(Above) Combine four Shamrock blocks to create a kaleidoscope effect. This combination creates a center circle that repeats as more blocks are added.

EASTER EGG

H46 Strip piece a 3¹/₂-inch square from 8 fabrics (A1-A8 pieces). Cut egg shape from the square and appliqué to the background block. Use decorative embroidery stitches to embellish as desired.

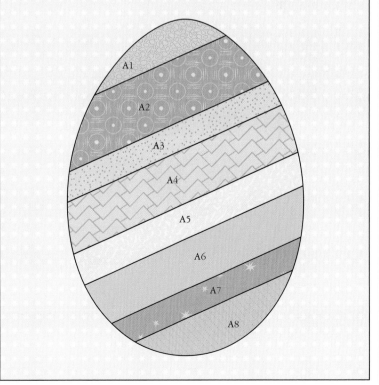

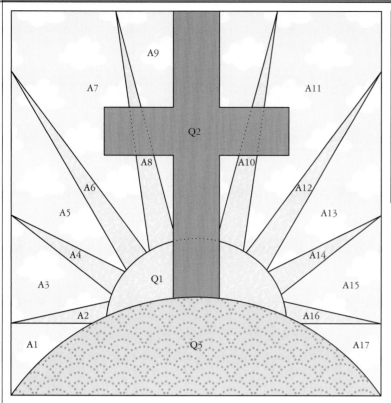

RISING SUN

H47 Piece background by joining the A pieces in numerical order. Appliqué the sun (Q1) piece in place. Appliqué Q2, then the Q3 piece.

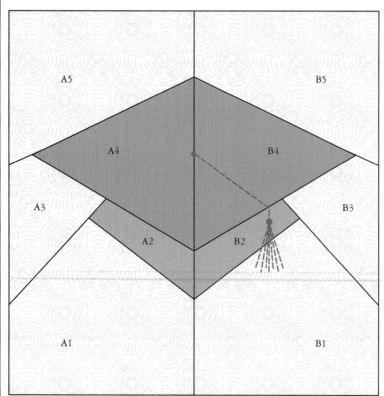

MORTARBOARD

H48 Make the A section by joining the A pieces in numerical order. Make the B section and join to the A section. Use stem stitch to make the cord, using a French knot for the button at the center. Attach a minitassel.

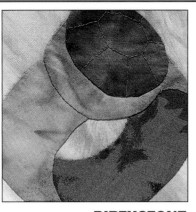

BIRTHSTONE

H49 Appliqué the Q pieces in numerical order to the background block. (Q2 is one piece continuing under Q3.) Use stem stitch to embroider detail on the ring and the stone.

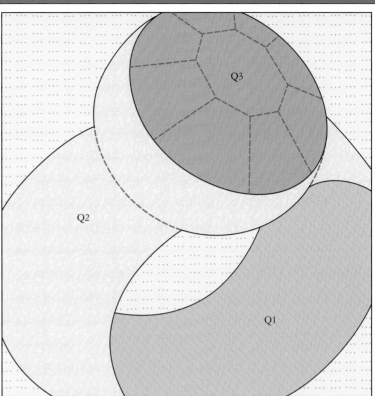

JANUARY

H50 Make the A section by joining the A pieces in numerical order. Make the B section and join to the A section. Make the C and D sections and join. Join the C-D unit to the A-B unit. Make the E and F sections and join. Join the E-F unit to the A-B-C-D unit. Appliqué the Q pieces to make the snowman's nose, eyes, and mouth.

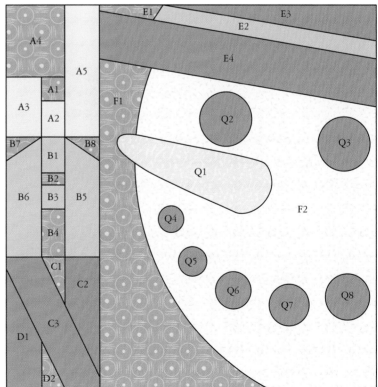

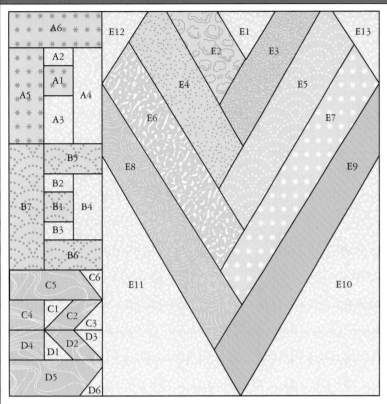

FEBRUARY

H51 Make the A section by joining the A pieces in numerical order. Make the B section and join to the A section. Make the C and D sections and join. Join the C-D unit to the A-B unit. Make the E section by joining the E pieces in numerical order. Join the E section to the A-B-C-D unit.

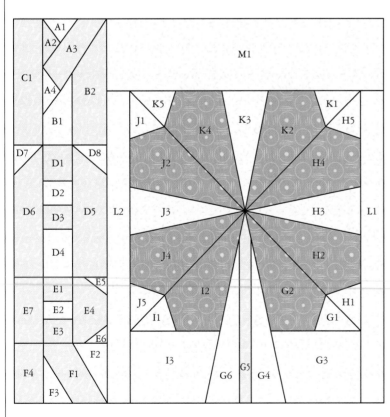

MARCH

H52 Make the A section by joining the A pieces in numerical order. Make the B section and join to the A section. Join the C1 piece. Make the D section and join to the A-B-C unit. Make the E and F sections and join. Join the E-F unit to the A-B-C-D unit. Make the G, H, and I sections and join. Make the J and K sections and join. Join the J-K unit to the G-H-I unit. Join the L pieces to opposite sides of the unit and the M1 piece to the top. Join the G-H-I-J-K-L-M unit to the A-B-C-D-E-F unit.

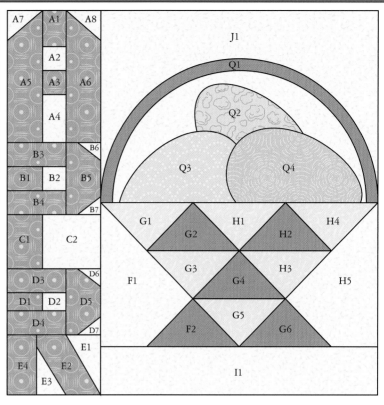

APRIL

H53 Make the A section by joining the A pieces in numerical order. Make the B and C sections and join. Join the B-C unit to the A section. Make the D and E sections and join. Join the D-E unit to the A-B-C unit. Make the F, G, and H sections and join. Join the I1 piece to the F-G-H unit. Appliqué the Q pieces in numerical order to the J1 piece. Join the completed appliqué unit to the F-G-H-I unit. Join the A-B-C-D-E unit to the F-G-H-I-J unit.

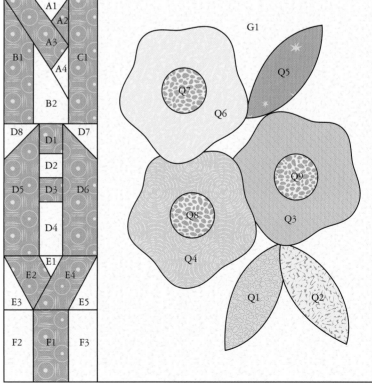

MAY

H54 Make the A section by joining the A pieces in numerical order. Make the B section and join to the A section. Join the C1 piece to the A-B unit. Make the D section and join to the A-B-C unit. Make the E and F sections and join. Join the E-F unit to the A-B-C-D unit. Appliqué the Q pieces in numerical order to the G1 piece. Join the appliqué unit to the A-B-C-D-E-F unit.

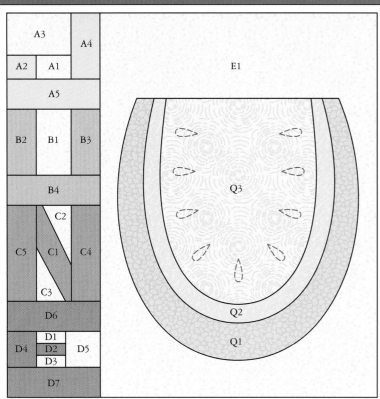

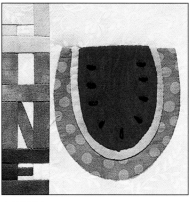

JUNE

H55 Make the A section by joining the A pieces in numerical order. Make the B section and join to the A section. Make the C and D sections and join. Join the C-D unit to the A-B unit. Appliqué the Q pieces in numerical order to the E1 piece. Join the appliqué unit to the A-B-C-D unit. Use lazy daisy stitch to embroider seeds on the watermelon.

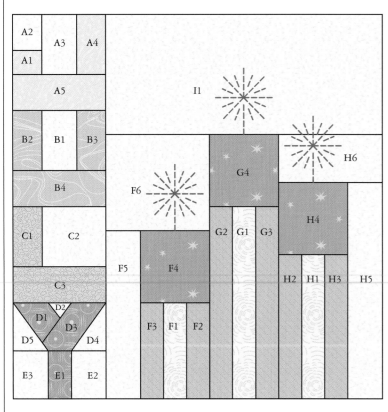

JULY

H56 Make the A section by joining the A pieces in numerical order. Make the B section and join to the A section. Make the C section and join to the A-B unit. Make the D and E sections and join. Join the D-E unit to the A-B-C unit. Make the F, G, and H sections and join. Join the I1 piece to the F-G-H unit. Join the A-B-C-D-E unit to the F-G-H-I unit. Use stem stitch to embroider wicks on the sparklers. Use metallic thread and straight stitches to add the fireworks.

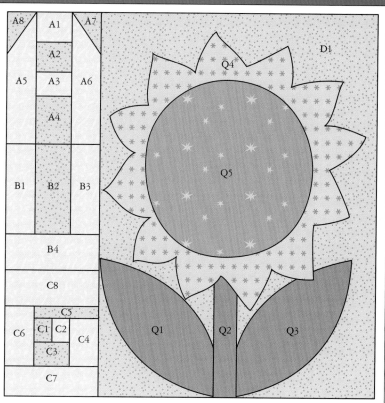

AUGUST

H57 Make the A section by joining the A pieces in numerical order. Make the B section and join to the A section. Make the C section and join to the A-B unit. Appliqué the Q pieces in numerical order to the D1 piece. Join the completed appliqué unit to the A-B-C unit.

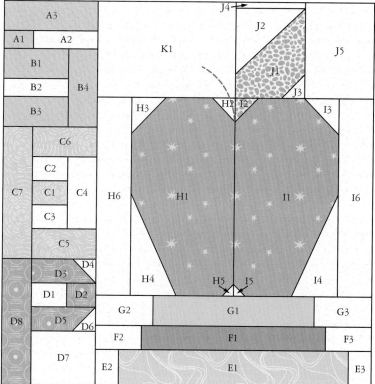

SEPTEMBER

H58 Make the A section by joining the A pieces in numerical order. Make the B section and join to the A section. Make the C and D sections and join. Join the C-D unit to the A-B unit. Make the E, F, and G sections and join. Make the H and I sections and join. Join the E-F-G unit to the H-I unit. Make the J section and join the K1 piece. Join the J-K unit to the E-F-G-H-I unit, then join to the A-B-C-D unit. Use stem stitch to embroider the apple stem. If desired, redesign lettering to include a T.

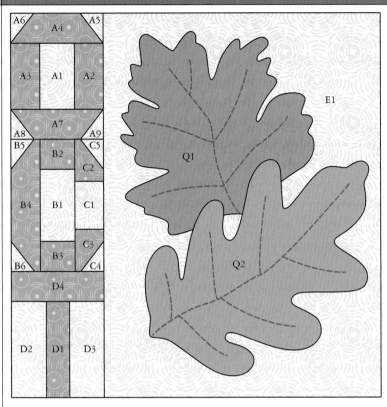

OCTOBER

H59 Make the A section by joining the A pieces in numerical order. Make the B and C sections and join. Join the B-C unit to the A section. Make the D section and join to the A-B-C unit. Appliqué the Q pieces in numerical order to the E1 piece. Join the E section to the A-B-C-D unit. Use stem stitch to embroider veins on the leaves as desired and decorative embroidery to embellish them.

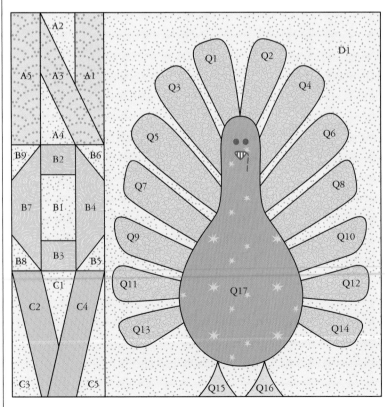

NOVEMBER

H60 Make the A section by joining the A pieces in numerical order. Make the B section and join to the A section. Make the C section and join to the A-B unit. Appliqué the Q pieces in numerical order to the D1 piece. Join the appliqué unit to the A-B-C unit. Use satin stitch to embroider the beak, stem stitch for the wattle, and French knots for the eyes.

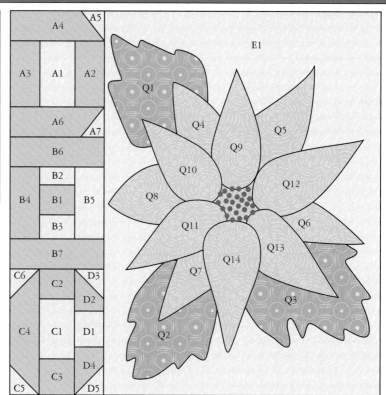

DECEMBER

H61 Make the A section by joining the A pieces in numerical order. Make the B section and join to the A section. Make the C and D sections and join. Join the C-D unit to the A-B unit. Appliqué the Q pieces in numerical order to the E1 piece. Join the appliqué unit to the A-B-C-D unit. Use French knots to fill the center of the poinsettia.

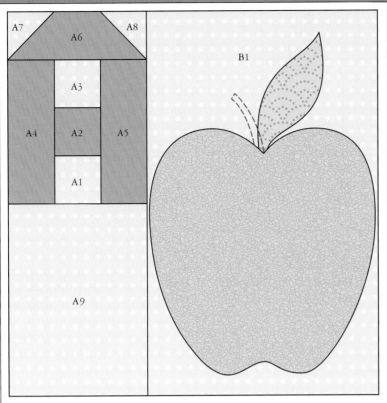

A—APPLE

I1 Make A section by joining pieces in numerical order. Join B1 piece to completed A section. Appliqué apple and leaf. Embroider stem on apple using stem stitch.

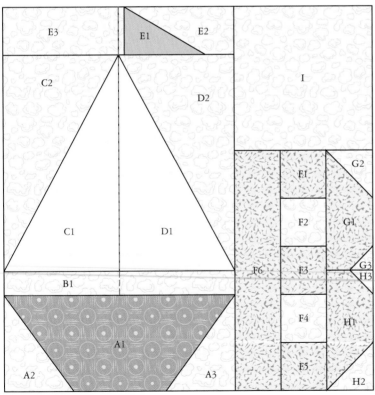

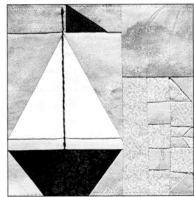

B—BOAT

I2 Make A section by joining pieces in numerical order. Join B1 to A section. Make C section and D section and join. Make E section. Join E section to C-D unit; join to A-B unit. Make F section. Make G and H sections and join. Join G-H unit to F section. Join I piece to F-G-H unit. Join the two completed units. Use stem stitch to embroider mast.

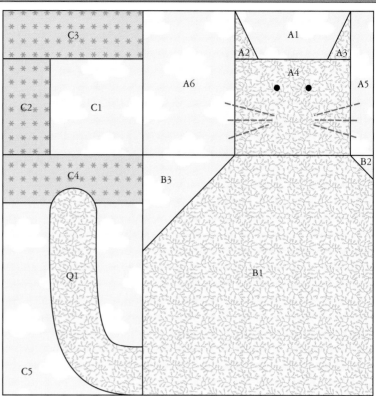

C—CAT

I3 Make A section by joining pieces in numerical order. Make B section and join to A section. Make C section; appliqué Q1 piece for tail, extending bottom of the tail to seam allowance of block. Join C section to A-B unit. Embroider whiskers using straight stitches. Make French knots for the eyes.

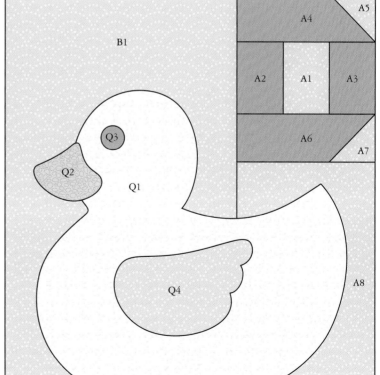

D—DUCK

I4 Make A section by joining pieces in numerical order. Join B1 piece to A section. Appliqué Q1 piece, extending piece to seam allowance of the block. Appliqué remaining Q pieces.

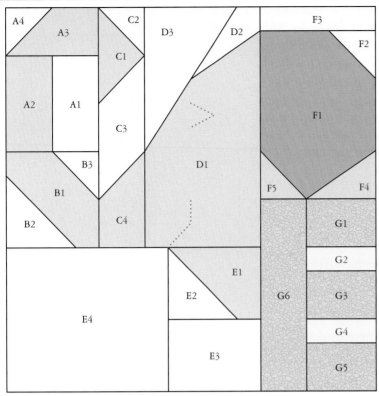

E—ELEPHANT

15 Make A section by joining pieces in numerical order. Make B section and join to A section. Make C section and join to A-B unit. Make D section and join to A-B-C unit. Make E section and join to A-B-C-D unit. Make F and G sections and join. Join F-G unit to A-B-C-D-E unit. Embroider eye and mouth on elephant using straight stitch.

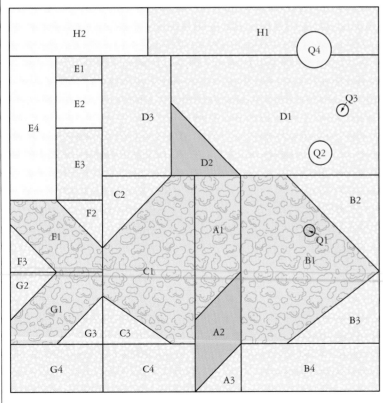

F—FISH

16 Make A section by joining pieces in numerical order. Make B section and join to A section. Make C section and join to A-B unit. Make D section and join to A-B-C unit. Make E, F and G sections and join. Join E-F-G unit to A-B-C-D unit. Make H section and join to A-B-C-D-E-F-G unit. Appliqué Q pieces to make fish eye and bubbles.

G—GRAPES

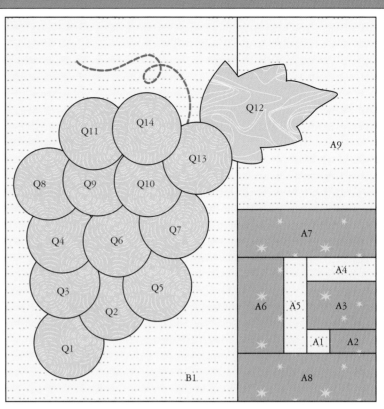

I7 Make A section by joining pieces in numerical order. Join A section to B1 piece. Appliqué Q pieces in numerical order to make grapes and grape leaf. Embroider vine using stem stitch.

H—HAT

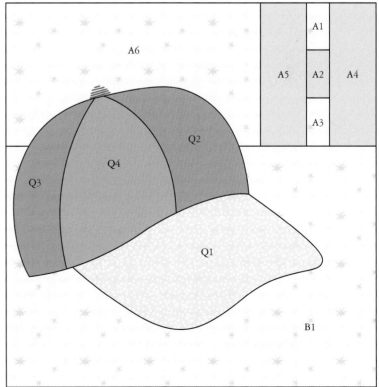

I8 Make A section by joining pieces in numerical order. Join A section to B1 piece. Appliqué hat pieces to block. Embroider a "button" on top of the hat using satin stitch.

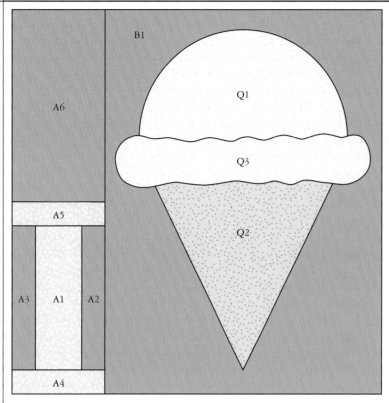

I—ICE CREAM

I9 Make A section by joining pieces in numerical order. Join A section to B1 piece. Appliqué Q pieces in numerical order to make ice cream and ice-cream cone.

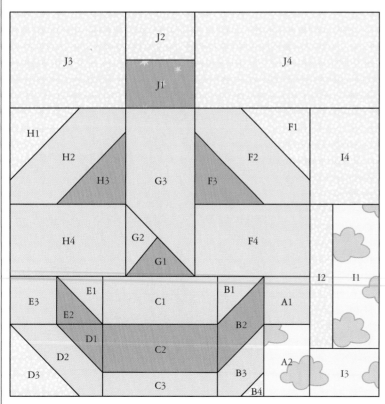

J—JACK-O'-LANTERN

I10 Make A section by joining A1 and A2. Make B section by joining pieces in numerical order; join to A section. Make C section and join to A-B unit. Make D section, then make E section and join to D section. Join D-E unit to A-B-C unit. Make F section, then make G section and join to F section. Make H section and join to F-G unit. Join F-G-H unit to A-B-C-D-E unit. Make I section and join to A-B-C-D-E-F-G-H unit. Make J section and join to the top to complete the block.

K—KITE

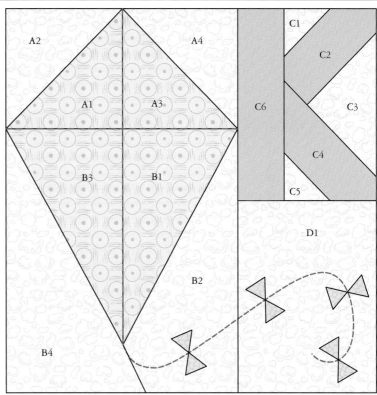

I11 Make A section by joining pieces in numerical order. Make B section and join to A section. Make C section and join to D1. Join C-D unit to A-B unit. Embroider kite tail and crossbars using stem stitch. Make 4 fabric "bows" and tack to kite tail.

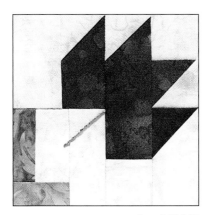

L—LEAF

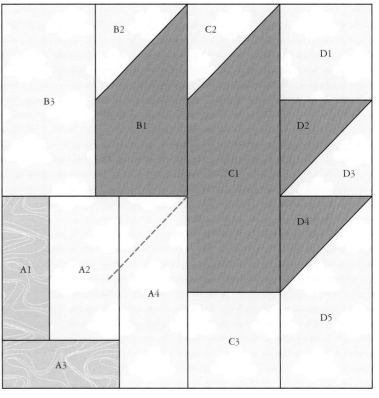

I12 Make A section by joining pieces in numerical order. Make B section and join to A section. Make C section, then make D section and join to C section. Join C-D unit to A-B unit. Embroider leaf stem using stem stitch.

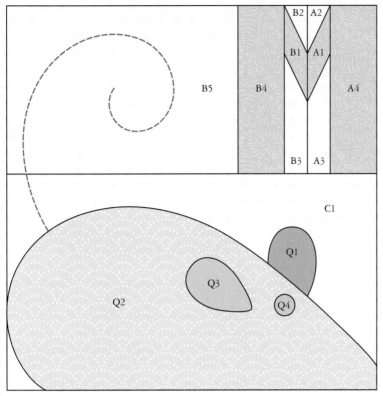

M—MOUSE

113 Make A section by joining pieces in numerical order. Make B section and join to A section. Join C1 piece to A-B unit. Appliqué Q pieces in numerical order to make mouse, mouse ears, and eye. Embroider tail using stem stitch.

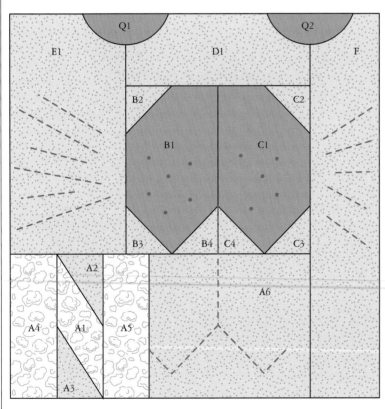

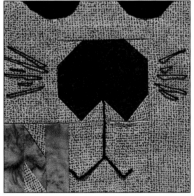

N—NOSE

114 Make A section by joining pieces in numerical order. Make B and C sections and join. Join D1 piece to B-C unit. Join E1 piece to B-C-D unit. Join B-C-D-E unit to A section. Join F1 piece to complete block. Appliqué Q pieces to the top of the block, extending eyes to seam allowance. Embroider face using straight stitches for whiskers, stem stitch for mouth, and French knots on nose.

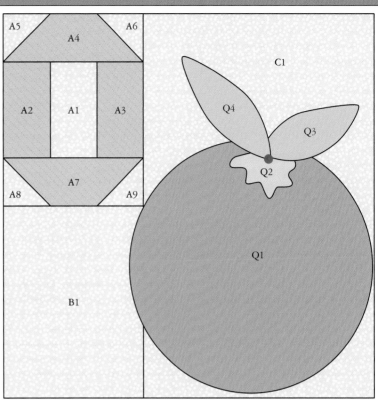

O—ORANGE

I15 Make A section by joining pieces in numerical order. Join B1 piece to A section. Join C1 piece to A-B unit. Appliqué Q pieces in numerical order. Embroider French knot on orange navel.

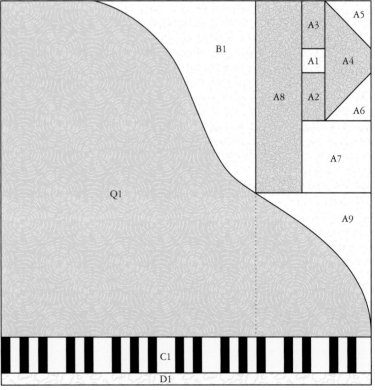

P—PIANO

I16 Make A section by joining pieces in numerical order. Join B1 piece to A section. Appliqué Q1 piece to A-B unit, extending it to seam allowance. Piece black and white pieces for C section and join to A-B unit. Join to D1 piece.

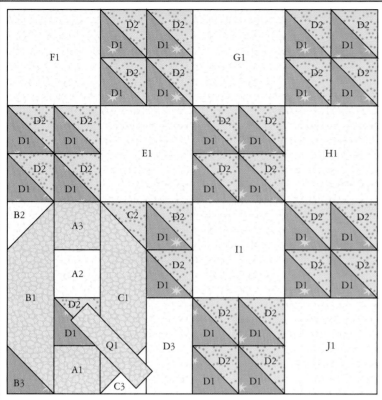

Q—QUILT

I17 Join D1 and D2 pieces to make a total of 27 squares. Use 1 square to make the A section. Make B section and join to A section. Make C section and join to A-B unit. Join 2 D1-D2 squares to D3 piece. Join D section to A-B-C unit. Join 4 D1-D2 squares to make a block as shown. Repeat to make 6 blocks. Using these blocks, add the E, F, G, H, I and J pieces as shown. Join all units to complete the block. Appliqué Q1 piece.

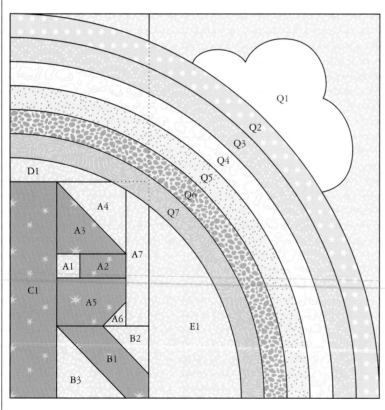

R—RAINBOW

I18 Make A section by joining pieces in numerical order. Make B section and join to A section; join C1 piece. Join D1 piece to A-B-C unit. Join E1 piece to complete block. Appliqué Q1 piece. Cut $3/4 \times 8$-inch bias strips for the rainbow. Appliqué rainbow pieces Q2–Q7, easing fullness.

S—STAR

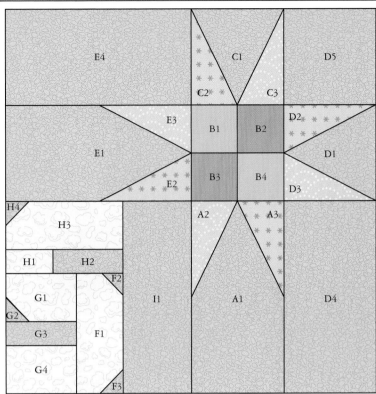

I19 Make A section by joining pieces in numerical order. Make B section and join to A section; make C section and join to A-B unit. Make D section and join to A-B-C unit. Make E section. Make F and G sections and join. Make H section and join to F-G unit, then add I1 piece. Join F-G-H-I unit to E section. Join the two units to complete the block.

T—TRUCK

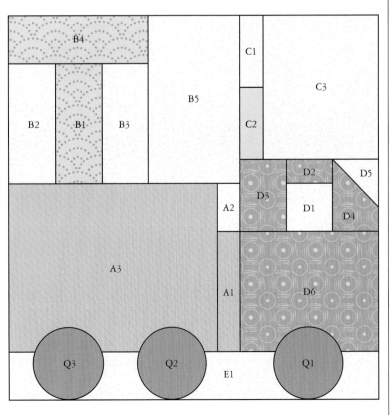

I20 Make A section by joining pieces in numerical order. Make B section and join to A section. Make C and D sections and join. Join C-D unit to A-B unit, then join E1 piece to the bottom. Appliqué Q pieces in place.

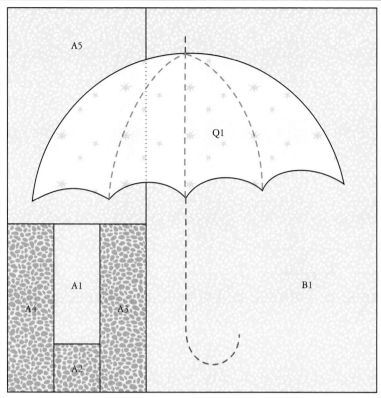

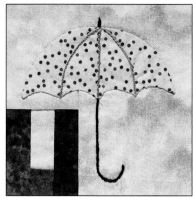

U—UMBRELLA

I21 Make A section by joining pieces in numerical order. Join B1 piece to complete block. Appliqué Q1 piece to make umbrella. Embroider ribs on the umbrella, handle, and point using stem stitch.

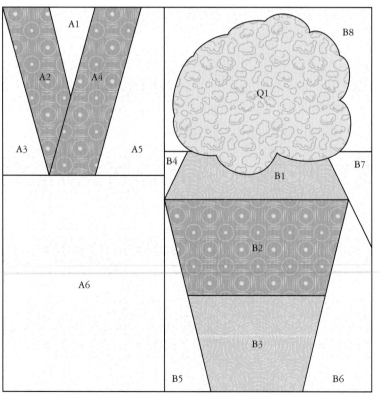

V—VASE

I22 Make A section by joining pieces in numerical order. Make B section and join to A section. Use floral fabric for Q1 piece and appliqué in place.

S—STAR

I19 Make A section by joining pieces in numerical order. Make B section and join to A section; make C section and join to A-B unit. Make D section and join to A-B-C unit. Make E section. Make F and G sections and join. Make H section and join to F-G unit, then add I1 piece. Join F-G-H-I unit to E section. Join the two units to complete the block.

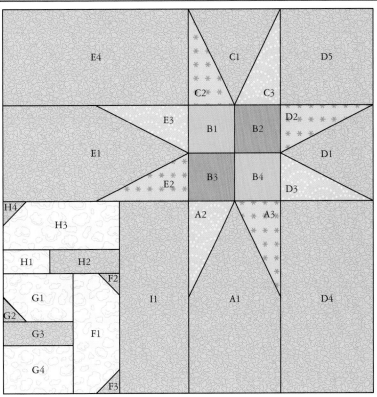

T—TRUCK

I20 Make A section by joining pieces in numerical order. Make B section and join to A section. Make C and D sections and join. Join C-D unit to A-B unit, then join E1 piece to the bottom. Appliqué Q pieces in place.

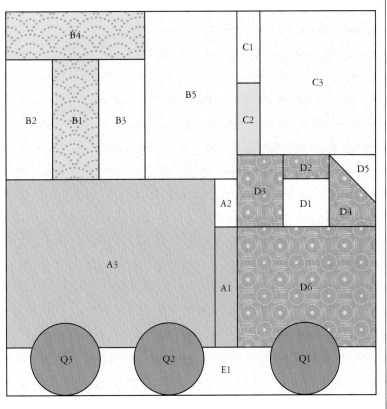

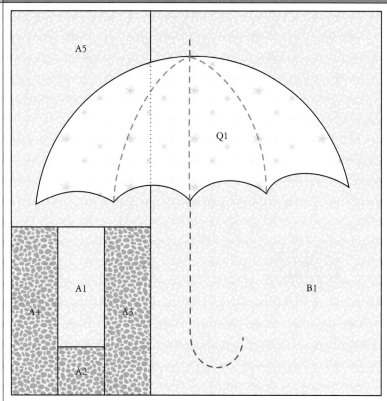

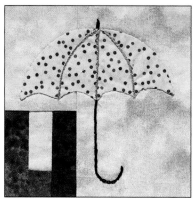

U—UMBRELLA

121 Make A section by joining pieces in numerical order. Join B1 piece to complete block. Appliqué Q1 piece to make umbrella. Embroider ribs on the umbrella, handle, and point using stem stitch.

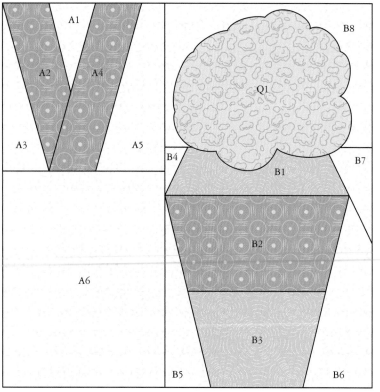

V—VASE

122 Make A section by joining pieces in numerical order. Make B section and join to A section. Use floral fabric for Q1 piece and appliqué in place.

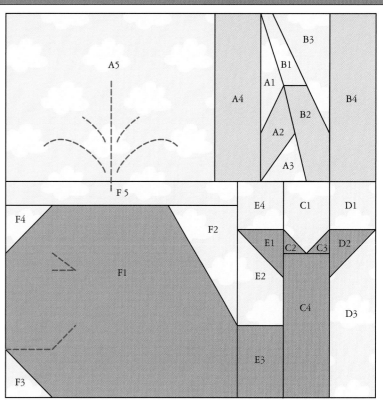

W—WHALE

123 Make the A section by joining the A pieces in numerical order. Make the B section and join to the A section. Make the C, D, and E sections and join. Make the F section and join to the C-D-E unit. Join the C-D-E-F unit to the A-B unit. Use stem stitch to embroider the whale's eye, mouth, and spout.

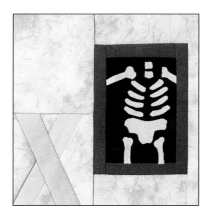

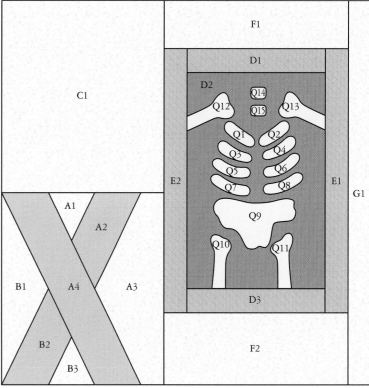

X—X-RAY

124 Fuse-appliqué or use fabric paint to make the D2 piece. Make the A section by joining the A pieces in numerical order. Make the B section and join to the A section. Join the C1 piece to the A-B unit. Using the appliquéd D2 piece, make the D section and join the E pieces to opposite sides. Join the F pieces to the D-E unit, then join the G1 piece. Join the D-E-F-G unit to the A-B-C unit.

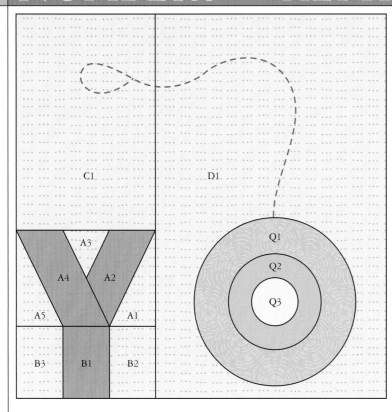

Y—YO-YO

125 Make A section by joining pieces in numerical order. Make B section and join to A section, then add C1 piece. Join D1 to A-B-C unit. Appliqué Q pieces in numerical order. Embroider yo-yo string using stem stitch.

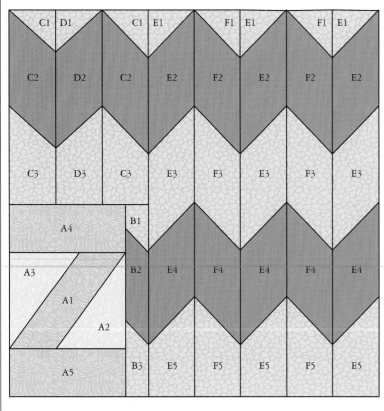

Z—ZIGZAG

126 Make the A section by joining the A pieces in numerical order. Make the B section and join to the A section. Make 2 C sections and 1 D section and join into the C-D-C unit. Join the C-D-C unit to the A-B unit. Make 3 E sections and 2 F sections. Join to make the E-F-E-F-E unit, then join to the A-B-C-D-C unit.

A

127 Make A section by joining pieces in numerical order. Make B section and join to A section. Join C1 and D1 pieces to the sides of A-B unit. Join E1 and F1 pieces to the bottom and top to complete the block.

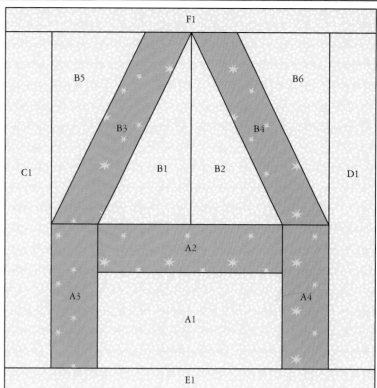

B

128 Make A section by joining pieces in numerical order. Make B section and join to A section. Make C section and join to the A-B unit. Join the D pieces to the A-B-C unit. Join E1 and F1 pieces to the bottom and top to complete the block.

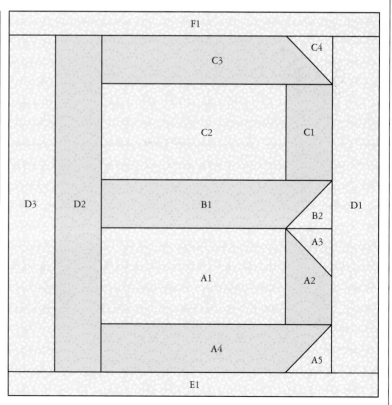

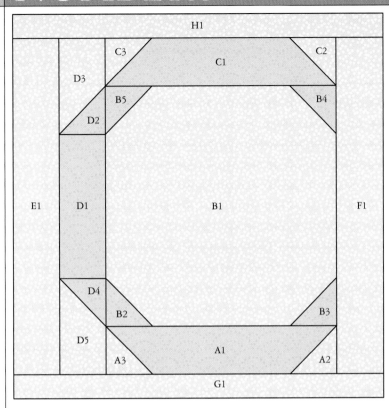

C

129 Make A section by joining pieces in numerical order. Make B section and join to A section. Make C section and join to A-B unit. Make D section and join to A-B-C unit. Join E1 and F1 pieces to the sides of A-B-C-D unit. Join G1 and H1 pieces to the bottom and top to complete the block.

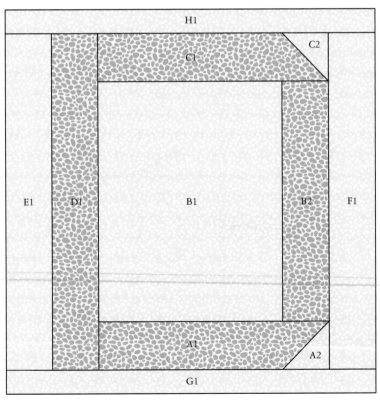

D

130 Make A section by joining A1 and A2. Make B section and join to A section. Make C section and join to A-B unit. Join D1 to A-B-C unit. Join E1 and F1 pieces to the sides of A-B-C-D unit. Join G1 and H1 pieces to the bottom and top to complete the block.

E

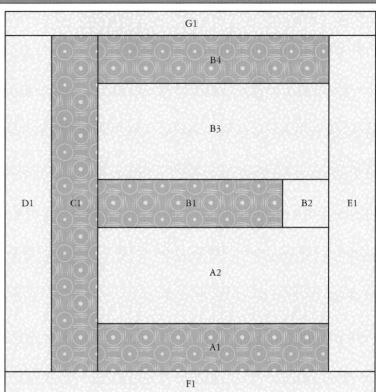

131 Make A section by joining A1 and A2. Make B section and join to A section. Join C1 to A-B unit. Join D1 and E1 pieces to the sides of A-B-C unit. Join F1 and G1 pieces to the bottom and top to complete the block.

F

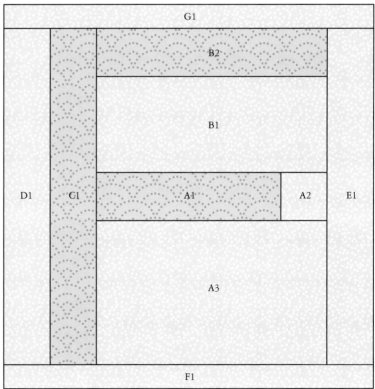

132 Make A section by joining pieces in numerical order. Make B section and join to A section. Join C1 piece to A-B unit. Join D1 and E1 pieces to the sides of A-B-C unit. Join F1 and G1 pieces to the bottom and top to complete the block.

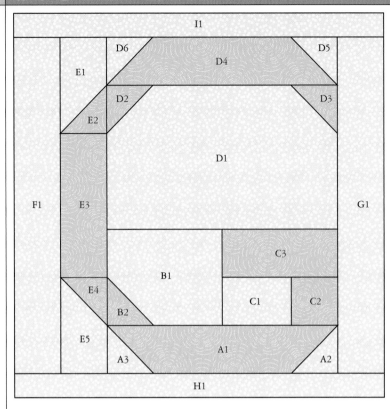

G

133 Make A section by joining pieces in numerical order. Make B and C sections and join. Join B-C unit to A section. Make D section and join to A-B-C unit. Make E section and join to A-B-C-D unit. Join F1 and G1 pieces to the sides of the A-B-C-D-E unit. Join H1 and I1 pieces to the bottom and top to complete the block.

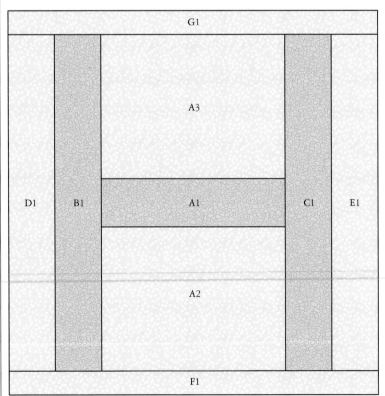

H

134 Make A section by joining pieces in numerical order. Join B1 and C1 pieces to each side of the A section. Join D1 and E1 pieces to the sides of A-B-C unit. Join F1 and G1 pieces to the bottom and top to complete the block.

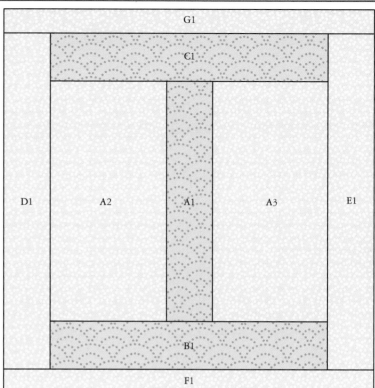

I35 Make A section by joining pieces in numerical order. Join B1 and C1 pieces to the top and bottom of the A section. Join D1 and E1 pieces to the sides of A-B-C unit. Join F1 and G1 pieces to the bottom and top to complete the block.

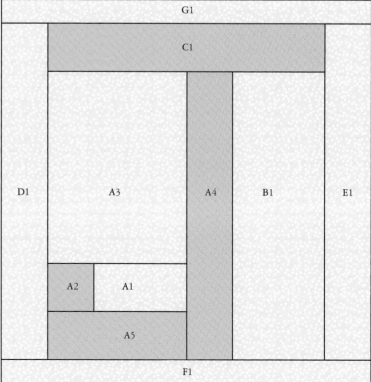

I36 Make A section by joining pieces in numerical order. Join B1 then C1 pieces to the A section. Join D1 and E1 pieces to the sides of A-B-C unit. Join F1 and G1 pieces to the bottom and top to complete the block.

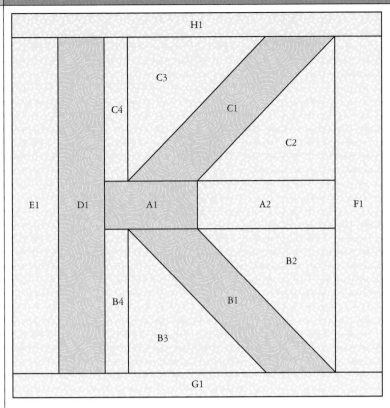

K

I37 Join A1 and A2 pieces. Make B section by joining pieces in numerical order; then join to A section. Make C section and join to A-B unit. Join D1 piece to A-B-C unit. Join E1 and F1 pieces to the sides of A-B-C-D unit. Join G1 and H1 pieces to the bottom and top to complete the block.

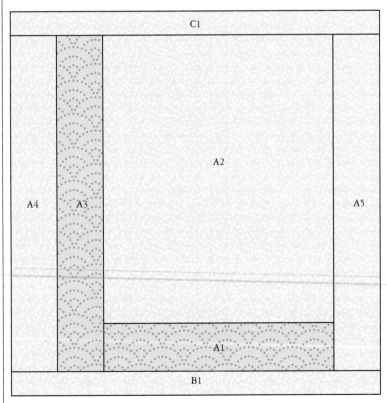

L

I38 Make A section by joining pieces in numerical order. Join B1 and C1 pieces to the bottom and top to complete the block.

M

139 Make A section by joining pieces in numerical order. Make B section; then join to A section. Join C1 piece to the A-B unit. Join D1 and E1 pieces to each side of the A-B-C unit. Join F1 and G1 to the A-B-C-D-E unit. Join H1 and I1 pieces to the bottom and top to complete the block.

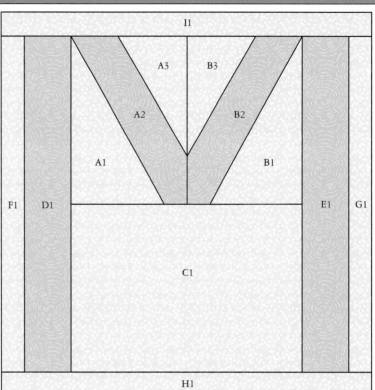

N

140 Make A section by joining pieces in numerical order. Make B and C sections, then join to A section. Join D1 and E1 pieces to each side of the A-B-C unit. Join F1 and G1 to the A-B-C-D-E unit. Join H1 and I1 pieces to the bottom and top to complete the block.

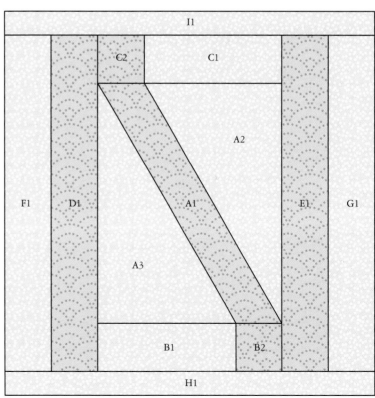

213

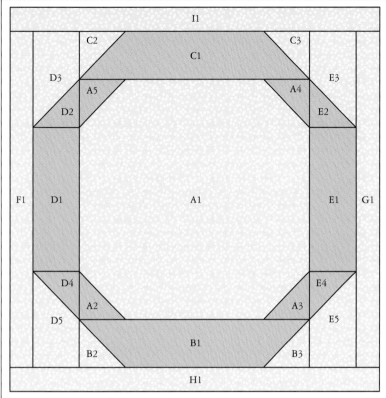

O

141 Make A section by joining pieces in numerical order. Make B and C sections; then join to A section. Make D and E sections and join to each side of the A-B-C unit. Join F1 and G1 to the A-B-C-D-E unit. Join H1 and I1 pieces to the bottom and top to complete the block.

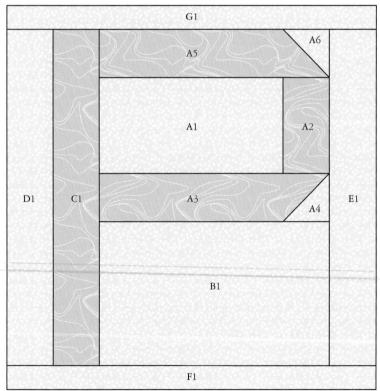

P

142 Make A section by joining pieces in numerical order; then join B1 piece. Join C1 piece to A-B unit. Join D1 and E1 pieces to each side of the A-B-C unit. Join F1 and G1 pieces to the bottom and top to complete the block.

Q

143 Make A section by joining pieces in numerical order. Make B section; then join to A section. Make C section and join to A-B unit. Make D section and join to A-B-C unit. Sew E1 to the bottom of the A-B-C-D unit. Make F and G sections and join to A-B-C-D-E unit. Join H1 and I1 pieces to each side of the A-B-C-D-E-F-G unit. Join J1 and K1 pieces to the bottom and top to complete the block.

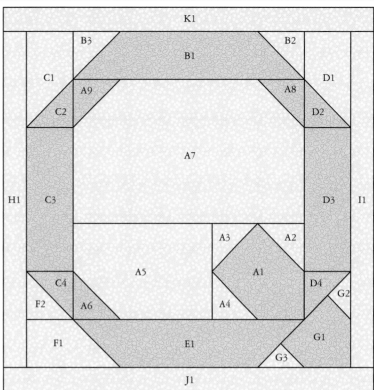

R

144 Make A section by joining pieces in numerical order. Make B section, then join to A section. Join C1 piece to the A-B unit. Join D1 and E1 pieces to each side of the A-B-C unit. Join F1 and G1 to the bottom and top to complete the block.

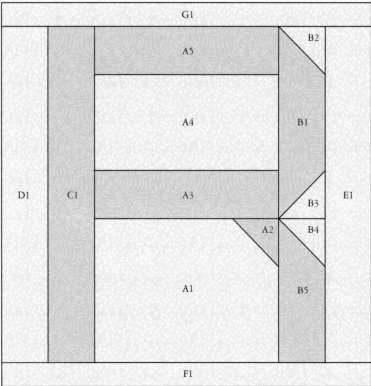

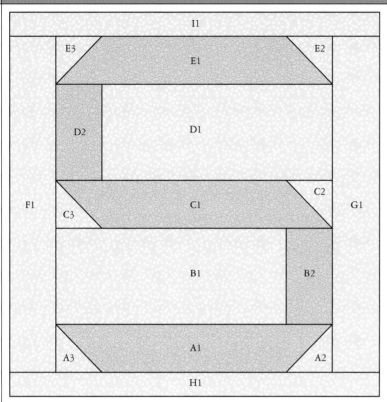

S

145 Make A section by joining pieces in numerical order. Make B section and join to A section. Make C section; join to A-B unit; make D and E sections and join to complete A-B-C-D-E unit. Join F1 and G1 pieces to each side; then join H1 and I1 pieces to the bottom and top to complete the block.

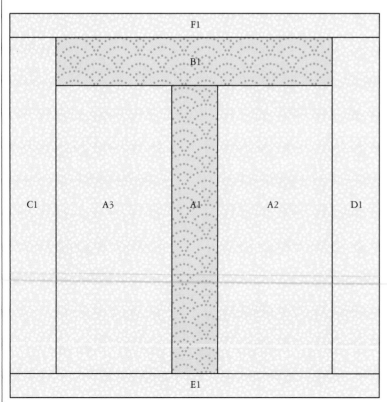

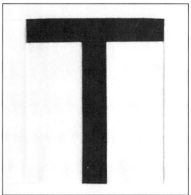

T

146 Make A section by joining pieces in numerical order. Join B1 piece to the A section. Join C1 and D1 pieces to each side of the A-B unit. Join E1 and F1 pieces to the bottom and top to complete the block.

U

147 Make A section by joining pieces in numerical order. Make B section and join to the A section. Join C1 and D1 pieces to each side of the A-B unit. Join E1 and F1 pieces to the bottom and top to complete the block.

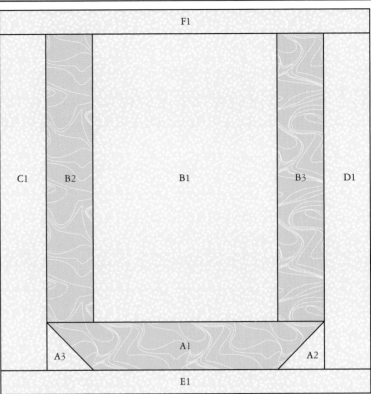

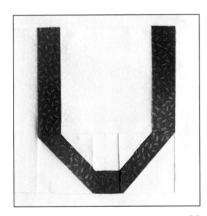

V

148 Make A section by joining pieces in numerical order. Make B and C sections and join to A section. Make D section and join to the A-B-C unit. Join E1 and F1 pieces to each side of the A-B-C-D unit. Join G1 and H1 pieces to the bottom and top to complete the block.

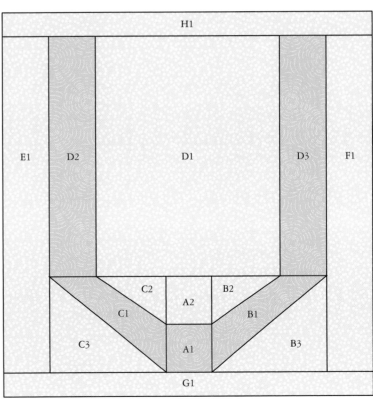

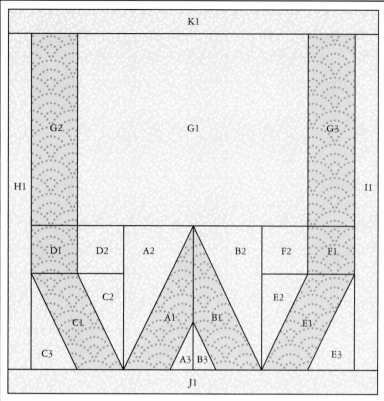

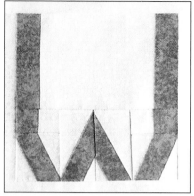

W

149 Make A section by joining pieces in numerical order. Make B section and join to A section. Make C and D sections, join. Join C-D unit to the A-B unit. Make E and F sections, join; then join to the A-B-C-D unit. Make G section and join to the A-B-C-D-E-F unit. Join H1 and I1 pieces to each side of the A-B-C-D-E-F-G unit. Join J1 and K1 pieces to the bottom and top to complete the block.

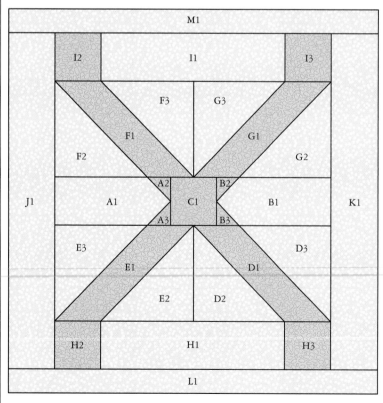

X

150 Make A section by joining pieces in numerical order. Join C1 to A section. Make B section and join to A-C unit. Make D and E sections and join. Join D-E unit to A-B-C unit. Make F and G sections, join; then join to A-B-C-D-E unit. Make H and I sections and join to top and bottom of completed unit. Join J1 and K1 pieces to each side of the A-B-C-D-E-F-G-H-I unit. Join L1 and M1 pieces to the bottom and top to complete the block.

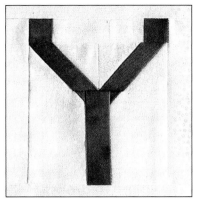

Y

I51 Join pieces to make B section and join to A1 piece. Make C section and join to A-B unit. Make D and E sections and join; then join to the A-B-C unit. Make F section and join to A-B-C-D-E unit. Join G1 and H1 pieces to each side of the A-B-C-D-E-F unit. Join I1 and J1 pieces to the bottom and top to complete the block.

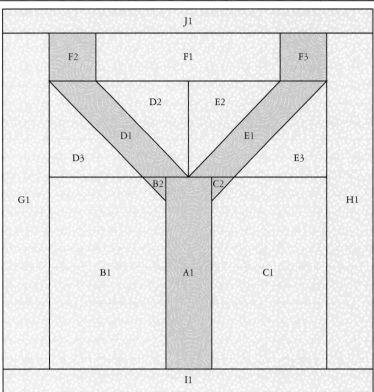

Z

I52 Make A section by joining pieces in numerical order. Join B1 and C1 pieces to the top and bottom of the A section. Join D1 and E1 pieces to each side of the A-B-C unit. Join F1 and G1 pieces to the bottom and top to complete the block.

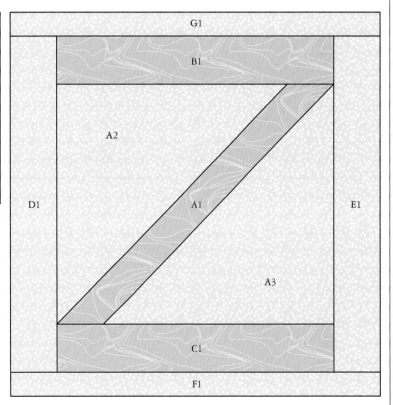

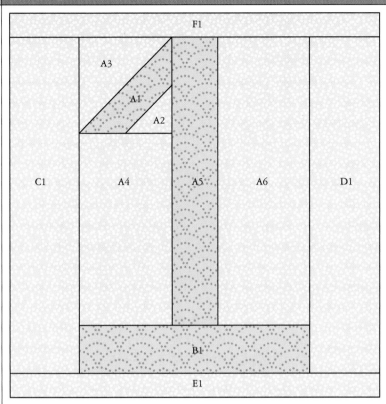

1

153 Make A section by joining pieces in numerical order. Join B1 piece to the bottom of the A section. Join C1 and D1 pieces to each side of the A-B unit. Join E1 and F1 pieces to the bottom and top to complete the block.

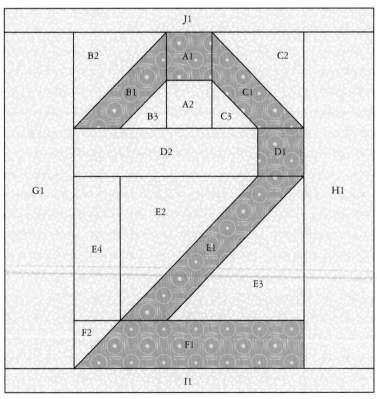

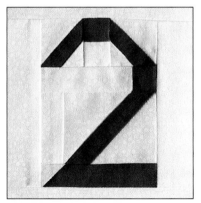

2

154 Join pieces to make A section. Make B and C sections and join to A section. Make D section and join to the A-B-C unit. Make E section and join to A-B-C-D unit. Make F section and join to the completed unit. Join G1 and H1 pieces to each side of the A-B-C-D-E-F unit. Join I1 and J1 pieces to the bottom and top to complete the block.

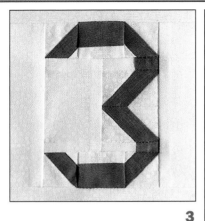

3

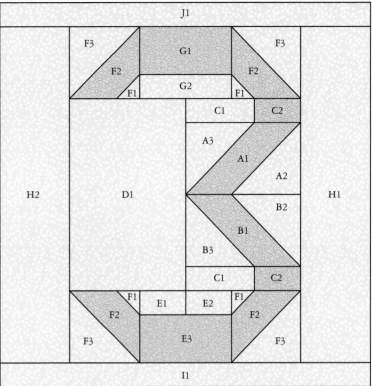

155 Make A section by joining pieces in numerical order. Make B section and join to A section. Make 2 C sections and join to the top and bottom of the A-B unit. Join the D1 piece. Make 4 F sections. Make E section and join 2 F sections. Make G section and join 2 F sections. Join E-F and G-F units to the A-B-C-D unit. Join H pieces to the sides and I1 and J1 pieces to the bottom and top to complete the block.

4

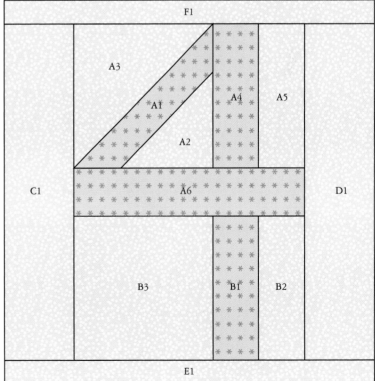

156 Make A section by joining pieces in numerical order. Make B section and join to A section. Join C1 and D1 to each side of the A-B unit. Join E1 and F1 pieces to the bottom and top to complete the block.

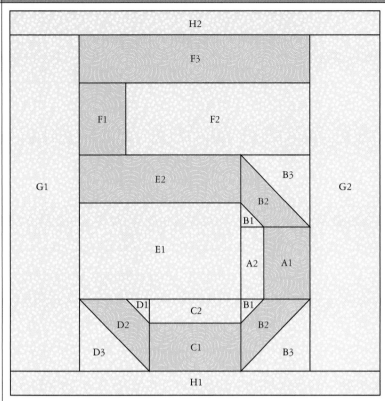

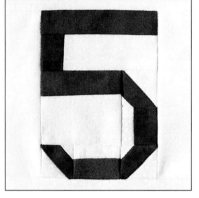

5

I57 Make A section by joining A1 and A2. Make 2 B sections and join to the A section. Make C and D sections and join. Make E section and join to the C-D unit. Join the C-D-E unit to the B-A-B unit. Make the F section and join to the completed unit. Join the G pieces to the sides and the H pieces to the bottom and top of the block.

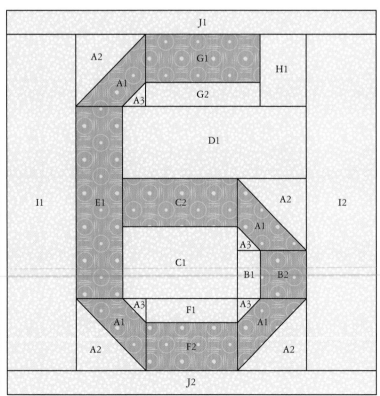

6

I58 Make 4 A sections. Make B section and join to one A section. Make C section and Join to A-B unit. Join D1 and E1 to the A-B-C unit. Make F section and join to 2 A sections; join to A-B-C-D-E unit. Make G section, join 1 A section and H1 piece. Join the A-G-H unit to the completed unit. Join I pieces to the sides and J pieces to the top and bottom.

7

159 Make A section by joining pieces in numerical order. Join B1 and C1 to each side of the A section. Join D1 and E1 pieces to the top and bottom to complete the block.

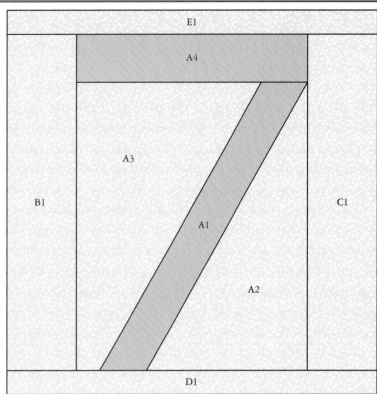

8

160 Make 4 A sections by joining pieces in numerical order. Join the 4 sections as shown to make center A unit. Make 2 B sections and join to the A unit. Make 2 C sections and 4 D sections. Join to make 2 D-C-D units and join to the top and bottom of the A-B unit. Join E pieces to the sides and F pieces to the top and bottom.

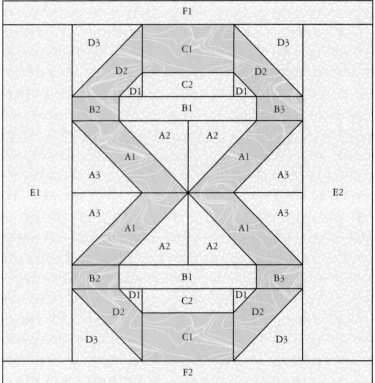

223

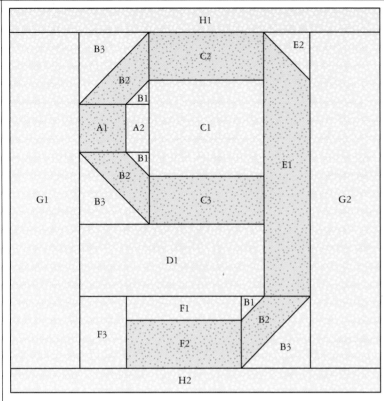

9

161 Make A section by joining the 2 A pieces. Make 3 B sections. Join 2 B sections to A section. Make C section and join to the B-A-B unit; then join the D1 piece. Make E section and join to A-B-C-D unit. Make F section and join to remaining B section. Join B-F unit to completed unit. Join G pieces to the sides and H pieces to the top and bottom.

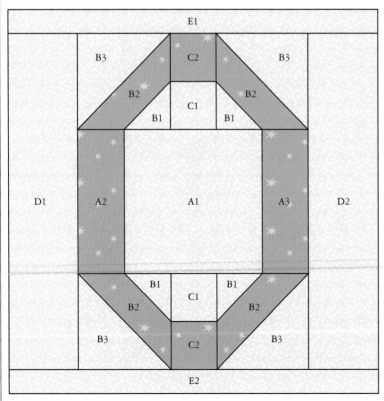

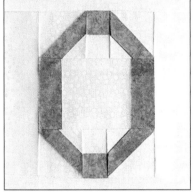

0

162 Make A section by joining pieces in numerical order. Make 4 B sections and 2 C sections. Join to make 2 B-C-B units and join to the top and bottom of the A section. Join D pieces to the sides and E pieces to the top and bottom.

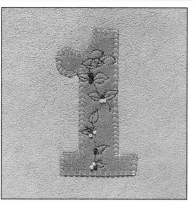

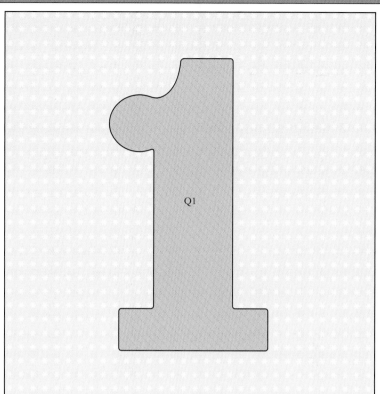

ONE

163 Appliqué the Q1 piece to the background block. Use blanket stitch to outline the numeral. With the photo as a guide, use stem stitch, lazy daisy stitches, and French knots to embellish as desired.

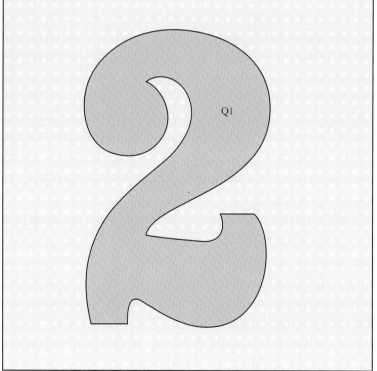

TWO

164 Appliqué the Q1 piece to the background block. Use blanket stitch to outline the numeral. With the photo as a guide, use stem stitch, lazy daisy stitches, and French knots to embellish as desired.

THREE

165 Appliqué the Q1 piece to the background block. Use blanket stitch to outline the numeral. With the photo as a guide, use stem stitch, lazy daisy stitches, and French knots to embellish as desired.

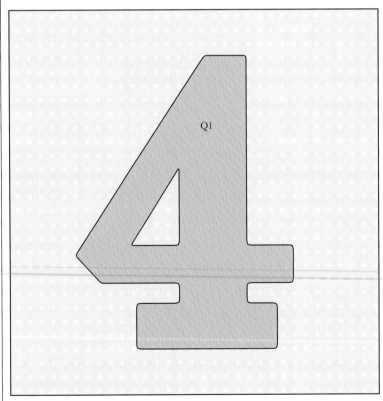

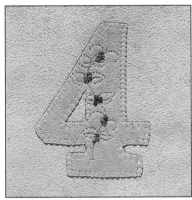

FOUR

166 Appliqué the Q1 piece to the background block. Use blanket stitch to outline the numeral. With the photo as a guide, use stem stitch, lazy daisy stitches, and French knots to embellish as desired.

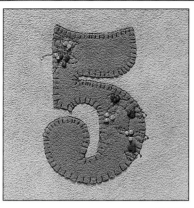

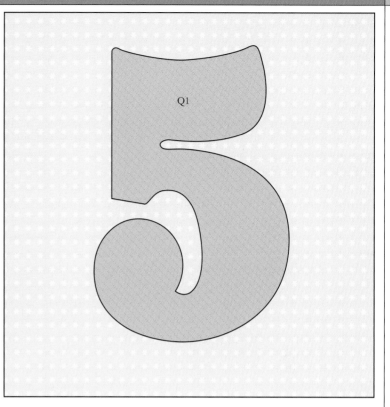

FIVE

167 Appliqué the Q1 piece to the background block. Use blanket stitch to outline the numeral. With the photo as a guide, use stem stitch, lazy daisy stitches, and French knots to embellish as desired.

SIX

168 Appliqué the Q1 piece to the background block. Use blanket stitch to outline the numeral. With the photo as a guide, use stem stitch, lazy daisy stitches, and French knots to embellish as desired.

227

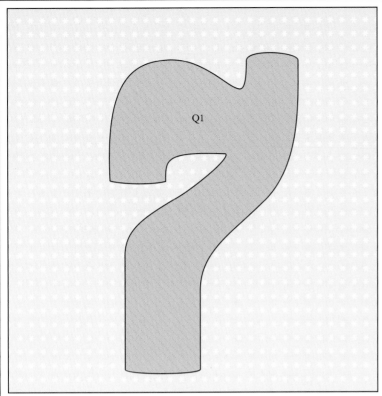

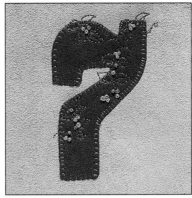

SEVEN

I69 Appliqué the Q1 piece to the background block. Use blanket stitch to outline the numeral. With the photo as a guide, use stem stitch, lazy daisy stitches, and French knots to embellish as desired.

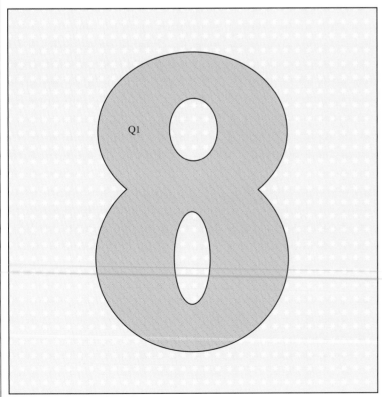

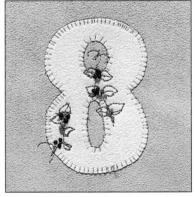

EIGHT

I70 Appliqué the Q1 piece to the background block. Use blanket stitch to outline the numeral. With the photo as a guide, use stem stitch, lazy daisy stitches, and French knots to embellish as desired.

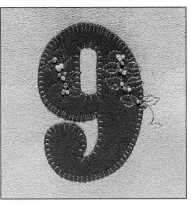

NINE

171 Appliqué the Q1 piece to the background block. Use blanket stitch to outline the numeral. With the photo as a guide, use stem stitch, lazy daisy stitches, and French knots to embellish as desired.

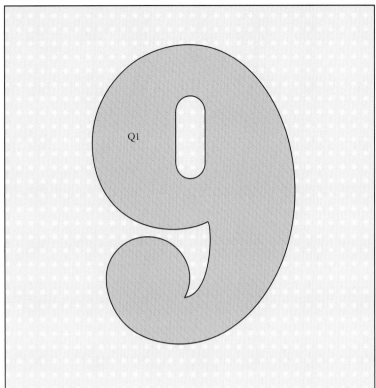

ZERO

172 Appliqué the Q1 piece to the background block. Use blanket stitch to outline the numeral. With the photo as a guide, use stem stitch, lazy daisy stitches, and French knots to embellish as desired.

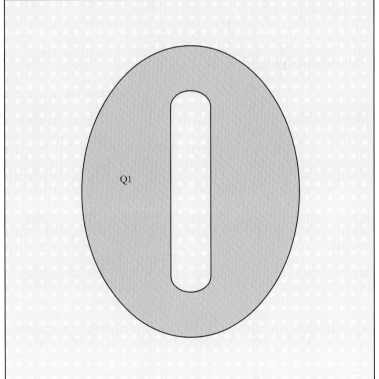

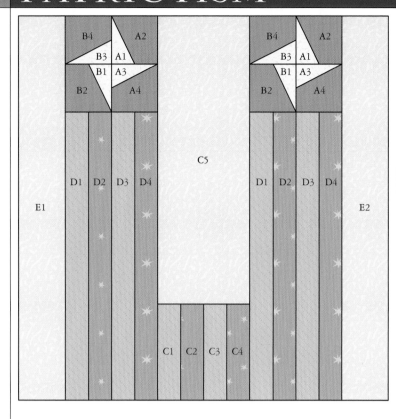

USA "U"

J1 Make 2 A sections by joining pieces in numerical order. Make 2 B sections. Join each B section to an A section. Make the C section. Make 2 D sections. Join an A-B unit to each D section. Join an A-B-D unit to each side of the C section. Join the E1 and E2 pieces to each side of the A-B-C-D unit.

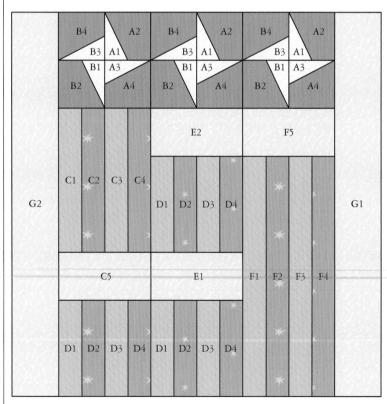

USA "S"

J2 Make 3 A sections by joining pieces in numerical order. Make 3 B sections. Join each B section to an A section. Make the C section and 3 D sections. Join 1 D section to C section then join to 1 A-B unit. Join 2 D sections with the E pieces, then join to 1 A-B unit. Make F section and join to 1 A-B unit. Join the 3 units, then join G pieces to the sides.

USA "A"

J3 Make 3 A sections by joining pieces in numerical order. Make 3 B sections. Join each B section to an A section. Make the C section and join to an A-B unit. Make the D section and join to an A-B unit. Make the E section and join to an A-B unit. Join the 3 completed units. Join the F1 and F2 pieces to each side to complete the block.

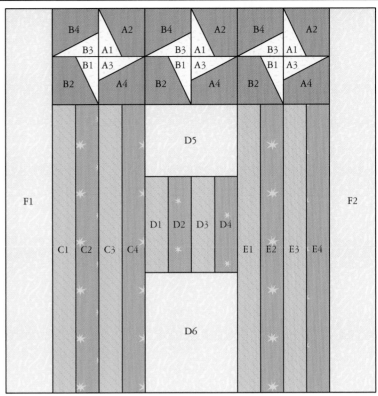

AMERICAN ROCKET

J4 Make the A section by joining pieces in numerical order. Make 2 B sections and 2 C sections and join into 2 B-C units. Join D pieces to one B-C unit. Make the E and F sections and join to each side of the B-C-D unit. Join G pieces to the other B-C unit. Make H and I sections and join to each side of the B-C-G unit. Join the B-C-G-H-I unit to one side of the A section and the B-C-D-E-F unit to the other side. Make the J section and join to the completed unit. Join the K piece to the opposite corner. Use stem stitch to embroider rocket trails.

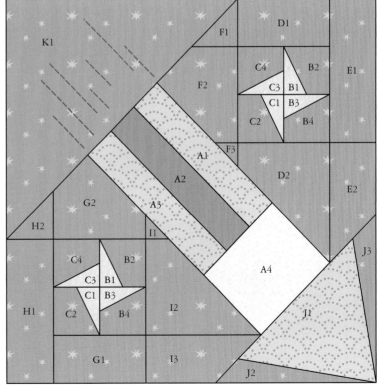

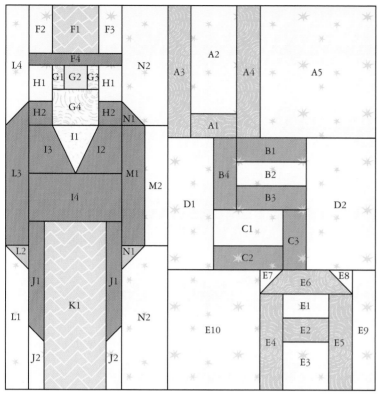

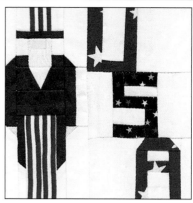

UNCLE SAM

J5 Make the A section by joining pieces in numerical order. Make the B and C sections and join, then join the D pieces to make the B-C-D unit. Make the E section. Join sections to make the A-B-C-D-E unit. Make the F, G, H, and I sections and join. Make the J-K unit and join to the F-G-H-I unit. Make the L section and join to the F-G-H-I-J-K unit. Make 2 N sections and join with 1 M section. Join all units.

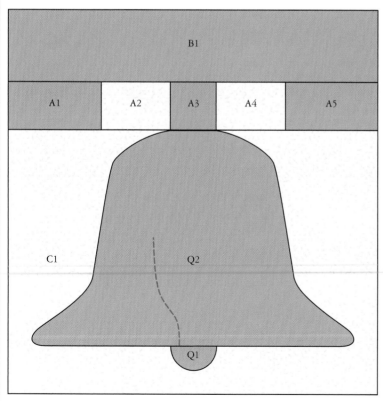

LIBERTY BELL

J6 Make the A section by joining the A pieces in numerical order. Join the B1 piece to the A section. Appliqué the Q1 and Q2 pieces to the C1 piece; then join to the A-B unit. Use stem stitch to embroider the crack in the bell.

EAGLE

J7 Appliqué Q pieces in numerical order on background block. Appliqué along lines indicated on wings and tail. Use satin stitch to embroider an eye on the eagle.

WAVING FLAG

J8 Use printed flag (or hand-painted) fabric for the Q1 piece. Turn under and hand-stitch a narrow hem around the piece. Appliqué in place on the background block, making a loose fold in the flag. For flag pole, use a darning needle to pull the cording through the background block at the top of the flag. Make a knot at that point. Tack the cording in place.

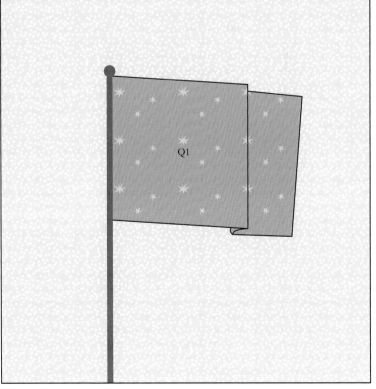

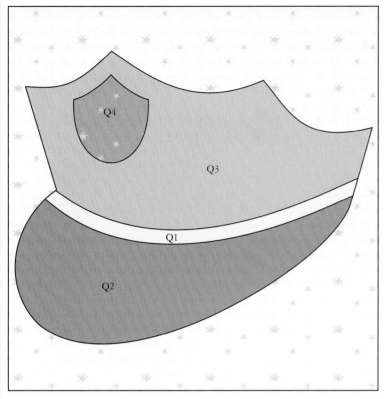

POLICE HAT

J9 Appliqué the Q pieces in numerical order to the background block.

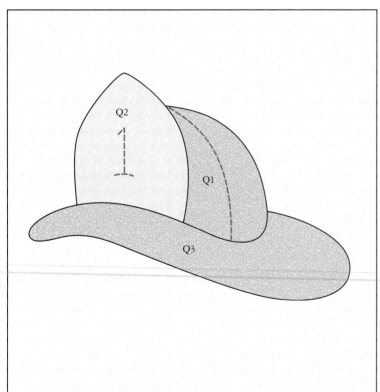

FIRE HAT

J10 Appliqué the Q pieces in numerical order to the background block. Use stem stitch to detail the Q1 piece and to embroider a number on the hat.

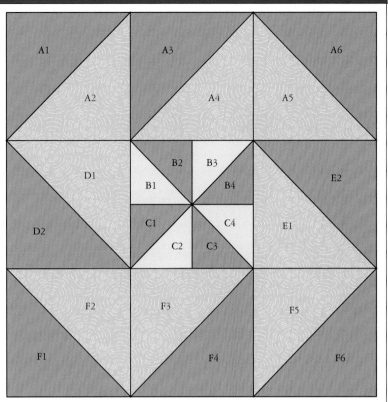

SPINNING SPARKLER

J11 Make the A section by joining the A pieces in numerical order. Make the B and C sections and join. Make the D section and join to the B-C unit. Make the E section and join to the B-C-D unit. Join the A section to the top of the B-C-D-E unit. Make the F section and join to the A-B-C-D-E unit.

Look Again

(Below) When Bunting blocks join as shown, left, a continuous chain of round links appears. Imagine changing the colors and adding straight-stitch spokes for a Halloween quilt spiderweb design.

BUNTING

J12 Make the A section by joining the A pieces in numerical order. Make the B section and join to the A section. Make the C and D sections and join. Join the C-D unit to the A-B unit.

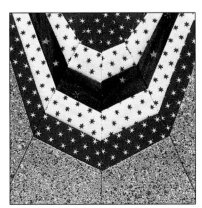

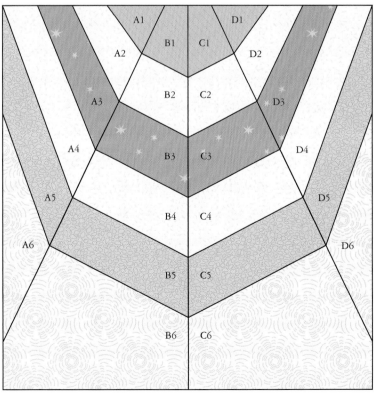

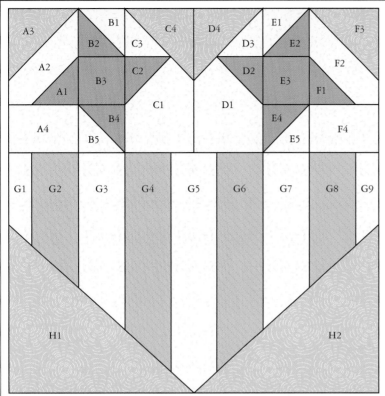

PATRIOTIC HEART

J13 Make the A section by joining pieces in numerical order. Make the B and C sections and join to the A section. Make the D, E and F sections and join. Join the A-B-C unit to the D-E-F unit. Make the G section; join H1 and H2 pieces to the G section. Join the G-H unit to the A-B-C-D-E-F unit.

Look Again

(Below) Combine Star in the Middle blocks to create movement in the design. While the stars remain prominent, the corner pieces come together to form interesting diamond patterns.

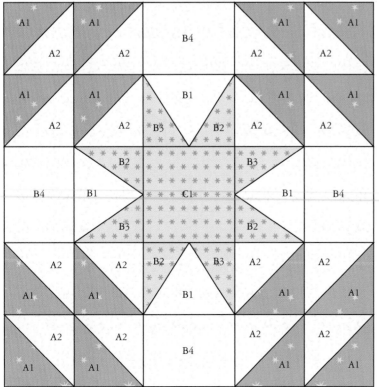

STAR IN THE MIDDLE

J14 Make 16 A sections. Join A sections into 4 squares. Make 4 B sections. Join an A square to each side of a B section. Repeat to make 2 A-B-A units. Join B sections to opposite sides of a C1 piece. Join the 3 rows (A-B-A, B-C-B, and A-B-A) to complete the block.

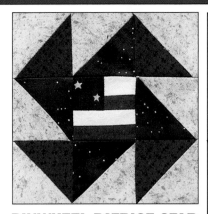

PINWHEEL PATRIOT STAR

J15 Make 4 A sections and 4 B sections in colors as shown. Make the C section by joining pieces in numerical order. Join B sections to opposite sides of the C section. Make 2 A-B-A units and join to the the top and bottom of the B-C-B unit.

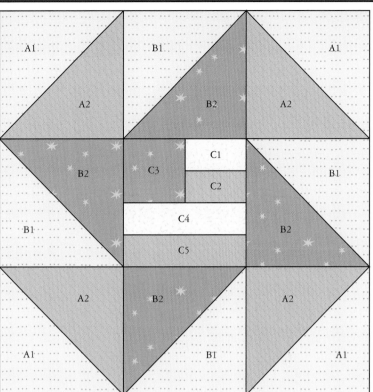

STAR PINWHEEL

J16 Using red, white, and blue-star fabrics, make 4 A sections by joining pieces in numerical order. Make 4 B sections. Join an A section to each B section for 4 A-B units. Sew the units together to complete the block.

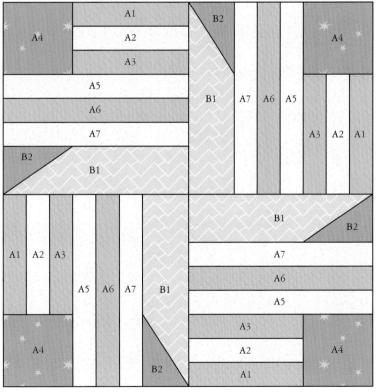

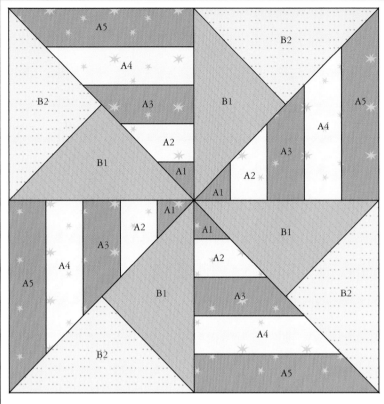

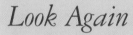

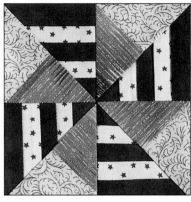

PINWHEEL

J17 Make 4 A sections by joining the A pieces in numerical order. Make 4 B sections. Join an A section to each B section for 4 A-B units. Join the 4 units to complete the block.

Look Again

(Above) For a lively patterned design, combine several Pinwheel blocks. Look closely and you'll see diamond-inside-diamond patterns created.

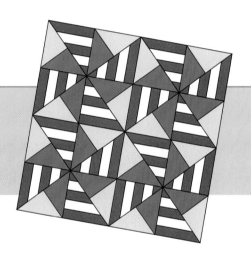

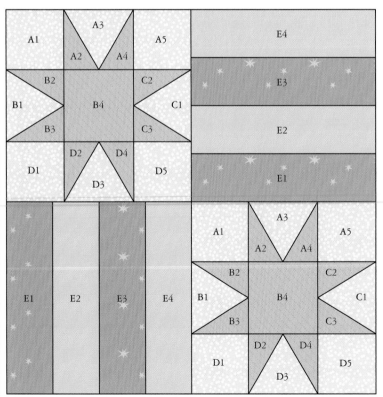

STARS AND STRIPES

J18 Make 2 A sections by joining pieces in numerical order. Make 2 B and 2 C sections and join to make 2 B-C units. Make 2 D sections. Join all to make 2 A-B-C-D units. Make 2 E sections. Join an E section to each A-B-C-D unit; join the 2 units.

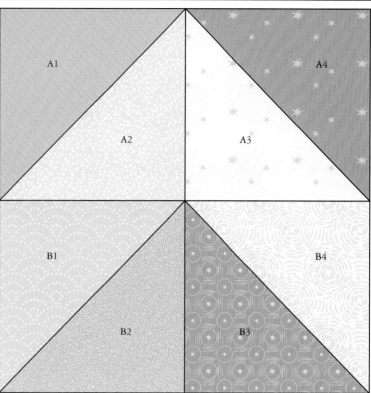

ROCKET

J19 Make the A section by joining pieces in numerical order. Make the B section and join to the A section to complete the block.

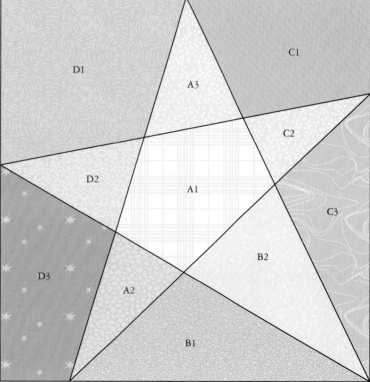

GOLD STAR

J20 Make the A section by joining pieces in numerical order. Make the B section and join to A section. Make the C section and join to the A-B unit. Make the D section and join to the A-B-C unit to complete the block.

PATRIOTISM

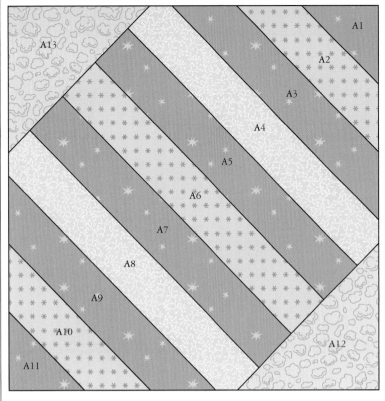

PATRIOTIC STRIPES

J21 Join the A pieces in numerical order to make the block. (The A1–A11 section can be strip pieced and trimmed to size. Then join the the A12 and A13 pieces.)

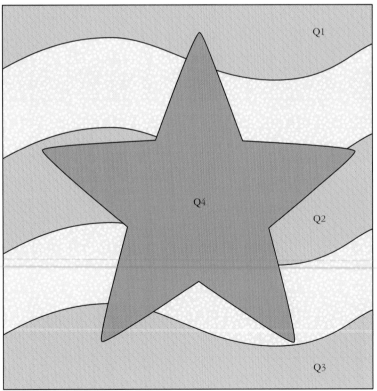

STAR ON STRIPES

J22 Appliqué the Q pieces in numerical order to background block. Outline the star with blanket stitch.

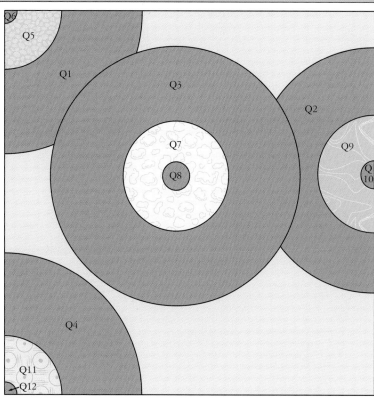

HIT PARADE

K1 Hand appliqué pieces in numerical order. The centers of each record (Q6, Q8, Q10, and Q12) may be embroidered, using satin stitch, or completed as reverse appliqué.

Look Again

(Above) The round record shapes in the Hit Parade block join to make layers of complete and overlapping circles.

WINDOW ON THE WORLD

K2 Hand-appliqué pieces in numerical order. If desired, buttons could be used for the "knobs" (Q4–Q8) rather than appliqué.

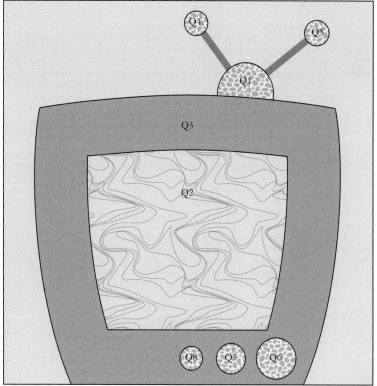

241

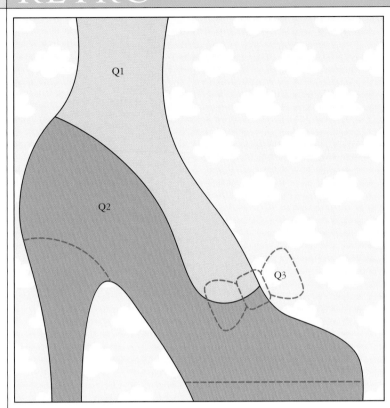

HERS

K3 Hand appliqué Q1 and Q2 pieces in place. Make a fabric bow for Q3 and tack in place. Use a running stitch to embroider heel and sole lines.

Look Again

(Below) Rotate four Poodle Skirt blocks and a full-circle skirt emerges. The poodles appear to be in motion, walking around the skirt edge.

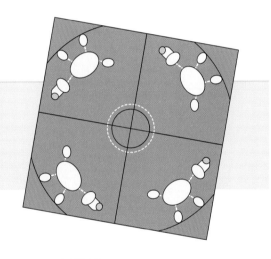

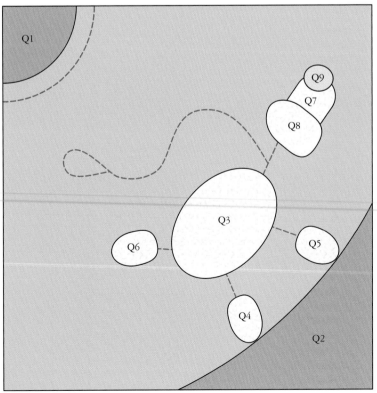

POODLE SKIRT

K4 Cut background block from "skirt" fabric. Appliqué Q1 and Q2 pieces. Cut Q pieces for poodle from felt and fuse or sew in place. Use stem stitch to embroider legs, tail, and neck of poodle and along skirt waistline. Tack on a decorative cord for leash. Add a seed bead to detail waistband.

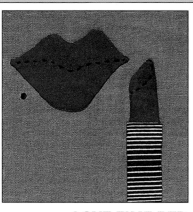

LOVE THAT RED

K5 Hand-appliqué Q1, Q2, and Q3 pieces. Use a running stitch to embroider lip lines and lipstick. Satin stitch a beauty mark.

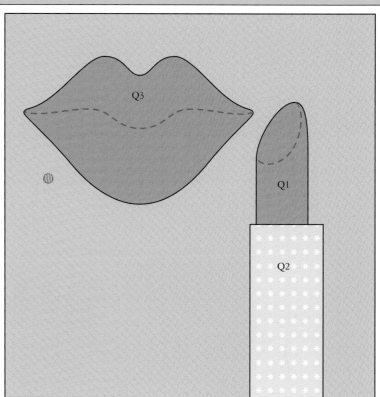

PROM NIGHT

K6 Appliqué Q1 and Q2 pieces. Necklace may be made of fabric appliqué, beads, or buttons.

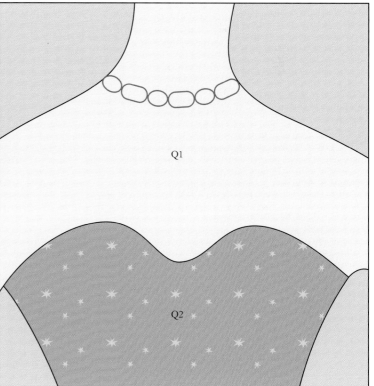

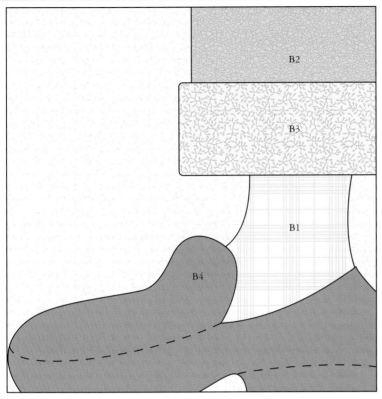

HIS

K7 Appliqué the Q pieces in numerical order to the background block. Use a running stitch to detail the shoe.

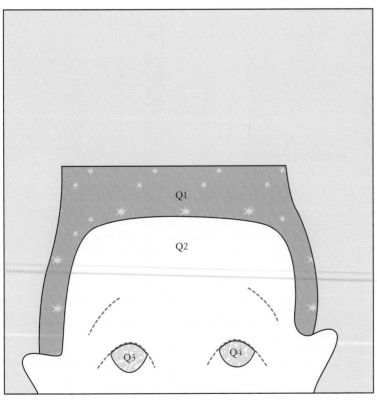

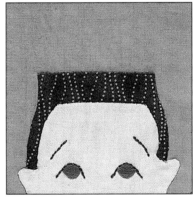

FLAT TOP

K8 Appliqué Q1 and Q2 pieces. Q3 and Q4 may be appliquéd fabric or felt or embroidered using satin stitch. Use stem stitch to embroider eyebrows and eyelids.

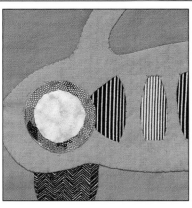

JALOPY

K9 Appliqué Q pieces in numerical order to background square.

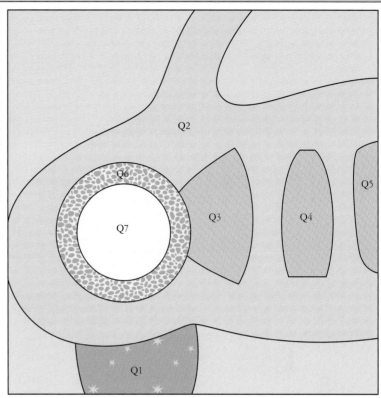

MALT SHOP

K10 Appliqué pieces in numerical order. Use a running stitch to embroider moisture on the side of the glass, and use stem stitch to make a cherry stem.

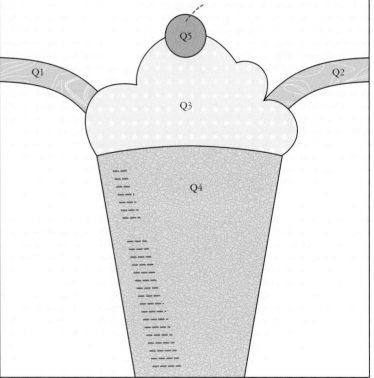

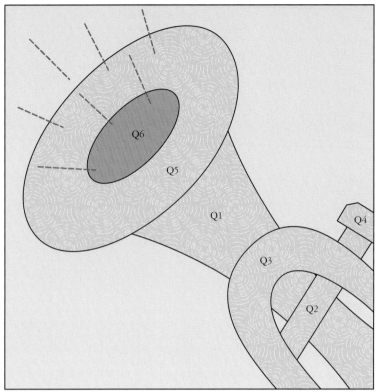

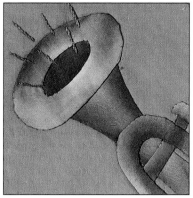

SWINGTIME

K11 Appliqué pieces in numerical order. Use stem stitch to embroider sound waves from the horn.

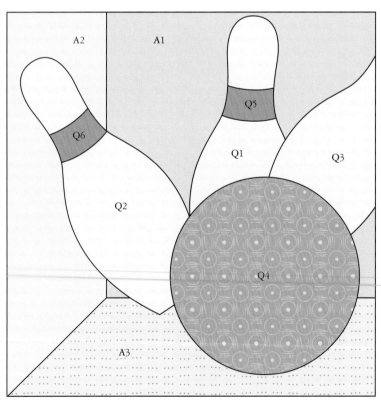

STRIKE

K12 Join A pieces to make background. Appliqué Q pieces in numerical order.

LOVE

K13 Appliqué or fuse letters onto background fabric, then blanket stitch around each letter.

BEEHIVE

K14 Appliqué Q1 and Q2 pieces. Appliqué a printed fabric butterfly or use a finished butterfly appliqué for Q3 piece. Use stem stitch to outline eyes and eyebrows. Use satin stitch for the eyes.

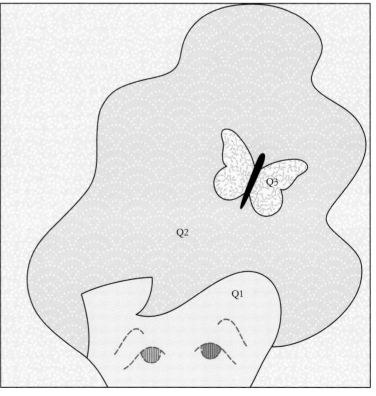

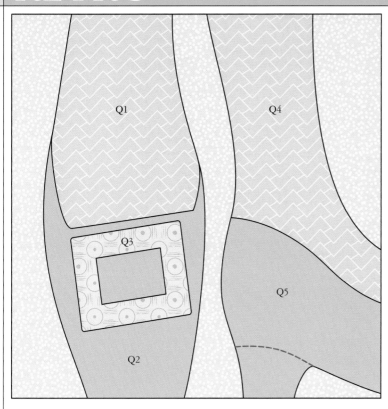

MOD

K15 Appliqué pieces in numerical order. Use a running stitch to embroider line on heel of shoe.

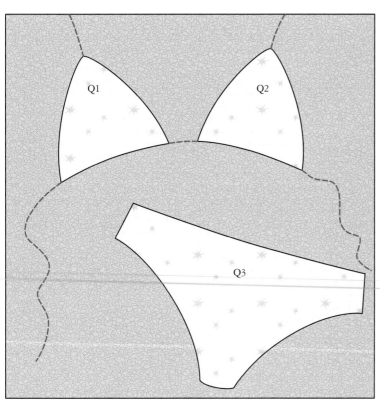

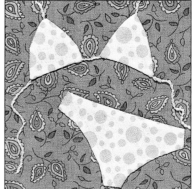

ITSY, BITSY

K16 Appliqué Q1, Q2, and Q3 pieces. Use stem stitch to embroider strings on suit top.

PORKPIE

K17 Appliqué Q1, Q2, and Q3 pieces. Use a running stitch to embroider mouth and hat detail.

MOON WALK

K18 Use "moon" fabric for block background. Appliqué pieces in numerical order. Use stem stitch to embroider "USA" and spaceship leg (connecting Q2 and Q9). A bead, button, or French knot can be used for the doorknob.

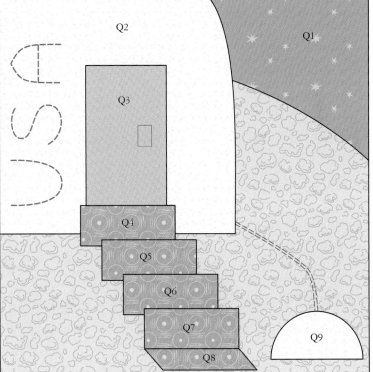

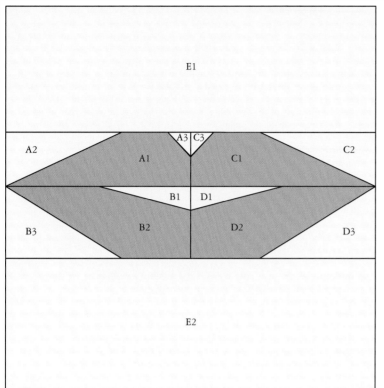

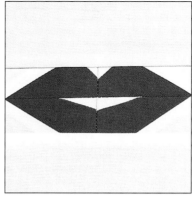

LIPS

K19 Make the A section by joining the A pieces in numerical order. Make the B section and join to the A section. Make the C and D sections and join. Join the C-D unit to the A-B unit. Join the E pieces to the top and bottom of the A-B-C-D unit.

FLOWER POWER

K20 Appliqué Q pieces in numerical order to the background block.

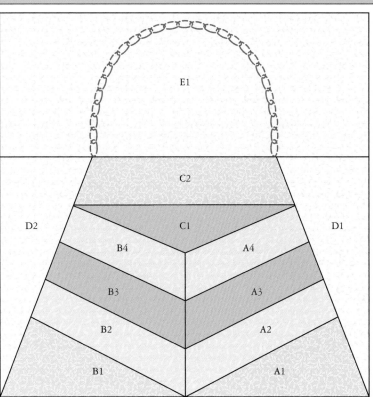

PRETTY PURSE

K21 Make the A section by joining the A pieces in numerical order. Make the B section and join to the A section. Make the C section and inset into the A-B unit. Join the D pieces to opposite sides of the A-B-C unit. Use chain stitch to crochet the handle; sew to the E1 piece. Join the E section to the A-B-C-D unit.

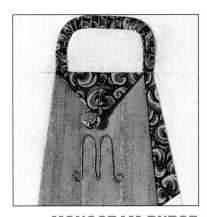

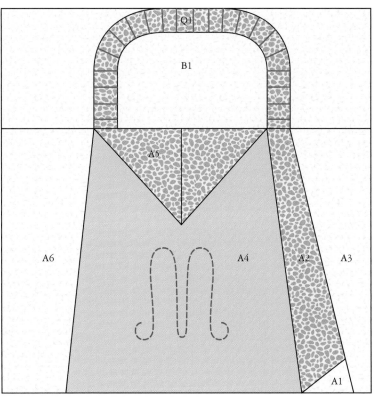

MONOGRAM PURSE

K22 Make the A section by joining the A pieces in numerical order. (The A5 piece is a prairie point. See page 313 for instructions.) Appliqué the Q1 piece to B1. Join the appliqué section to the A section. Use stem stitch to embroider a monogram. Use straight stitches on the handle. Tack a charm to the prairie point.

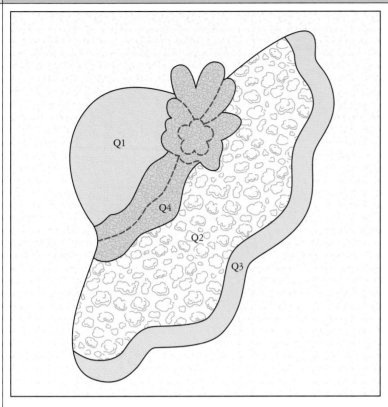

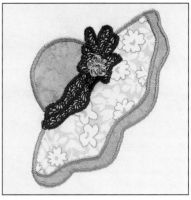

FLOWER HAT

K23 Appliqué the Q pieces in numerical order to the background block. Use machine appliqué or stem stitch to embellish hat band as shown. Sew a button or bead to the flower center.

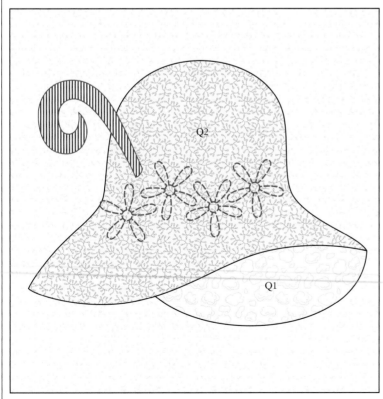

FEATHERED HAT

K24 Appliqué the Q pieces in numerical order to the background block. Use straight stitches and stem stitch to embroider the feather. Use lazy daisy stitches for the flowers. Sew a bead to the center of each flower.

STOPWATCH

L1 Appliqué the Q pieces in numerical order on the background block. Use stem stitch to embroider detail on the stem, the 4 numerals, and the hands. Use satin stitch at the center of the hands. Sew beads between numerals.

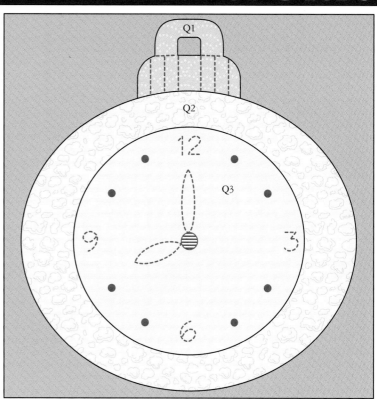

STAR MEDAL

L2 Piece the block by joining the A pieces in numerical order. Appliqué the Q1 pieces in numerical order.

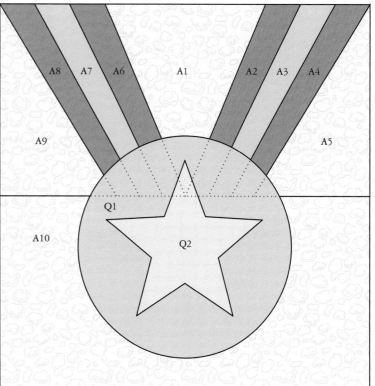

SPORTS

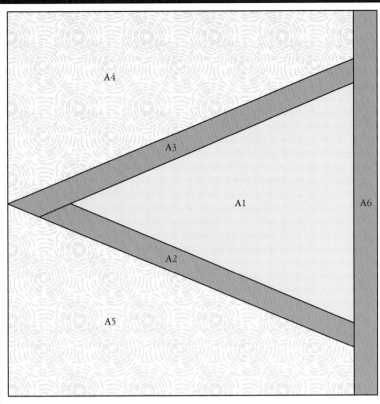

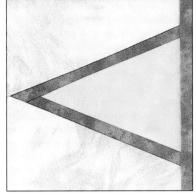

PENNANT

L3 Join the A pieces in numerical order to complete the block.

Look Again

(Below) Reverse the colors for the B1 and D1 pieces to create a mirror image. Make 2 blocks of each configuration, place as shown at right, and a wonderful pattern emerges that is reminiscent of Frank Lloyd Wright designs.

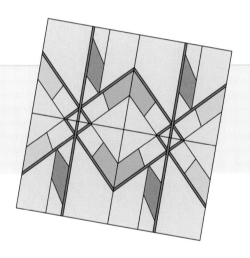

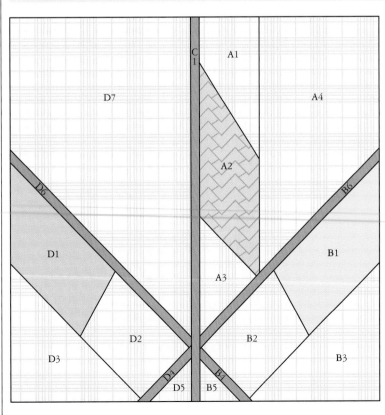

RACING FLAGS

L4 Make the A section by joining the A pieces in numerical order. Make the B section and join to the A section. Join the C1 piece to the A-B unit. Make the D section and join to the A-B-C unit.

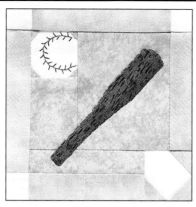

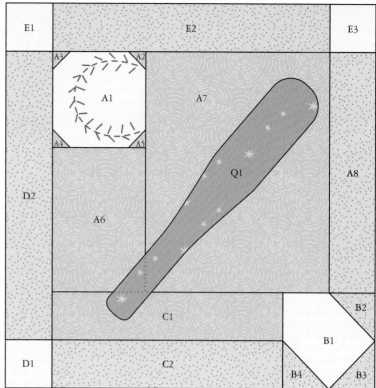

BASEBALL

L5 Make the A section by joining the A pieces in numerical order. Make the B and C sections and join. Join the B-C unit to the A section. Make the D section and join to the A-B-C unit. Make the E section and join to the top of the A-B-C-D unit. Appliqué the Q1 piece in place. Use feather stitch to embroider the baseball.

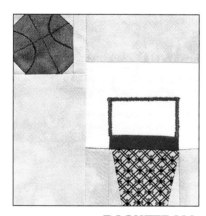

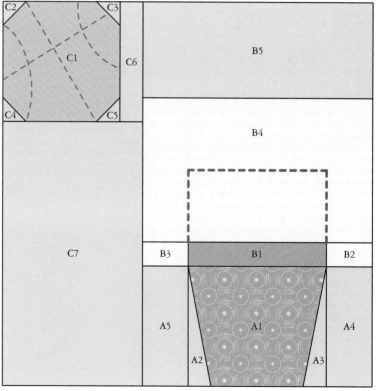

BASKETBALL

L6 Make the A section by joining the A pieces in numerical order. Make the B section and join to the A section. Make the C section and join to the A-B unit. Use stem stitch to embroider lines on the basketball. Machine-satin-stitch lines on the backboard.

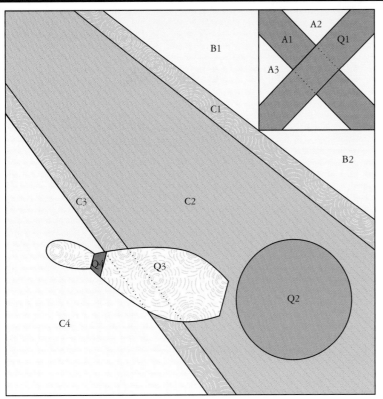

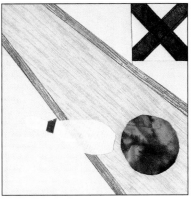

BOWLING

L7 Make the A section by joining the 3 A pieces. Appliqué the Q1 piece on the A section. Join the B pieces to the A section. Make the C section and join to the A-B unit. Appliqué the Q2, Q3, and Q4 pieces in place.

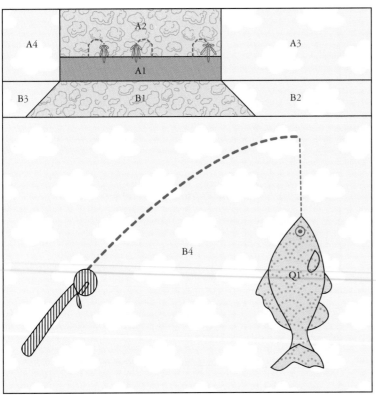

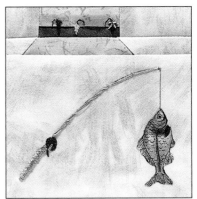

FISHING

L8 Make the A section by joining the A pieces in numerical order. Make the B section and join to the A section. Appliqué printed fabric fish Q1 to the B4 piece. Use satin stitch to make the handle of the fishing pole. Couch strands of embroidery floss to make the fishing pole. Use a straight stitch for the fishing line. Use stem stitches and straight stitches to embroider fishing flies in the hat brim.

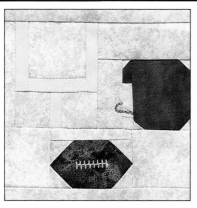

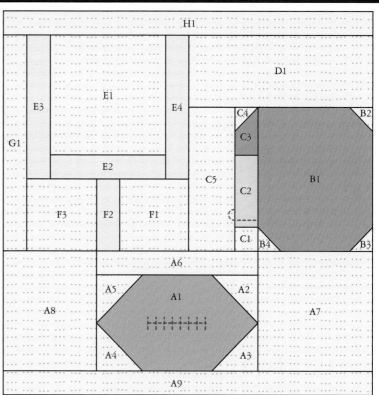

FOOTBALL

L9 Make the A section by joining the A pieces in numerical order. Make the B and C sections and join. Join the D1 piece to the B-C unit. Make the E and F sections and join. Join the G1 piece to the E-F unit. Join the E-F-G unit to the B-C-D unit. Join the A section to the B-C-D-E-F-G unit. Join the H1 piece to the top of the block. Use stem stitch and straight stitches to embroider the football. Use stem stitch for helmet strap.

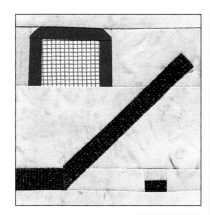

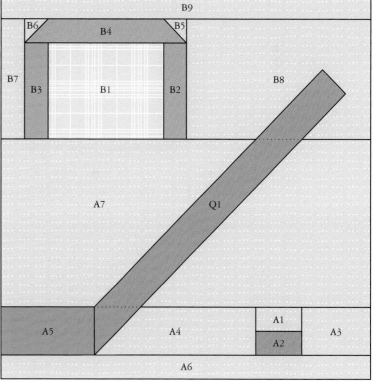

HOCKEY

L10 Make the A section by joining the A pieces in numerical order. Make the B section and join to the A section. Appliqué the Q1 piece in place.

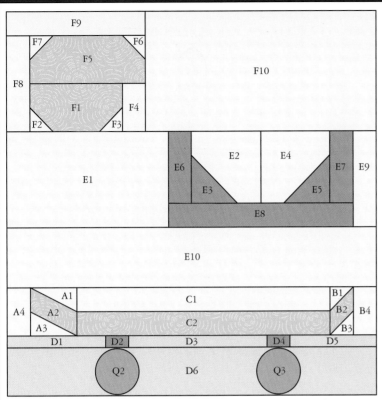

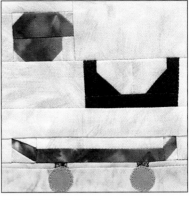

SKATEBOARD

L11 Make the A section by joining the A pieces in numerical order. Make the B and C sections. Join the sections to make the A-B-C unit. Make the D section and join to the A-B-C unit. Make the E section and join to the A-B-C-D unit. Make the F section and join to the top of the A-C-B-D-E unit. Appliqué the Q pieces in place.

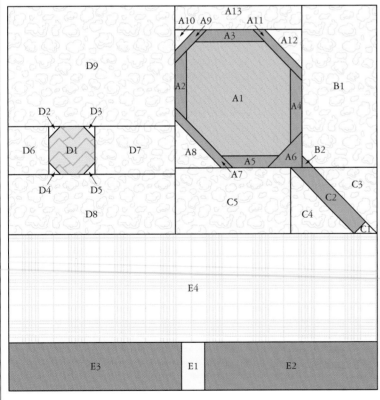

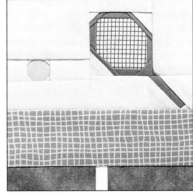

TENNIS

L12 Make the A section by joining the A pieces in numerical order. Make the B section and join to the A section. Make the C section and join to the A-B unit. Make the D section and join to the A-B-C unit. Make the E section and join to the A-B-C-D unit.

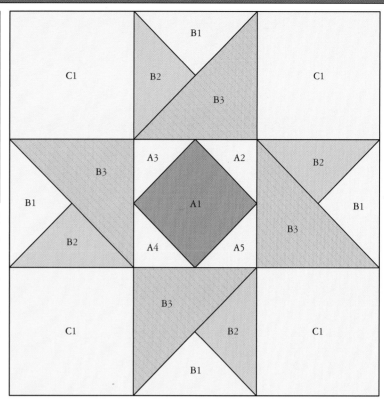

CROSSED STAR

M1 Make the A section by joining the A pieces in numerical order. Make 4 B sections. Join 2 B sections to opposite sides of the A section. Join C1 pieces to each end of 2 B sections. Join the C-B-C units to opposite sides of the B-A-B unit.

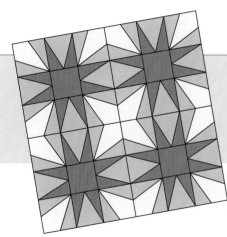

Look Again

(Below) New four-pointed stars and large background diamonds are created when Spring Star blocks are joined.

SPRING STAR

M2 Make 4 A sections by joining the A pieces in numerical order. Join 2 A sections to opposite sides of the B1 piece. Make 4 C sections. Make 2 C-A-C units. Join the C-A-C units to the A-B-A unit.

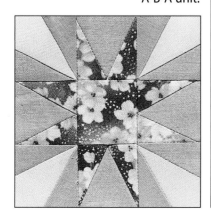

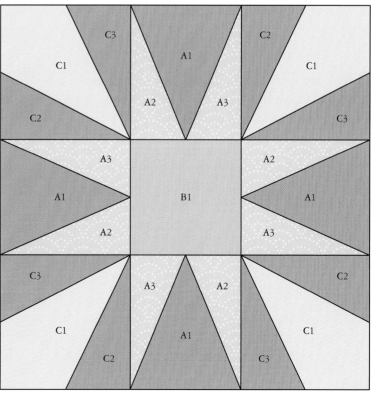

259

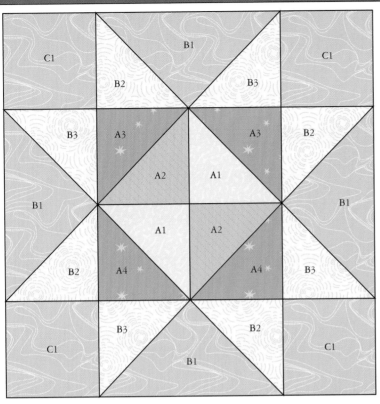

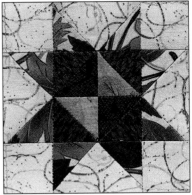

AUTUMN STAR

M3 Make 2 A sections by joining the A pieces in numerical order. Join the 2 A sections. Make 4 B sections. Join 2 B sections to opposite sides of the A-A unit. Join C1 pieces to opposite ends of 2 B sections. Join the C-B-C units to the top and bottom of the center B-A-B unit.

Look Again

(Below) Rotate Stars blocks to make unified blocks of smaller stars. When only four blocks are joined, a ring of stars encircles the center grouping. When more blocks are added, like colors sit side-by-side to make the pattern appear less busy.

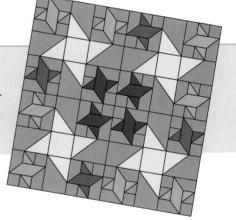

FIVE STARS

M4 Make the A section by joining the A pieces in numerical order. Make 2 B sections. Make 4 C, 4 D, and 4 E sections. Join the C, D, and E sections into 4 C-D-E units. Join C-D-E units to opposite sides of the B sections to make 2 C-D-E-B-C-D-E units. Join these units to opposite sides of the A section.

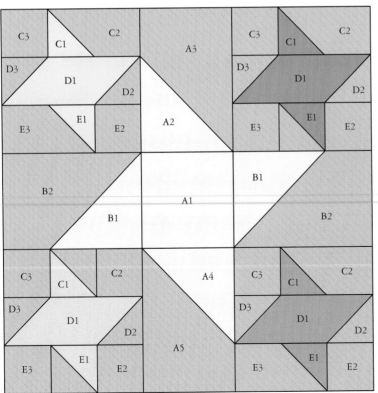

FOUR-POINTED CHECKED STAR

M5 Make 4 A sections by joining the A pieces in numerical order. Make 2 B-C units. Make 2 D-E units. Make 1 F-G unit. Assemble block in 3 rows. Make a B-C-A-D-E row, an A-F-G-A row and a D-E-A-B-C row. Join the rows to complete the block.

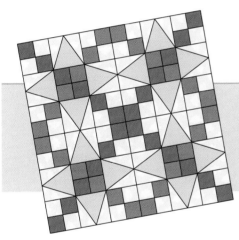

Look Again

(Above) A lively checkerboard pattern appears when Four-Pointed Checked Star blocks are combined.

STAR PATCH

M6 Join the A1 and A2 pieces twice; join to make the A section. Make 4 B sections. Make 4 C sections and 8 D sections. Join to make 4 D-C-D units. Join 2 B sections to opposite sides of A section. Join D-C-D units to opposite sides of remaining 2 B sections. Join the 3 rows of units to complete the block.

261

STARS

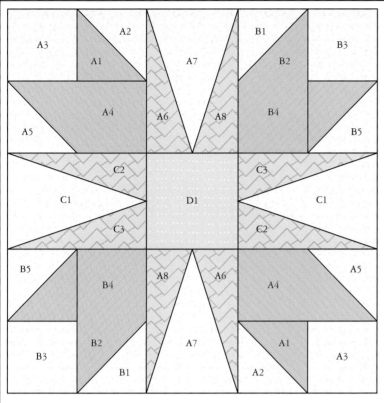

STARBURST

M7 Make 2 A sections by joining the A pieces in numerical order. Make 2 B sections and join a B section to each A section. Make 2 C sections and join to opposite sides of the D1 piece. Join the A-B units to opposite sides of the C-D-C unit.

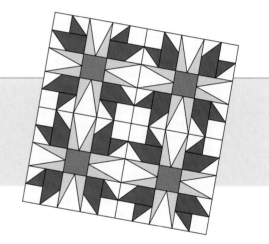

Look Again

(Above) For a pattern full of energy, combine Starburst blocks. Diamond and square patterns take shape where the star points meet.

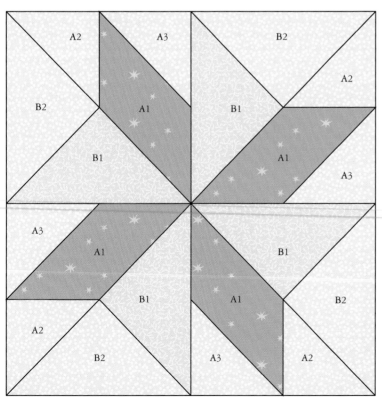

TWISTED STAR

M8 Join A1, A2, and A3. Make 4 A sections. Join B1 and B2. Make 4 B sections. Join A and B sections to make 4 squares. Join the 4 A-B units to complete the block.

STAR IN THE CENTER

M9 Make 4 A sections by joining the A pieces in numerical order. Make 4 B sections and join each B section to an A section. Make 4 C sections. Join 2 C sections to opposite sides of the D1 piece. Join 2 A-B units to opposite sides of a C section twice. Join the 3 rows.

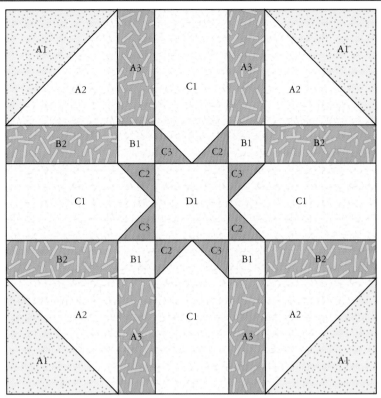

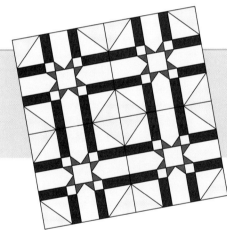

Look Again

(Above) Join Star in the Center blocks and a bold grid appears in the foreground while a large diamonds repeat in the background.

WIND BLADE STAR

M10 Join A1, A2 and A3. Make 4 of these A sections. Join the A sections to make the center square. Make 2 B sections and join to the top and bottom of the completed A section. Make 2 C sections and join to each side of the A-B unit.

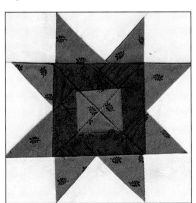

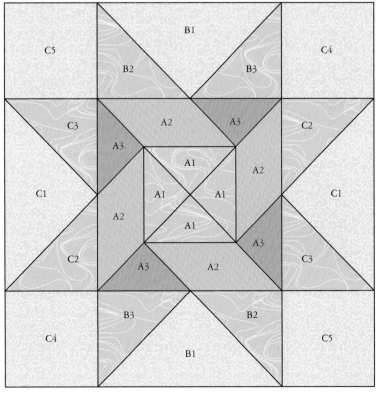

263

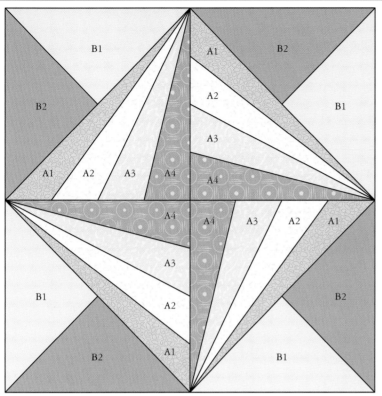

ROTATING STAR

M11 Make 4 A sections by joining pieces in numerical order. Make 4 B sections. Join a B section to each A section. Join the 4 A-B units to complete the block.

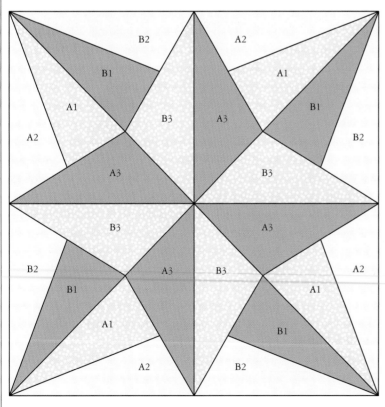

3-D STAR

M12 Make 4 A sections by joining the A pieces in numerical order. Make 4 B sections. Using pattern as a guide, join each A section to a B section. Join the 4 A-B units to complete the block.

GEOMETRIC STAR

M13 Make 2 A sections by joining the A pieces in numerical order. Make 2 B sections. Join an A section to a B section twice to make 2 A-B units. Join the 2 units to complete the block.

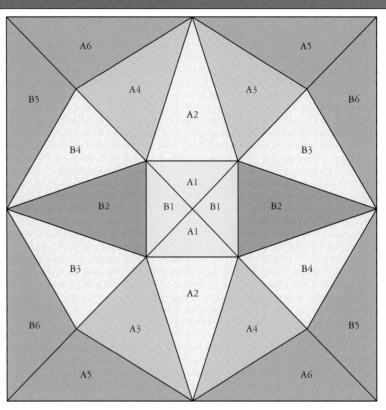

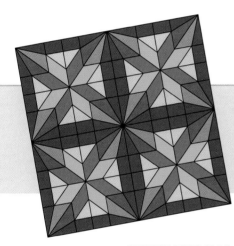

Look Again

(Below) *Dimensional Star blocks combine to create a beautiful pattern that appears to be layers deep. The star points meet to create windmill blades in a square.*

DIMENSIONAL STAR

M14 Make 4 A sections by joining pieces in numerical order. Maker 4 B sections and join each to an A section. Make 4 C sections; then 4 D sections and join each C section to a D section. Join each A-B unit to a C-D unit. Repeat to make a total of 4 A-B-C-D units. Join the 4 units to complete the block.

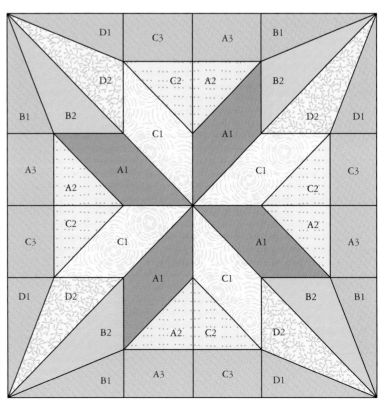

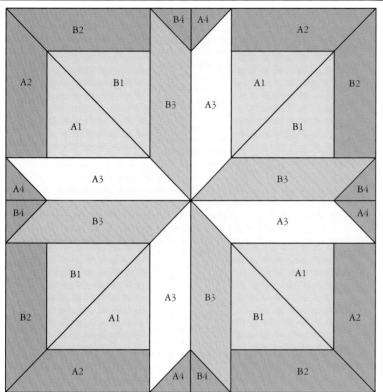

EIGHT-POINTED COUNTRY STAR

M15 Make 4 A sections and 4 B sections. Join each A section to each B section along diagonal line to make a square. Join the 4 A-B units to complete the block.

Look Again

(Below) Rotate four Chain Star blocks to make an eight-pointed center star. As more blocks are joined, the corners meet to create more star designs.

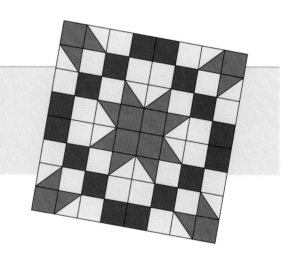

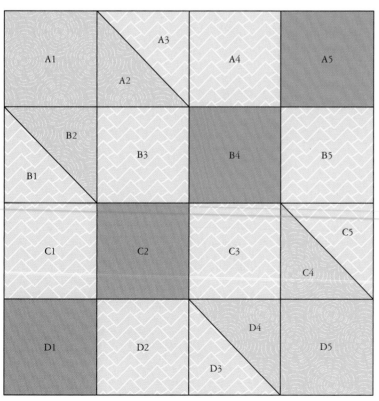

CHAIN STAR

M16 Make the A section by joining the A pieces in numerical order. Make the B section and join to the A section. Make the C section and join to the A-B unit. Make the D section and join to the A-B-C unit.

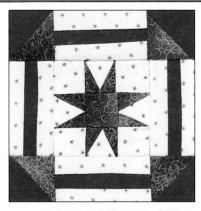

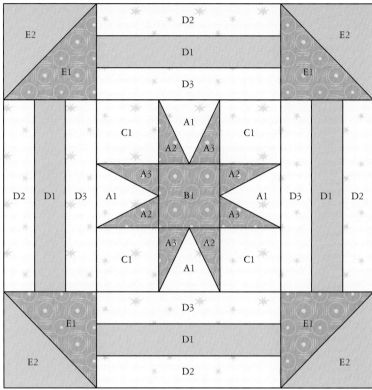

EIGHT-POINTED STAR

M17 Make 4 A sections by joining the A pieces in numerical order. Join 2 A sections to opposite sides of B1 piece. Join a C1 piece to opposite sides of 2 A sections. Join the C-A-C, A-B-A, and C-A-C units to make the center square. Make 4 D sections and 4 E sections. Join 2 D sections to opposite sides of the A-B-C unit. Join E sections to opposite ends of the remaining 2 D sections. Join the E-D-E units to the top and bottom of the D-A-B-C-D unit.

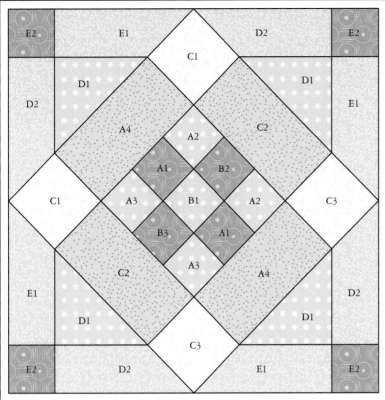

AMISH NINE-PATCH

N1 Make 2 A sections by joining the A pieces in numerical order. Make the B section. Join an A section to each side of the B section. Make 2 C sections and join to opposite sides of the A-B-A unit. Make 4 D sections and 4 E sections. Join these sections into 4 D-E units. Join a D-E unit to each side of the center A-B-C unit.

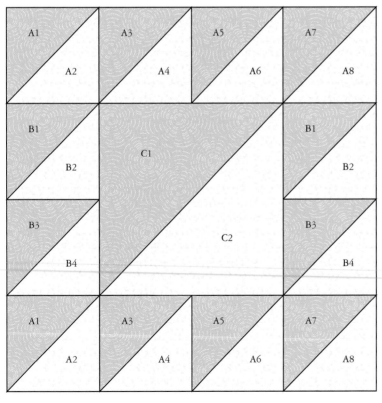

ANVIL

N2 Make 2 A sections by joining the A pieces in numerical order. Make 2 B sections. Join the C1 and C2 pieces. Join a B section to each side of the C section. Join the A sections to the top and bottom of the B-C-B unit.

SQUARES IN THE CORNER

N3 Make the A section by joining the A pieces. Make the B and C sections. Join the B section to the A section. Join the C section to the A-B unit.

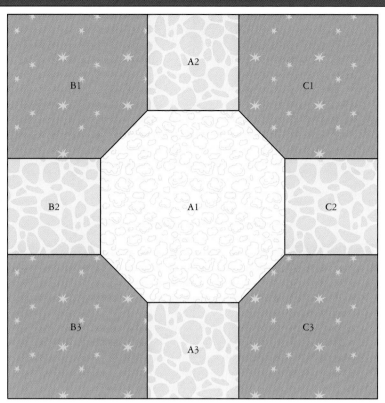

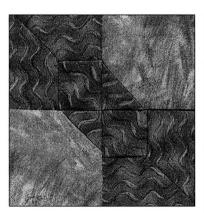

BOW TIE VARIATION

N4 Make 2 A sections by joining pieces in numerical order. Make 2 B sections. Join each A section to a B section. Join the 2 A-B units to complete the block.

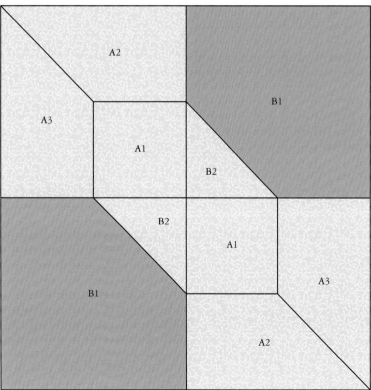

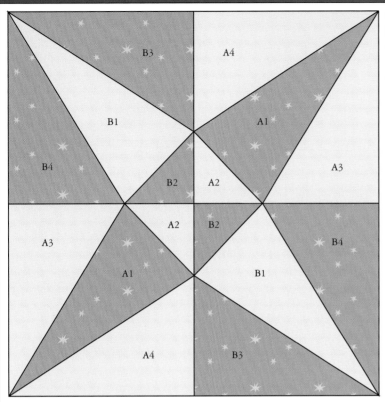

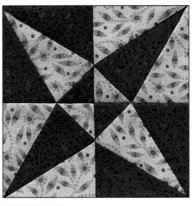

CANOES

N5 Make 2 A sections by joining pieces in numerical order. Make 2 B sections. Join to make 2 A-B units. Join the 2 units.

Look Again

(Above) Join several two-color Canoes blocks, and an overlapping circular pattern and checkerboard background is revealed.

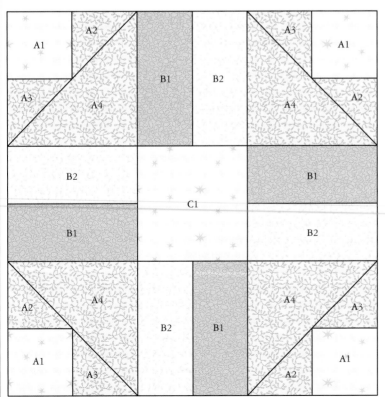

CENTER STRIPES

N6 Make 4 A sections by joining the A pieces in numerical order. Make 4 B sections. Join A sections to opposite sides of B sections to make 2 A-B-A rows. Join B sections opposite sides of the C1 piece to make the B-C-B row. Join the 3 rows to complete the block.

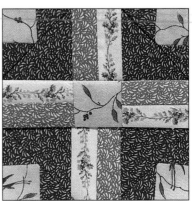

CENTER SQUARE

N7 Make A section by joining pieces in numerical order. Make 4 B sections. Make 4 C sections. Join a C section to 2 opposite sides of A section. Join B section to each end of the remaining 2 C sections. Join B-C-B sections to top and bottom of C-A-C unit.

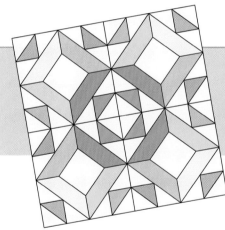

Look Again

(Below) Dimension square and diamond patterns seem to almost dance when Charm blocks are rotated.

CHARM

N8 Make 4 A sections by joining pieces in numerical order. Make B section and join 1 A section to each end of B section. Join C piece to each of the other 2 A sections. Join the A-C units to each side of the A-B unit.

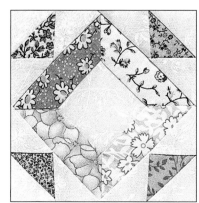

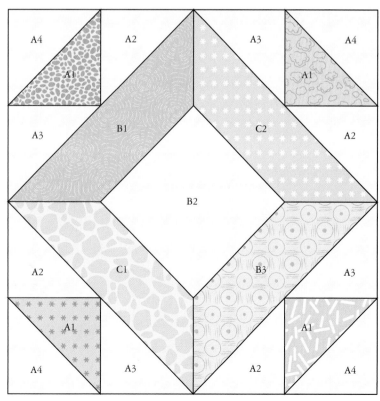

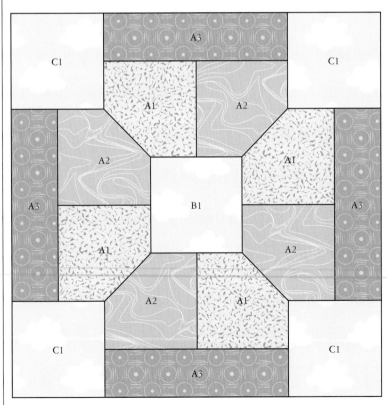

CHECKERED CROSS

N9 Join A 1 and A 2 pieces to make 6 A sections. Join into 3 A-A units. Make 4 B sections and join into 2 B-B units. Make 4 C sections. Join into 3 rows (A-C-B, C-A-C, and B-C-A). Join rows.

CORNER FLOWERS

N10 Make 4 A sections by joining the A pieces in numerical order. Join 2 A sections to the B1 piece. Join C1 pieces to each end of both remaining A sections. Join the C-A-C units to opposite sides of the A-B-A unit.

CORNER NINE PATCH

N11 Join pieces into 3 rows (A1-A2-A3, B1-B2-B3, C1-C2-C3). Join the 3 rows.

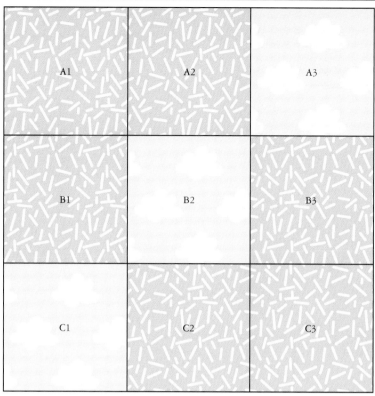

CRAZY HOUSE
(SQUARES IN THE MIDDLE)

N12 Join A1 and A2 to make 8 A sections. Join into 4 A-A units. Make 4 B sections. Join sections into 3 rows (A-B-A, B-C-B, A-B-A). Join the 3 rows.

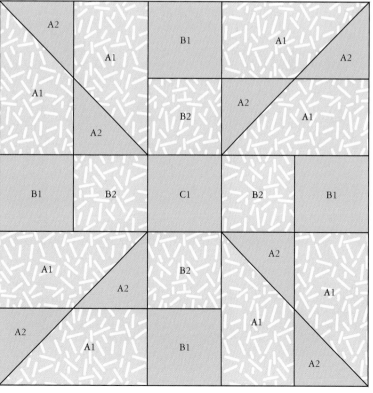

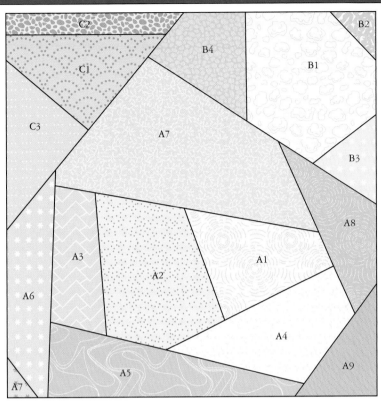

CRAZY PATCH

N13 Make the A section by joining the A pieces in numerical order. Make the B section and join to the A section. Make the C section and join to the A-B unit. Embellish the block with decorative embroidery, using the photo for a guide. Use blanket stitches, feather stitches, lazy daisy, straight stitches, and French knots as desired.

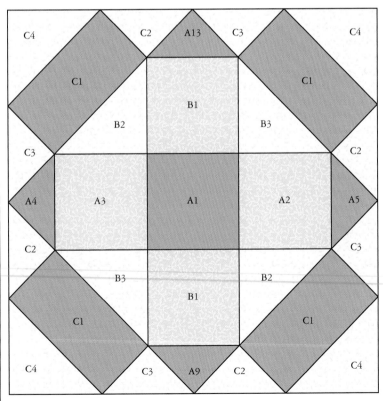

CROSS

N14 Make A section by joining the A pieces in numerical order. Make 2 B sections and join to opposite sides of the A section. Make 4 C sections and join to the 4 sides of the B-A-B unit.

FLYING GEESE VARIATION

N15 Make 4 A sections by joining pieces in numerical order. Make B-C-D unit 2 times. Make E-F-G unit 2 times. Join G-E-F unit to A section, then join B-C-D unit. Join 2 A sections to H1 piece. Join B-C-D unit to A section, then join G-E-F unit. Join the 3 units to complete the block.

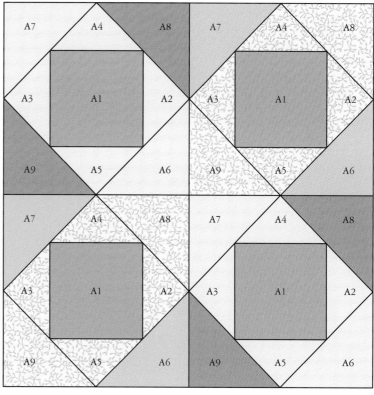

Look Again

(Above) Join Flying Geese Variation blocks and intricate overlapping grids appear. Placing the dark and light fabrics in different areas of each block will change the pattern dramatically.

CROSSED STRIPES

N16 Make 4 A sections by joining pieces in numerical order. Join 2 A sections, then join the remaining 2 A sections. Join the 2 A-A units to complete the block.

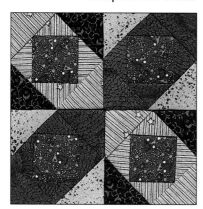

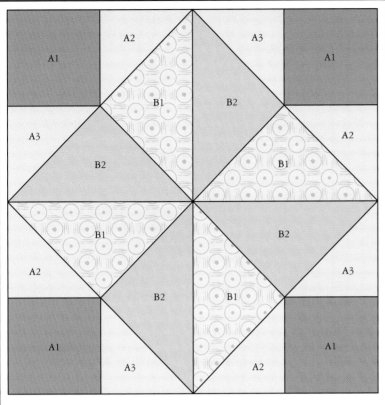

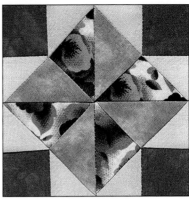

DOUBLE PINWHEEL

N17 Make 4 A sections by joining the A pieces in numerical order. Make 4 B sections by joining B1 and B2. Join the 4 B sections into a square. Join an A section to each side of the B square.

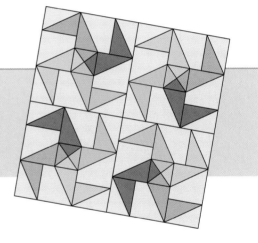

Look Again

(Below) Rotate and join four Fan Blades blocks to add movement to these lively blocks. The color positioning makes the blades appear to turn.

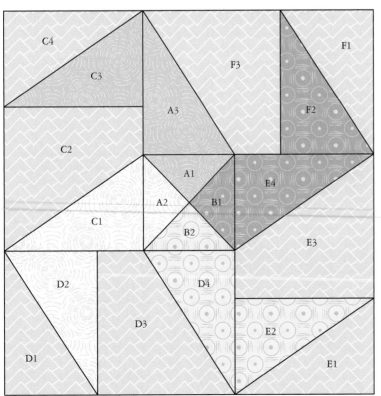

FAN BLADES

N18 Make the A section by joining the A pieces in numerical order. Make the B section and join to the A section. Make the C section and join to the A-B unit. Make the D section and join to the A-B-C unit. Make the E and F sections and join. Join the E-F unit to the A-B-C-D unit.

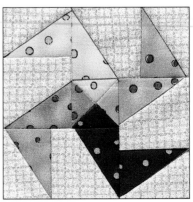

CROSSROADS

N19 Make 4 A sections. Join A units with D pieces to make 2 A-D units. Join B and C pieces to make 2 B-C units. Join the 4 units to complete the block.

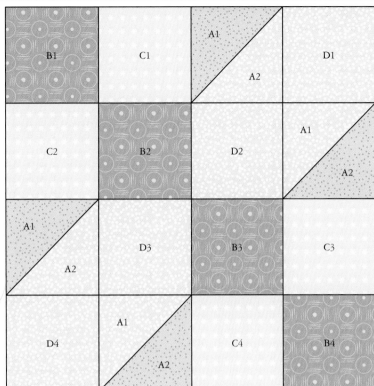

FOUR CORNERS BRIGHT

N20 Make 4 A sections. Make 2 B sections. Make 2 C sections. Make 1 D section. Join 2 A-C-A units. Join B-D-B unit. Join the 3 units to complete the block.

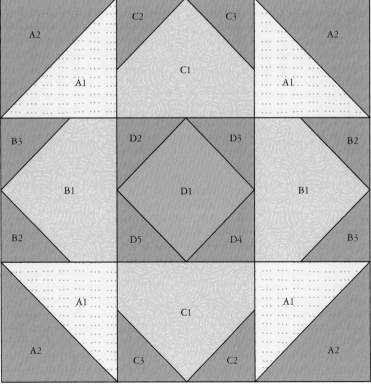

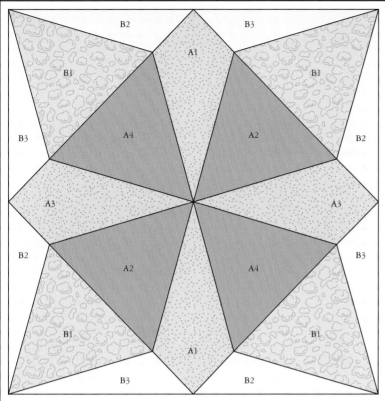

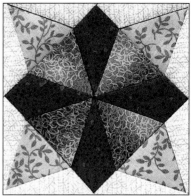

FOUR POINTS IN THE MIDDLE

N21 Make 2 A sections by joining pieces in numerical order, Join the 2 A sections. Make 4 B sections. Join a B section to each side of the A section.

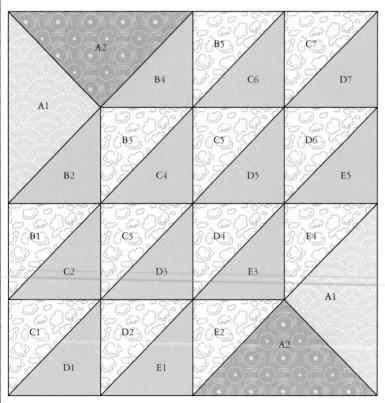

GARDEN PATH

N22 Make 2 A sections by joining A1 and A2 pieces. Make the B and C sections and join. Make the D and E sections and join. Join the B-C unit with the D-E unit. Join the A sections to opposite sides of the B-C-D-E unit.

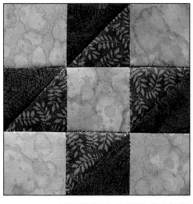

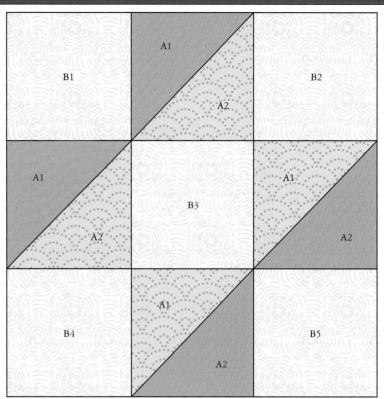

GREEN AND BLUE

N23 Join A pieces to make 4 squares. Join A sections with B pieces in rows. Join the 3 rows.

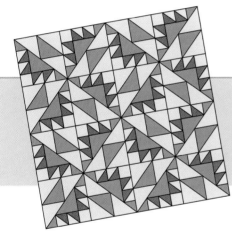

Look Again

(Below) No rotation of Kansas Troubles Variation blocks is needed to create this ornate squares-in-squares pattern.

KANSAS TROUBLES VARIATION

N24 Make 4 A sections by joining the A pieces in numerical order. Make 4 B sections and 4 C sections. Join the B sections to the C sections. Join an A section to each B-C unit. Join 2 A-B-C units twice. Then join the 2 A-B-C-A-B-C units.

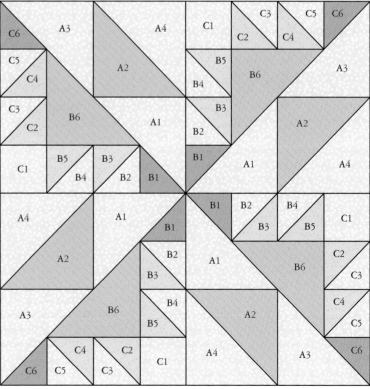

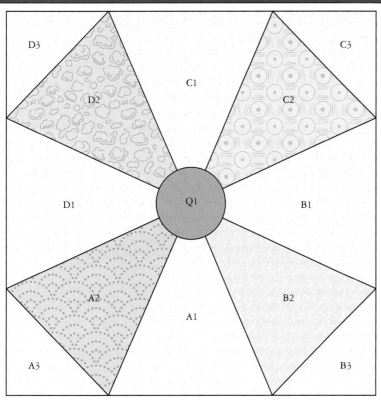

KALEIDOSCOPE

N25 Make A section by joining pieces in numerical order. Make B, C, and D sections. Join A and B sections; join C and D sections. Join A-B unit to C-D unit. Appliqué Q1 piece to the center of the block.

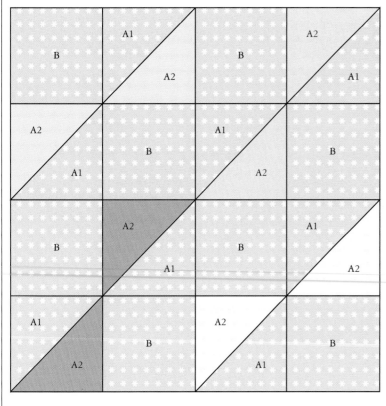

KITE TAILS

N26 Make 8 A sections using photo for color guide. Join A sections to B pieces in 4 square blocks using the pattern as a placement guide. Join the 4 units to complete the block.

LINKED SQUARES

N27 Make A section by joining pieces in numerical order. Repeat to make a second A section. Make 2 B sections. Join 1 A section to C1 piece, leaving the end of the seam open. Working clockwise, join B section to A-C; then join A section. Join final B section and complete the first seam.

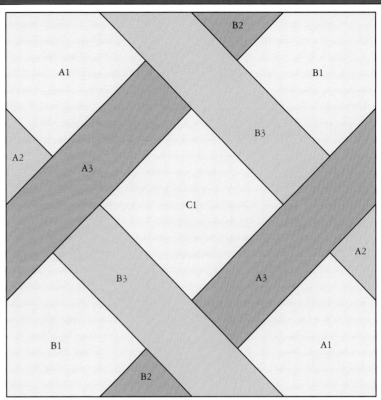

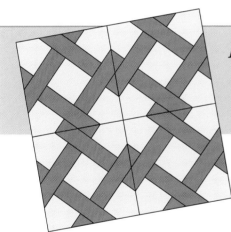

Look Again

(Above) A single Linked Squares block looks quite plain until it is joined to more blocks with the same design. As blocks are added, an interesting pattern of interlocking square links appears to create a geometric quilt design.

PATCHED GEESE

N28 Make 4 A sections by joining pieces in numerical order. Join to make 2 A-A units, then join the units.

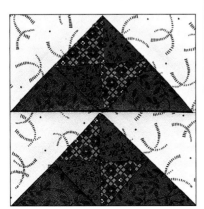

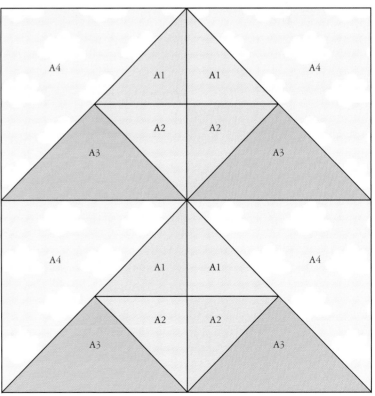

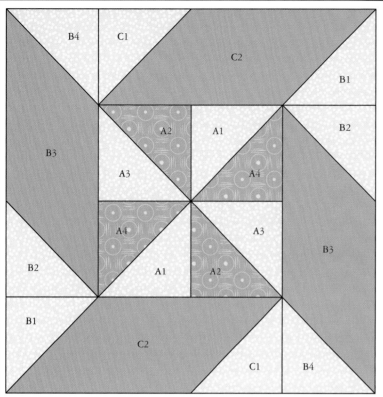

PINWHEEL BLADES

N29 Make 2 A sections by joining the A pieces in numerical order. Make 2 B sections and 2 C sections. Join a C section and a B section to an A section twice to make 2 A-B-C units. Join the 2 units.

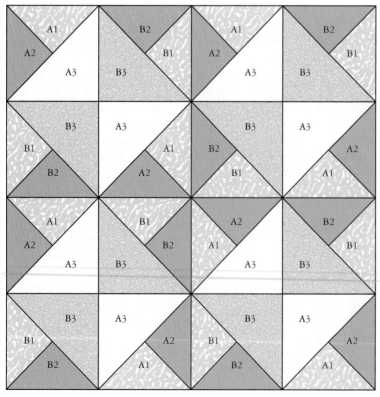

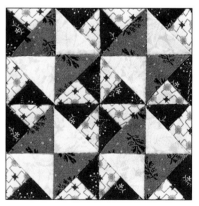

PINWHEEL CORNERS

N30 Make 8 A sections by joining A pieces in numerical order. Make 8 B sections. Using pattern as a guide, join the sections into 4 rows of 4 squares each. Join the rows to complete the block.

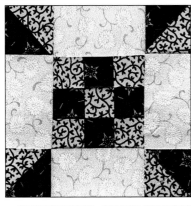

PINWHEEL NINE PATCH

N31 Make the A section by joining the A pieces. Make the B and C sections and join. Join the A section to the B-C unit. Make 2 D sections and join to opposite sides of the A-B-C unit. Make the E and F sections and join to the top and bottom of the A-B-C-D unit.

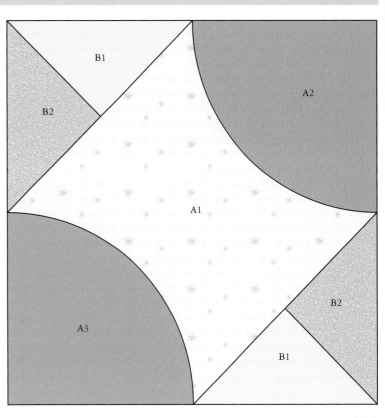

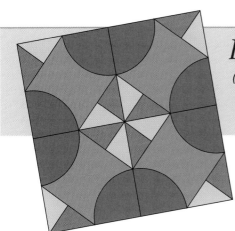

Look Again

(Below) The Spools block takes on a new look when joined as shown at left. Small and large background diamonds take shape. As more blocks are added, large circles become part of the interesting pattern.

SPOOLS

N32 Make the A section by joining the A2 and A3 pieces to A1. Make 2 B sections and join to opposite sides of the A section.

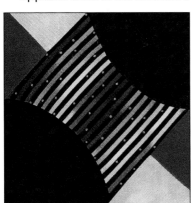

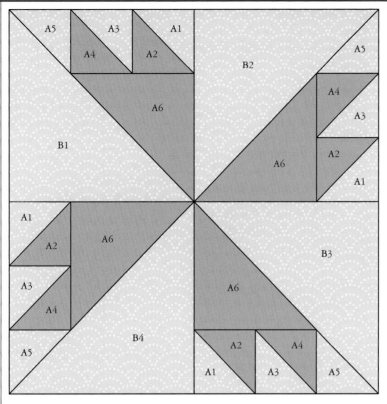

PINWHEEL VARIATION

N33 Make 4 A sections by joining pieces in numerical order. Join each A section to a B piece. Make 2 rows by joining 2 A-B units. Join the 2 rows.

Look Again

(Below) As pretty as a stained glass window, Pointing Inward blocks create pretty patterns when the border motifs are joined.

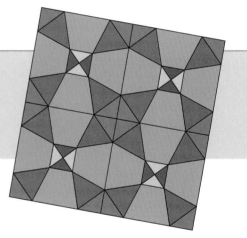

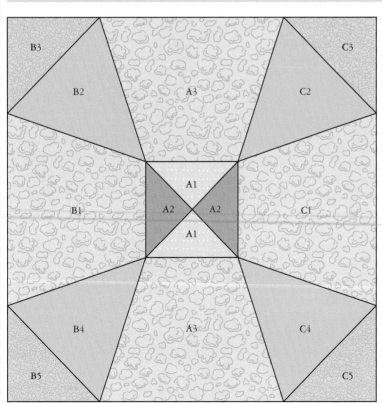

POINTING INWARD

N34 Make 2 A sections by joining pieces in numerical order. Join the A sections. Make B section and join to A-A unit. Make C section and join to A-B unit.

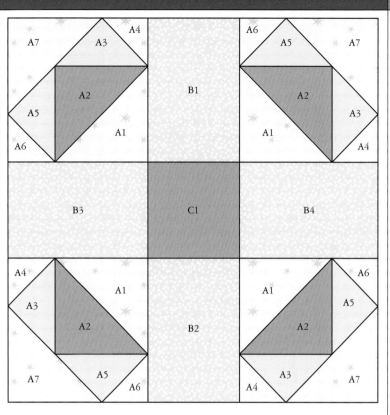

RECTANGLE POINTS

N35 Make 4 A sections by joining pieces in numerical order. Join 2 A sections with B1 piece; join 2 A sections with B2 piece. Join B3 and B4 to C piece. Join the 3 completed rows.

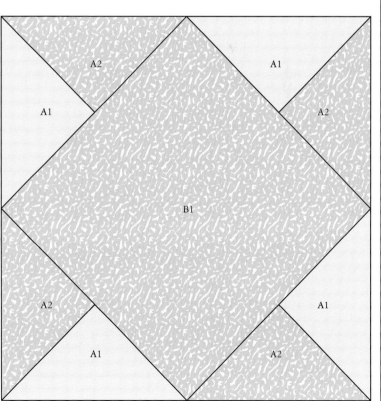

RIGHT AND LEFT
(SQUARE IN THE MIDDLE)

N36 Make 4 A sections. Join an A section to each side of the B1 piece.

285

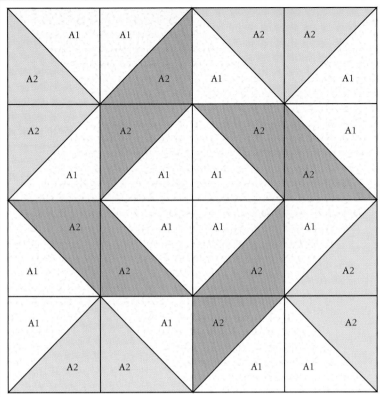

ROUND YOU GO

N37 Make 16 A1-A2 sections using photo for a color guide. Join A sections into 4 blocks of 4 squares each. Join the 4 blocks.

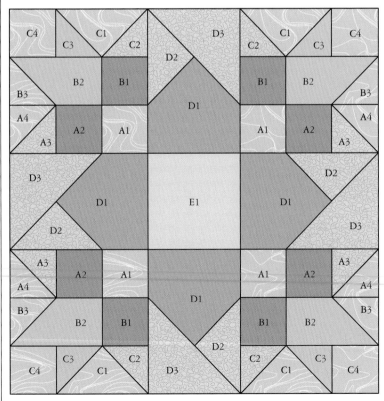

SPRING BURST
(SQUARES IN THE MIDDLE)

N38 Make 4 A sections by joining A pieces in numerical order. Make 4 B sections and 4 C sections. Join these sections into 4 A-B-C units. Make 4 D sections. Join 2 A-B-C units to opposite sides of a D section for top row. Join D sections to opposite sides of E1 piece for middle row. Join 2 A-B-C units to opposite sides of a D section for bottom row. Join the 3 rows to complete block.

SUGAR BOWL

N39 Make the A section by joining the 2 A pieces. Make the B section and join to the A section. Make the C section and join to the A-B unit. Make the D section and join to the A-B-C unit. Make 2 E sections and join to adjacent sides of the A-B-C-D unit. Join the F1 piece to complete the block.

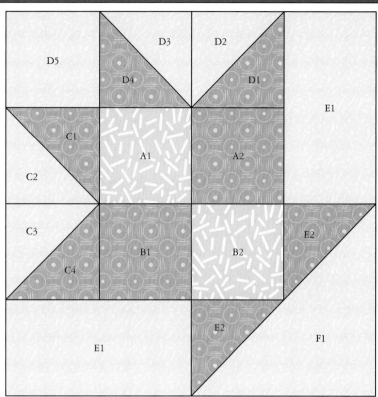

SQUARE IN A CURVE

N40 Make 4 A sections by joining the A pieces in numerical order. Join 2 A sections twice to make 2 A-A units. Join the 2 units to complete the block.

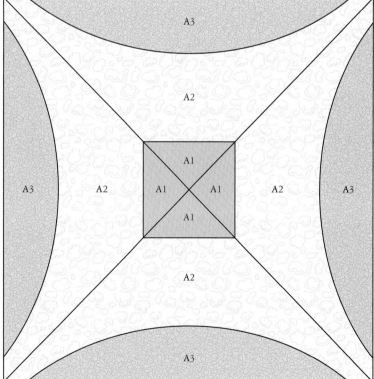

TRADITIONAL

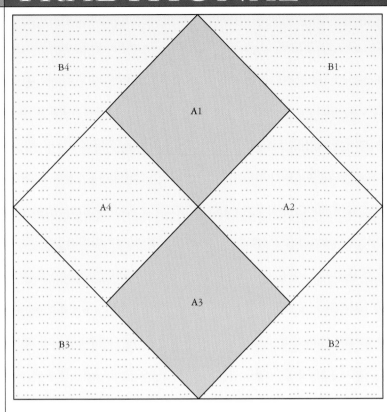

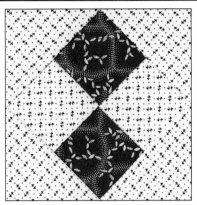

TWO SQUARES

N41 Join A1 and A2; Join A3 and A4. Join A1-A2 to A3-A4. Join a B piece to each side of the center square.

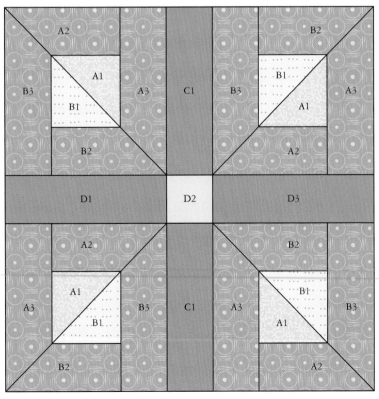

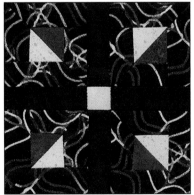

SQUARE IN SQUARE

N42 Make 4 A sections by joining the A pieces in numerical order. Make 4 B sections. Join A and B sections into 4 A-B units. Join 2 A-B units with a C1 piece twice. Make the D section and use it to join the 2 completed A-B-C-A-B units.

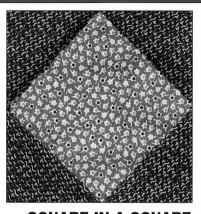

SQUARE IN A SQUARE

N43 Join A2, A3, A4, and A5 pieces to A1.

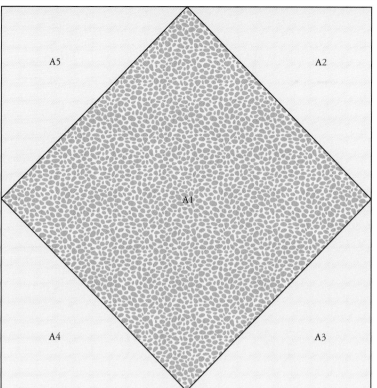

SQUARES AND TRIANGLES

N44 Make A section by joining pieces in numerical order. Join B pieces to the sides of A section. Make 4 C sections. Join C sections to the sides of A-B unit. Join D pieces to complete the block.

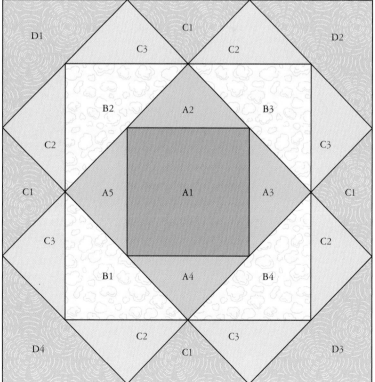

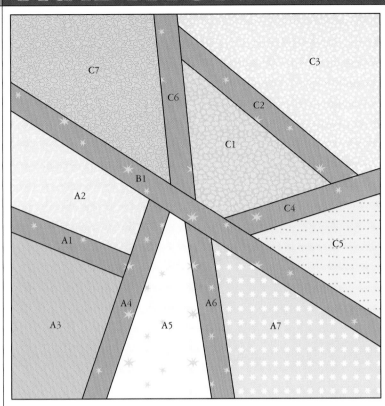

STAINED GLASS

N45 Make the A section by joining the A pieces in numerical order. Join the B1 piece to the completed A section. Make the C section and join to the A-B unit.

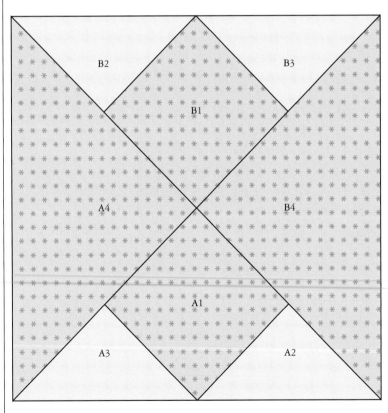

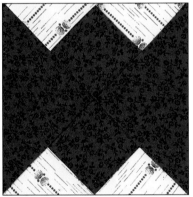

FOUR TRIANGLES

N46 Make A section by joining pieces in numerical order. Make B section. Join A and B sections.

TRIANGLES ALL AROUND

N47 Make 4 A sections by joining pieces in numerical order. Make 4 B sections. Make 2 A-B-A units. Make 1 B-C-B unit. Join the 3 units.

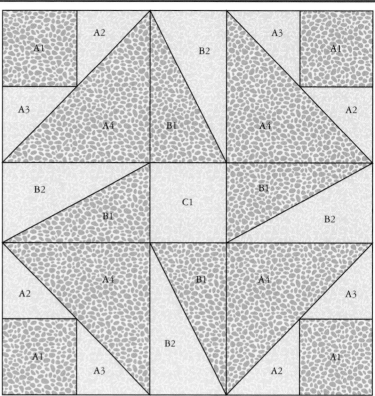

TRIANGLE CHECK

N48 Make 4 A sections and 4 B sections. Join into 4 A-B units. Join C pieces to each side of each unit to make 4 A-B-C units. Make 4 D sections. Join a D section to each side of an A-B-C unit twice for 2 rows of the block. Join 2 A-B-C units to the E1 piece to make the center row. Join the 3 rows to complete the block.

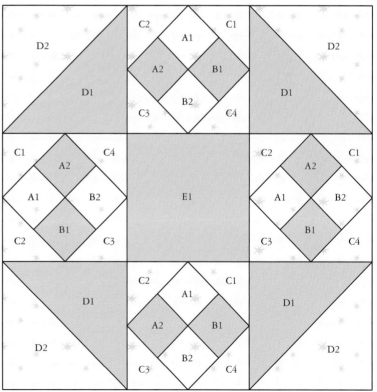

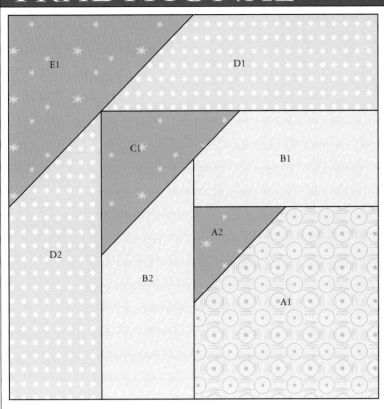

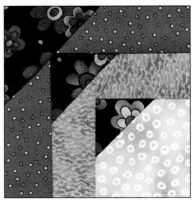

TRIANGLE LOGS

N49 Join pieces to make A section; join B1, then B2 pieces. Join C1 piece to make A-B-C unit. Join D1 and D2 pieces to the A-B-C unit. Join E1 piece to complete the block.

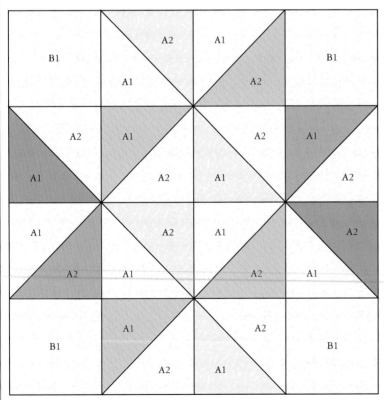

TRIANGLE IN A CIRCLE

N50 Make 12 A sections by joining A1 and A2 pieces following block photo for color selection. Join 2 A sections with B1 pieces on each end to make the top and bottom rows. Follow pattern to make 2 center rows. Join rows to complete the block.

TRIANGLE SPIN

N51 Make 4 A sections by joining the A1 and A2 pieces. Make 4 B sections. Join each A section to a B section. Join 2 A-B units twice. Join the 2 units to complete the block.

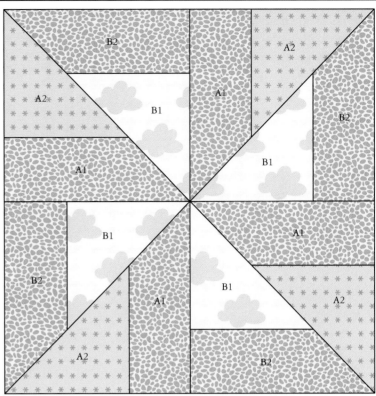

TURKEY TRACKS VARIATION

N52 Make 4 A sections by joining the A pieces in numerical order. Make 2 rows by joining A sections with a B1 square in the middle. Make the C section. Join B1 squares to opposite sides of the C section. Join the A-B-A units to the top and bottom of the B-C-B unit.

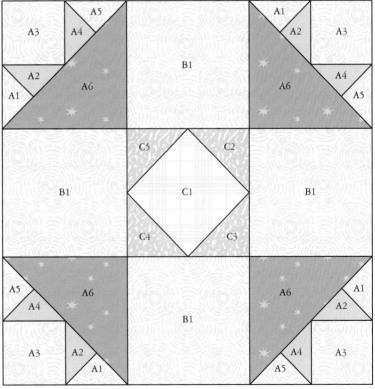

TRADITIONAL

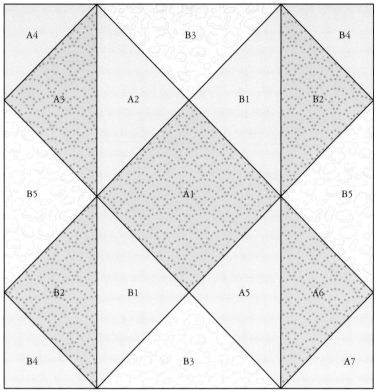

VERTICAL SQUARES

N53 Make A section by joining pieces in numerical order. Make 2 B sections. Join B sections to each side of A section.

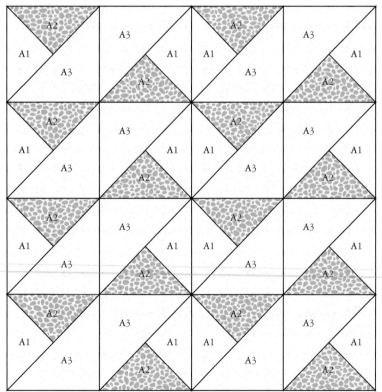

WAVES

N54 Make A section by joining pieces in numerical order. Repeat to make a total of 16 A sections. Join as shown into 4 rows of 4 squares. Join the rows to complete the block.

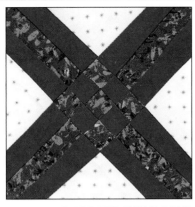

WOVEN RIBBONS

N55 Make center A section by joining squares in 3 rows of 3 squares; join the rows. Join A10, A11, and A12 to center A section. Repeat with A13, A14, and A15. Make B section and join to A section. Make C section and join to A-B unit.

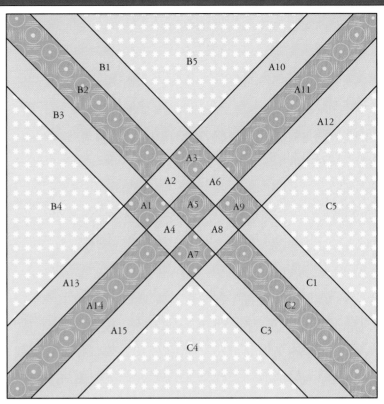

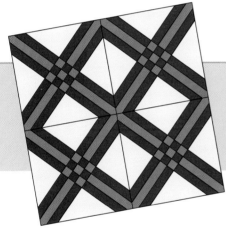

Look Again

(Above) Join Woven Ribbons blocks to make a tri-colored lattice design.
The triangular background pieces come together to form repetitive diamonds.

YO-YO WINDOW

N56 Make 3 A sections by joining the A pieces in numerical order. Make 2 B sections. Join the A and B sections as shown. Make 4 yo-yos from 2¼-inch fabric circles. (See page 313 for instructions.) Sew yo-yos to block with a button at each center.

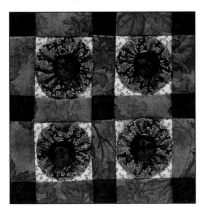

TRADITIONAL

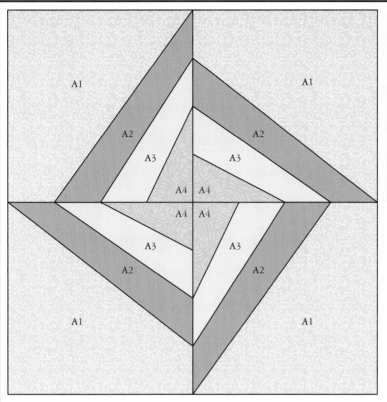

COOL PINWHEEL

N57 Make 4 A sections by joining pieces in numerical order. Join the completed sections as shown.

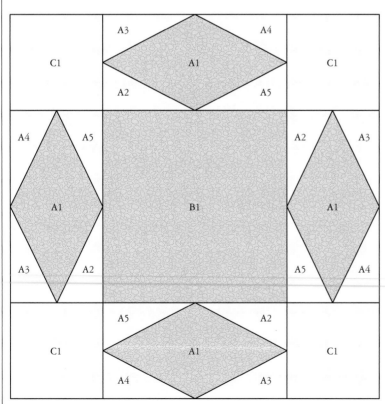

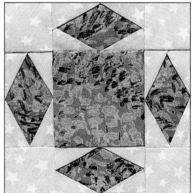

CORNER SQUARES

N58 Make 4 A sections by joining the A pieces in numerical order. Make 3 rows by joining 2 A sections to opposite sides of the B1 piece and joining C1 pieces to opposite ends of 2 A sections. Join the 3 rows to complete the block.

SUNBONNET SUE

N59 Appliqué the Q pieces in numerical order to the background block. Use satin stitch, outlined with stem stitch to embroider the band and bow on the bonnet and the hand. Use straight stitches and French knots to embroider flowers on the apron.

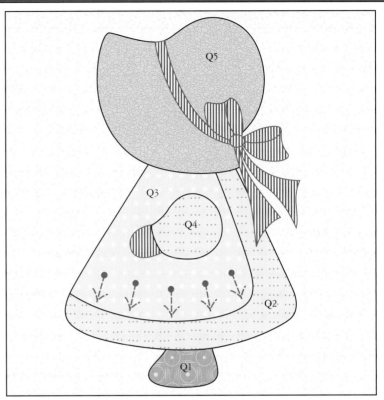

SUNBONNET SAM

N60 Appliqué the Q pieces in numerical order to the background block. Use satin stitch to embroider hat band and suspenders. Use stem stitch to stitch line on the overalls.

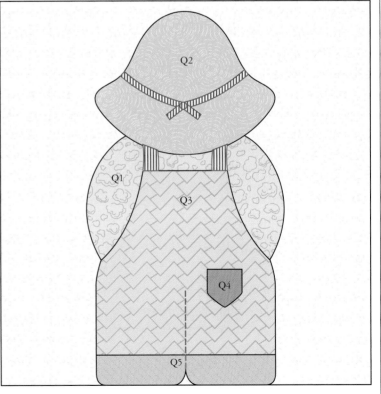

297

PARASOL SUNBONNET

N61 Appliqué the Q pieces in numerical order to the background block. Use buttonhole stitch to outline the skirt border. Use satin stitch, outlined with stem stitch, to embroider the bow, the cuff on the sleeve, the arm, the handle, and trim on the parasol. Use stem stitch to embroider detail on the bonnet and for the feet.

POSY SUNBONNET

N62 Appliqué the Q pieces in numerical order to the background block. Use buttonhole stitch to outline the bonnet. Use satin stitch, outlined with stem stitch, to embroider the bow, the cuff on the sleeve, and the arm. Use stem stitch for the feet, detail on the bonnet, and the flower stems. Use lazy daisy stitches for the flowers. Make French knots on skirt border and for center of each flower.

SUNBONNET BALLOONS

N63 Appliqué the Q pieces in numerical order to the background block. Use buttonhole stitch to outline each piece. Use stem stitch to embroider apron ties, detail on apron, detail on dress, pantaloons, feet, arm, and balloon strings. Use satin stitch, outlined with stem stitch, for the balloons and the knot on the apron bow.

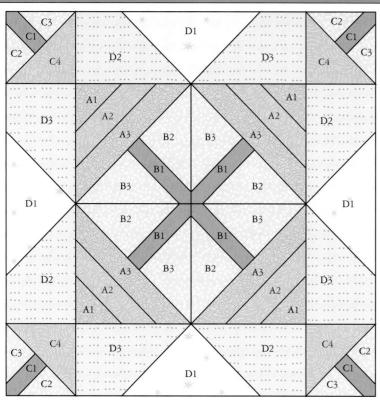

TREE SQUARE

01 Make 4 A sections by joining the A pieces in numerical order. Make 4 B sections. Join A and B sections to make 4 A-B units. Join the 4 units to make the center square. Make 4 C sections and 4 D sections. Join C sections to opposite ends of 2 D sections. Join the other 2 D sections to opposite sides of the A-B square. Join the 3 units to complete the block.

Look Again

(Above) Join Tree Square blocks and watch the diamond motifs multiply. The corners come together to resemble the larger diamonds with crosses in the center of each block.

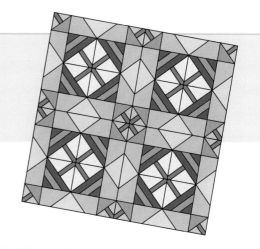

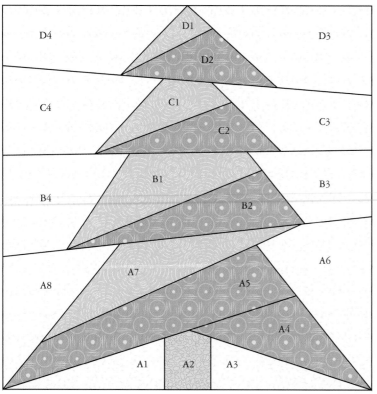

SNOW-CAPPED PINE TREE

02 Make the A section by joining the A pieces in numerical order. Make the B section and join to the A section. Make the C and D sections and join. Join the C-D unit to the A-B unit.

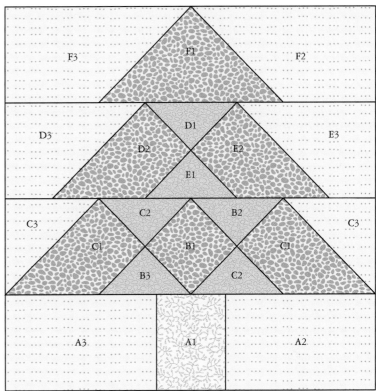

COUNTRY TREE

03 Make the A section by joining the A pieces in numerical order. Make the B section. Make the 2 C sections and join to each side of the B section. Join the B-C unit to the A section. Make the D and E sections and join. Join the D-E unit to the A-B-C unit. Make the F section and join to the A-B-C-D-E unit to complete the block.

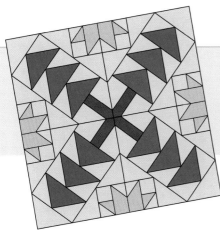

Look Again

(Below) Once a single tree, the Tall Tree with Corner Stars blocks rotate and join to take on a graphic, almost Native American, appearance. As more blocks are added, star patterns emerge between the central motifs.

TALL TREE WITH CORNER STARS

04 Make 3 A sections by joining the A pieces in numerical order. Join the A sections. Make the B section and join to the A sections. Make the C and D sections and join to opposite sides of the A-B unit. Join the E1 piece to the A-B-C-D unit.

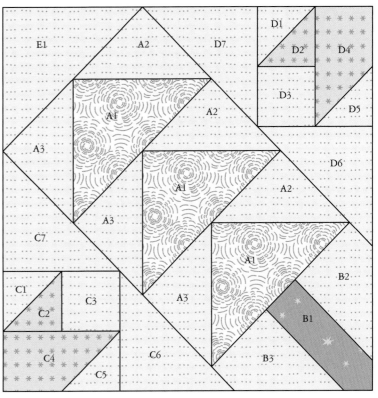

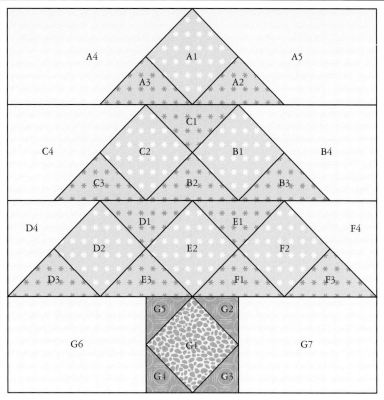

ZIG-ZAG TREE

05 Make the A section by joining the A pieces in numerical order. Make the B and C sections and join to make the B-C unit. Join the B-C unit to the A section. Make the D, E, and F sections and join. Join the D-E-F unit to the A-B-C unit. Make the G section and join to the bottom of the block.

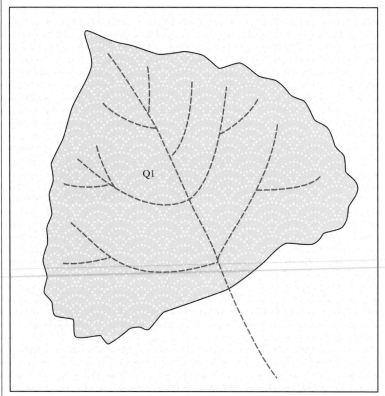

COTTONWOOD LEAF

06 Appliqué the Q1 piece to the background block. Machine-appliqué or hand-embroider stem stitch to make the leaf stem and the veins on the leaf.

MAPLE LEAF

07 Appliqué the Q1 piece to the background block. Machine-appliqué or hand-embroider stem stitch to make the leaf stem and the veins on the leaf.

STRIPED MAPLE LEAF

08 Appliqué the Q1 piece to the background block. Machine-appliqué or hand-embroider stem stitch to make the leaf stem and the veins on the leaf.

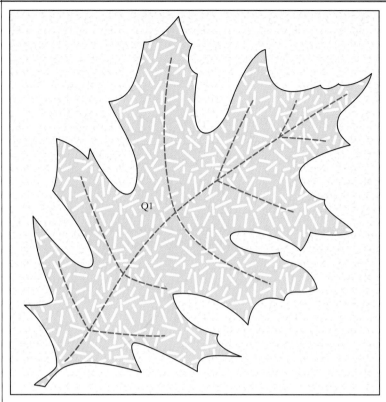

PIN OAK LEAF

O9 Appliqué the Q1 piece to the background block. Machine-appliqué or hand-embroider stem stitch to make the leaf stem and the veins on the leaf.

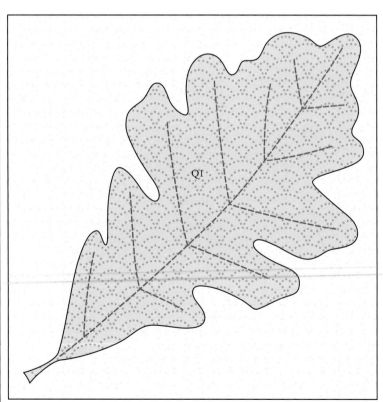

WHITE OAK LEAF

O10 Appliqué the Q1 piece to the background block. Machine-appliqué or hand-embroider stem stitch to make the leaf stem and the veins on the leaf.

ACORN

011 Appliqué the Q pieces in numerical order to the background block. Stem-stitch the vein on the leaf.

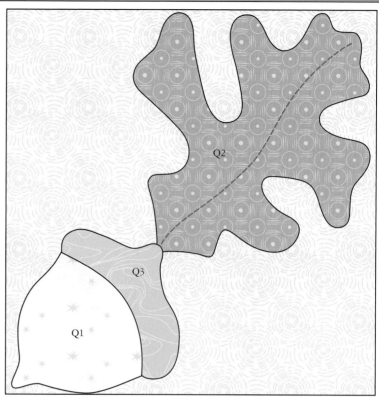

Q2

Q3

Q1

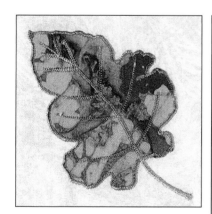

POPLAR LEAF

012 Appliqué the Q1 piece to the background block. Machine-appliqué or hand-embroider stem stitch to make the leaf stem and the veins on the leaf.

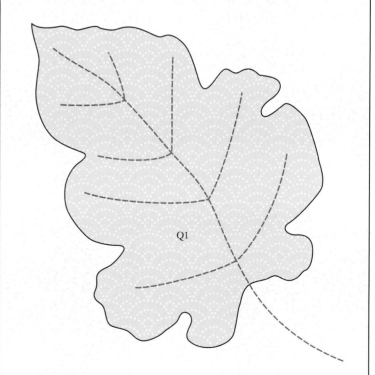

Q1

TIPS & TECHNIQUES

FABRICS, TOOLS, & SUPPLIES

Before beginning a quilt project, in your work area assemble all the fabric, tools, and supplies you'll be using. Experienced stitchers may have all the necessary equipment and some specialized tools; novice and beginning sewers will learn along the way what tools make cutting, sewing, piecing, and finishing easier and more pleasant. New and improved tools and supplies, adapted especially for quilting, are regularly introduced in quilting and fabric stores and in quiltmaking and sewing classes.

FABRICS

One-hundred-percent cotton fabric remains the best choice for quiltmaking. Cotton minimizes seam distortion, presses crisply, and has a nice finish for hand- and machine-quilting. Project yardage requirements often specify 42-inch or 44/45-inch-wide fabrics, which are common in the industry. After removing the selvages from the fabric, the width is closer to 42 inches. The projects in this book allow for enough extra yardage to compensate for minor fabric flaws, shrinkage, and slight cutting errors.

Prewashing fabrics is recommended. Prewashing fabrics offers quilters certainty as its main advantage. Although fabrics manufactured today resist bleeding and shrinkage, some of both occur in some fabrics, which is an unpleasant prospect for finished quilts. We suggest prewashing fabrics for most sewing and quilting projects for several reasons:
1) to prevent shrinkage and puckering in finished quilts,
2) to prevent dyes from running in finished quilts, 3) to remove excess sizing, and 4) to remove dust collected during shipping, handling, and storage. Prewashing also softens fabric for handling, and some quilters believe it is easier to quilt.

To prewash fabric, unfold it to a single layer, washing only like colors together, and allowing the fabric ample room in the washer. Place fabric pieces that measure less than one-half yard in zippered pillowcases or mesh bags to prevent them from tangling and twisting in the washer. Wash the fabric in warm water on delicate cycle. If the dyes from the fabric run, rinse the fabric until the water is clear. Or, use a product that traps excess dyes in the pre-wash to prevent color transfer from one fabric to another. Do not use fabrics that have not stopped running or bleeding in quilts. Do not use fabric softener in the final rinse of the fabrics. Hang the fabric to dry, or tumble it in the dryer until just slightly damp. Steam press the fabric before measuring, marking, and cutting.

If you choose not to prewash fabrics, the following will be helpful. Some quilters prefer piecing crisp, unwashed fabrics. When quilts are made with fabrics that have the same fiber content and thread count throughout, the fabrics will likely shrink uniformly with the first washing, giving the quilt a slightly puckered and antique look, which some quilters like. Also, for quilted projects that will never be laundered, such as wall hangings that can be vacuumed or shaken to remove the dust, prewashing may seem unnecessary; although a spill on the finished project may cause shrinkage and puckering or dyes to run. Using lighter color fabrics eliminates the fear of color running, if not the issue of shrinkage. To test fabric to determine whether to prewash or not, cut two identical size and shape pieces from each fabric, including selvage edges. Soak one of each piece in water for several hours. Rinse the fabric until the water runs clear, lay it to dry, and press it smooth. Compare the fabric pieces for shrinkage and color.

BATTING

- ◆ Thin cotton batting is a good choice for small or beginning projects because it adheres to fabric, requires less basting, and is easy to stitch through. Follow the stitch density (the distance between rows of quilting stitches that prevents the batting from shifting and bunching) for each batting type. Recommendations for stitch density are printed on packaging and are available at stores that sell batting by the yard. Cotton batting, a good choice for garments, conforms well to the body.

◆ Polyester batting is lightweight and inexpensive. In general, it springs back to its original height when compressed and adds puffiness to quilts. As it is quilted it tends to "beard" (work out between the weave of the fabric) more than natural fibers. Polyester fleece is denser and works well for quilting pillow tops and place mats.

◆ Wool batting is warm, has loft retention, and absorbs moisture, making it ideal for cool, damp climates. Wool batting also provides a flatter, natural, or antique look to quilts. Some wool batts require special care; read packaging labels carefully or check with sales people at quilting stores before purchasing wool batting for quilt projects.

TOOLS & SUPPLIES

◆ **TABLE OR OTHER LARGE, STABLE WORK SURFACE:** The work surface should be a comfortable height for reaching and cutting the fabric. A table, portable or stationary, adjacent to a sewing machine or quilting hoop is also useful for supporting the weight of the quilt while machine- or hand-quilting.

◆ **CUTTING MAT, ACRYLIC RULER, AND ROTARY CUTTER:** These tools, which have revolutionized quilting, allow for several fabric layers to be cut accurately and easily. The fabric is laid on the mat, the ruler is held firmly on the fabric in position for cutting, and the sharp wheel-like blade of the rotary cutter is rolled along the edge of the ruler to make straight cuts.

A self-healing cutting mat provides a surface for the cutting blade and prevents fabric from shifting as it is being cut. To allow for adjusting, layering, and cutting fabric, the recommended mat minimum size is 24×36 inches, with 1-inch grids marked along the surface.

Place the cutting mat on a firm surface at approximately table or counter height.

Acrylic rulers vary in sizes and shapes, from small to large rectangles, squares, and triangles. For a basic ruler, choose a 6×24-inch ruler that has $\frac{1}{8}$-inch markings and a 45-degree angle marking. Some rulers have 30- and 60-degree angle markings as well as specialized angles for cutting triangles and other shapes.

Several styles of rotary cutters and replaceable cutting blades are available. Quilters usually find the style that best fits their grip. Additionally, some rotary cutters have blades for cutting more than straight cuts.

◆ **SCISSORS:** Designate a sharp pair for cutting fabric only. Designate a pair for general purpose to cut paper, plastic, and template material. Also, small nippers or embroidery scissors are useful for clipping into seam allowances, clipping threads, and precisely cutting small irregular shapes.

◆ **PINS AND PINCUSHION OR PINHOLDER:** Select good quality, rustproof, long quilter's pins that have round heads for easy visibility and grasping. Use a stuffed pincushion or magnetic pinholder (if you don't have a computerized sewing machine) that you can transport between your cutting, sewing, and pressing areas.

◆ **MARKING TOOLS:** Marking fabrics with specially made markers for sewing and quilting ensures that the marks will be removable when the project is finished. Depending on fabric content and color, look for chalks, pencils, water- and air-soluble markers with quilting supplies at fabric and quilt stores. Test marking tools on fabric scraps before using on your quilt.

◆ **TEMPLATE PLASTIC:** Use this material to trace and cut fabric shapes that cannot be cut using an acrylic ruler and rotary cutter or as an option to using a rotary cutter and acrylic ruler. The material comes in sheets about $\frac{1}{16}$ inch thick and appears slightly frosted. Use general purpose scissors to cut the material.

continued on page 308

TIPS&TECHNIQUES *continued*

◆ **SEWING MACHINE:** Use a clean sewing machine that is in good working order, sews reliably straight stitches, and has even tension. Have a supply of sewing machine needles that fit the machine, and change the needle regularly to ensure good stitches and against needle breakage during sewing. A nice added feature is a ¼-inch sewing foot for sewing precise seam allowances; an alternative is marking the needle plate with masking tape at the precise ¼-inch width between the stitched seam and the raw edge of the fabric. Wind several bobbins with thread before beginning each project to have them ready when you need them.

◆ **WALKING FOOT:** This sewing machine accessory frees the feed dogs to allow the backing, batting, and quilt top layers to remain smooth and even rather than bunching while machine-quilting.

◆ **DARNING FOOT, HOPPER FOOT, OR FREE-MOTION FOOT:** This sewing machine accessory is used for free-motion stitching through single or layered fabrics. Some machines are equipped with this accessory; to purchase one for your machine, have available the machine brand and model.

◆ **THREADS:** For hand- or machine-piecing, use 100-percent-cotton or cotton-covered polyester thread. For hand-quilting, use 100-percent-cotton or cotton-covered polyester quilting thread, which is stronger than hand- or machine-sewing threads. For machine-quilting, use 100-percent-cotton or cotton-covered polyester quilting thread, fine nylon thread, or threads specifically made for machine-quilting.

◆ **HAND-SEWING NEEDLES:** The needles used for piecing, appliquéing, and quilting are sharps and betweens; the larger the number, the finer the needle. Betweens are short with a narrow eye to sew through fabric layers without leaving marks. Common needle sizes are #11 and #12 sharps for hand-sewing and appliqué, and sizes #8, #9, and #10 betweens for hand-quilting, with #9 suggested for beginning quilters. Often quilters like to sew with fine needles to obtain tiny stitches and larger needles for obvious stitches.

◆ **THIMBLES:** Use metal, plastic, or leather thimbles, or adhesive strips on fingertips to help push the needle through fabric, relieving some of the pressure and preventing skin punctures. The wide variety of sizes, styles, and materials allows for selecting thimbles for multiple purposes.

◆ **SAFETY PINS:** Use brass or nickel-coated, rust-proof safety pins to temporarily hold together fabrics, to hold together the quilt layers for basting, or to use instead of basting threads for machine-quilting. Size 1 is a common size to use with sewing. To pin-baste a large quilt for machine-quilting, use between 350 to 500 Size 1 safety pins placed approximately 6 inches apart; remove the pins as you quilt.

◆ **IRON AND IRONING BOARD:** A good quality steam iron and a sturdy ironing board or pressing table are important for pressing throughout the piecing process to ensure accurate piecing and finished size of units, blocks, rows, and the quilt top. Press along each step of the way whether hand-sewing or machine-sewing. When pressing, lay the hot iron on the fabric, press firmly, and lift. Avoid sliding or pushing the iron across the fabric, which distorts seams and shapes, affecting the finished project.

◆ **FUSIBLE ADHESIVE MATERIAL:** Available packaged and by the yard, this fusible adhesive is bonded to the wrong side of fabric for fusing two layers of fabric together. The adhesive has a paper side for drawing or tracing shapes and stabilizing the fabric for cutting. After cutting out the shape, the paper is removed, and the adhesive side is pressed to the right side of another fabric. The edges of the fabric shape can be hand- or machine-stitched, left unfinished, or finished with other techniques.

◆ **FREEZER PAPER:** Press the waxed side of this slightly stiff paper to the wrong side of fabric as an option to needle-turning the raw edges of fabric shapes that may distort during stitching, or use it as an alternative to stiff adhesive-backed material. Freezer paper can be cut to shape, minus seam allowances, and pressed to the wrong side of fabric. Cut fabric beyond the freezer paper shape for a seam allowance, then turn and press under the fabric edges toward the freezer paper. Pin or baste the shaped piece in place, appliqué most of the shape, insert the needle between the appliqué and base fabric to loosen the freezer paper from the shape, pull out the paper, and finish stitching the shape in place. Freezer paper also can be used as a stabilizer for writing on fabric, such as making labels to sew to a finished quilt or for signing fabric to make into a signature or album quilt.

◆ **QUILTING FRAME OR HOOP:** A variety of sizes and shapes of frames, from room-size to portable handheld sizes, support the size, weight, and layers of the quilt. Stretching the sandwiched quilt top, batting, and backing in a frame or hoop before quilting creates tension and a firm surface in order to take small, even stitches by hand, and allows freedom for working with both hands. Quilting hoops, made of wood or sturdy plastic, are deeper than embroidery hoops to accommodate the quilt layers. A portable handheld or tabletop 14-inch to 18-inch circular wooden hoop is adequate for quilting even a large quilt.

SELECT A FIRST PROJECT

Choosing a project is the first step in successful quilting, whether you're new to quilting or have quilted for years. With the array of fabrics, projects, patterns, books, and ideas available, settling on one project to see through to completion may seem daunting. If you need help, follow these tips:

◆ **FIND A FRIENDLY PLACE.** A quilt supply store or fabric store where employees are knowledgeable about quilting is a good place to start. Often the staff at quilting stores are quilters and eager to share their knowledge and excitement about the craft.

◆ **START SMALL.** Making a wall hanging, table runner, pillow cover, or baby quilt that takes less time than a full-size quilt allows you to experience success and look forward to a new project.

◆ **TAKE CLASSES.** Quilting shops and fabric stores offer a variety of classes—from beginner to advanced—and offer timesaving tips along the way. Taking classes with peers

allows you to benefit from one another's experiences and share your excitement for all the little successes.

◆ **PURCHASE KITS.** Sometimes selecting all the fabrics for a project seems daunting. By purchasing a kit that contains pattern, fabrics, and instructions, a major hurdle is already accomplished, and you can get started sooner.

◆ **BE SQUARE.** Projects that are made by piecing squares, right triangles, and rectangles are easier for beginners than piecing odd shapes and angles. Appliqué shapes, as long as the technique is kept simple, also is a good beginning project.

◆ **LOVE IT.** Encourage yourself to finish each project by choosing designs and fabrics that you're eager to finish, share, show off, and use.

MACHINE-PIECING

Cut the pattern pieces from fabric, including seam allowances. Place two cut pieces of fabric, right sides together, aligning raw edges, and pin them together. Place the layered pieces under the presser foot of the sewing machine, lower the needle, and sew an exact ¼-inch seam allowance to join pieces of the unit.

To chain-piece several units without breaking the thread between each unit, pin together and feed another unit right behind the finished unit, and begin stitching. After chaining several units, raise the presser foot, and clip the threads between each unit. Press the seam allowances of each unit, using an up and down motion with the iron rather than a sliding motion to avoid distorting the seams.

HAND-PIECING

Mark pattern pieces on wrong sides of fabric, drawing around the finished size of the patterns and allowing space between pattern pieces to draw and/or cut ¼-inch seam allowances. Draw a ¼-inch seam allowance around each pattern piece, or

continued on page 310

cut out the pieces gauging a ¼-inch seam allowance by eye. Pin together pattern pieces, right sides together, aligning pieces along the drawn finished line, which is the sewing line.

Insert a threaded needle at the seam line; back-stitch to lock the stitch in place. Hand-sew the pieces together, weaving the needle in and out to take 4 to 6 stitches at a time and sewing 8 to 10 stitches per inch. Back-stitch and end the last stitch with a loop knot; cut the thread. Press the seams to one side.

APPLIQUÉ

If you're a beginner, select an appliqué design with straight lines and gentle curves. Learning to make sharp points and tiny stitches takes practice. Some appliquéd motifs are pieced then appliquéd. The project instructions may suggest marking the position of each piece on a foundation block before cutting and piecing the design.

◆ **BASIC HAND-APPLIQUÉ METHOD:** Pin and baste appliqué shapes to foundation fabrics, overlapping multiple pieces if required, following position markings on illustrations and referring to photographs. For hidden stitching, appliqué the shapes in place using matching thread and small stitches, using a hand-quilting needle or a long milliner's needle to catch a few threads of the folded edge of the shape and a few threads of the foundation fabric. Use the point of the needle to work the fabric, tucking in the seam allowance and adjusting points and V-shapes of the appliqué. Finish stitching by taking an extra slip-stitch at the end of the appliqué shape; carry the needle and thread to the inside of the shape or the underside of the foundation fabric, and clip the thread close to the fabric. A short tail of thread will remain hidden in a seam or behind the appliqué. When appliquéing lightweight fabrics and the foundation fabric shows through the appliqué, carefully cut away the foundation fabric behind the appliqué to within ¼ inch of the hand stitching.

For decorative appliqué stitches, use heavier weight and contrasting color threads, allowing the project size and motif to guide the thread selection.

◆ **MACHINE-HEMSTITCH APPLIQUÉ METHOD:** Sewing machines that have a setting or attachment for hemstitching or blind-stitching can be used to appliqué shapes to foundation fabrics. Use the freezer paper method, *below,* to prepare the appliqué shape for stitching, and follow the instructions with your sewing machine for setting the stitch length and width to appliqué.

◆ **FUSIBLE ADHESIVE METHOD:** To fuse fabric shapes to foundation fabric without turning under a seam allowance, apply fusible adhesive to the appliqué fabric, trace and cut out a shape on the paper side of the fusible adhesive, remove the paper, and fuse the shape to the foundation fabric. Finish the appliqué by hand or machine, leave it unfinished, or use fabric glue to finish the edges.

To fuse large appliqué shapes to foundation fabric and eliminate the stiffness of the fusible adhesive, trace and cut out the design ¼ to ½ inch along the outer edge of the design. Fuse only the outline of the design to the appliqué fabric, then to the foundation fabric. The piece will be secure enough for finish stitching without the stiffness or bulk of the adhesive.

◆ **FREEZER PAPER METHOD:** To turn neat seam allowances on appliqué shapes for hand- or machine-appliqué, trace the pattern shapes on freezer paper. Press the waxed side of the paper to the wrong side of the fabric. Turn under and press the seam allowance along the paper edge, clipping and trimming tight inner and outer corners and working them neatly to the underside with a needle or quilting pin. For hand-appliqué, baste the shape to the foundation fabric and stitch in place until a small section remains unstitched. Insert the needle in the opening, loosen the freezer paper, remove it, and finish stitching. For machine-appliqué, press the freezer-paper lined shape from the front and back side to set the seams. Remove the freezer paper, hand-baste the seam allowance in place, trimming and clipping as needed for the shape to lie flat. Position the appliqué shape on the foundation fabric, and stitch in place. Remove the basting stitches.

- **NEEDLE-TURN METHOD:** Freezer paper in the shape of the appliqué can be fused to the back of the fabric first to help in turning under crisp edges. Cut out the appliqué shape ⅛ inch beyond the finished design. Baste or pin the shape to a foundation fabric. Use matching thread and a small needle to turn under the seam allowance and blind-stitch along the edge of the shape.

- **DOUBLE-APPLIQUÉ METHOD:** To ease the challenge of turning curved edges, face the appliqué shape before sewing it to foundation fabric. Trace an appliqué shape to fabric; cut out the shape, allowing a ¼-inch seam allowance. Place the shape facedown on a piece of sheer nonwoven interfacing. Sew around the shape for a ¼-inch seam allowance; grade the seams and clip the curves. Make a small clip in the center of the interfacing and turn the appliqué shape to the right side through the opening. Press the shape from the right side, rolling under the seam line toward the interfacing side. Stitch the appliqué shape to foundation fabric.

- **MAKING BIAS STEMS AND VINES:** For singlefold bias strips, cut fabric on the bias approximately twice the finished width and slightly longer than required. If necessary, piece together bias strips for long vines. With the wrong side of the strip facing up, press the long raw edges toward the center of the strip. Pin or baste the bias strips to the foundation fabric and appliqué in place.

For doublefold bias strips, cut strips approximately two and one-half the finished width. Fold the strip in half wrong sides together; sew a ⅛- to ¼-inch seam along the raw edges. Press the seam and raw edges to finish under the fold. Pin, baste, and appliqué the strip to the foundation fabric. For making bias strips easier, bias bar sewing tools are available.

MACHINE PAPER PIECING

This method of machine piecing allows for sewing small pieces of fabric into intricate designs because the fabrics are stabilized by the paper or fabric foundation. A block design is traced onto lightweight paper or other purchased stabilizer; fabric pieces are then sewn to the underside of the design in numerical order. Sewing the fabrics to the underside creates an identical design to that traced rather than a mirror image, which would be created by sewing fabrics to the traced side of the design. Sew the fabrics along the corresponding seam lines using short stitches, approximately 18 to 20 stitches per inch. The tight stitches perforate the foundation paper so it can be torn away after the design is stitched.

Trace a foundation paper design onto lightweight paper, including the numbered sections of the design; draw a ½-inch border around all edges of the design. The tracing side of the foundation paper design will be face up while the fabric pieces are sewn to the underside of the design. Use fabric pieces that measure approximately ¾ inch larger all around than the corresponding design sections.

Place and pin the first piece of fabric on the underside of the paper, right side up and extending at least ¼ inch beyond the first section. Trim seams after they are sewn. Having them extend more at this time ensures good design coverage. Hold the paper up to a light source to ensure the design is covered. Place and pin the fabric for the second section facedown on the the first fabric at the adjoining seam line. Insert the foundation paper right side up under the sewing machine needle. Holding the fabric in place, and removing the pin if it is in the way, sew on the line between the first two sections, sewing a couple of stitches beyond the seam line.

Remove the paper and fabric from the machine, clip the threads, and turn the design to the fabric side. Open out the fabric and finger-press it. Trim excess seam allowance to a scant ¼ inch. Holding the foundation piece to a light source, place and pin the fabric for the third section. Sew on the seam line between the second and third sections. Fingerpress and trim the seam allowance. Continue sewing on pieces until the design is covered. Press the design from the fabric side. Carefully tear away the perforated paper. Use a rotary cutter and ruler to trim the seam allowance around the block to ¼ inch all around.

continued on page 312

TIPS&TECHNIQUES *continued*

Many of the blocks in this book can be adapted to paper piecing. Look for blocks and sections of blocks that have straight seams. Piece units; then sew the units together.

PIECED BLOCK TEMPLATES

All of the patterns in this book are finished-size to make creating templates easy and frustration-free. Use template plastic that is slightly frosted. You can see through it, spot it easily, and can mark on it without smearing or smudging. For the blocks in this book avoid template plastic with printed grid, and avoid using cardboard for templates; it doesn't hold its shape with continuous use.

Using a ruler and fine-line permanent marker, trace block pieces onto the plastic. You'll add ¼-inch seam allowances when you cut out the pieces. (See information at right for making appliqué templates.) Cut plastic on marked lines.

It is not necessary to move the template plastic when tracing each template. When several pieces are grouped together, draw them together, then cut them apart.

Note how the block patterns are labeled using letters. Use a permanent marking pen to label your templates with these same letters. The letters in each block are for that block only; piece B in one block isn't the same as B used in another block.

Instructions for making the blocks occasionally include the direction 4 times; this means to create the unit described a total of four times.

As you draw templates, note edges that will be on the outer edge of the block. Mark template with an arrow along this edge to remind you to cut the fabric with arrow on the straight of grain, which helps prevent your block from stretching. Also mark which edges are to be sewn together.

To store blocks and templates, use small, clear zipper-type plastic bags to help keep items separate and easy to find. These easy-to-label bags are available at quilting and crafts stores as well as at the supermarket.

APPLIQUÉ BLOCK TEMPLATES

Trace the entire design onto template plastic as described above. Letter the design pieces on the template plastic. Cut out the template pieces.

Place templates face up on the right side of fabric. Trace around the template. Make a dotted line on the template to indicate areas that will be covered by another shape.

TRANSFERRING THE PATTERN FROM TEMPLATE TO FABRIC

Lay out your fabric smoothly, wrong side up. Try to use fabric print elements to enhance the block design, centering a flower or stripe, for example. Position the template face down on the wrong side of the fabric.

For appliquéd blocks, mark fabric on the right side. Add the seam allowance (between ⅛ and ¼ inch) when you cut out each piece.

Trace around the template onto the fabric using a No. 2 pencil. This is the sewing line. Mechanical pencils are excellent, because they stay sharp. Don't choose one with lead that is too thin—the 0.7mm size is large enough. If using dark fabrics, choose light color leads.

For pieced blocks, use a ruler to add a ¼-inch seam allowance to all sides. You'll need a clear ruler printed with a fine-line ⅛-inch grid. Many rulers are not 100 percent accurate—the ¼-inch mark may be different from opposite sides of the ruler. If you own one of these, choose one edge and use only that edge.

You also can use the red ruler, which is exactly ¼-inch thick. This useful alternative to the clear ruler is about 1 inch high, so it lifts your fingers, keeping them out of the way as you trace. Its bright red color makes it easy to spot on your sewing table.

Transfer the template marks, indicating which edges are to be sewn together for the seam allowances. This is especially helpful when, for example, a triangle has two similar length sides.

PRAIRIE POINTS

To make prairie points for the projects in this book, fold the square in half lengthwise with wrong sides together; press. With fold at top, fold and press each bottom corner up to the center, forming a triangle.

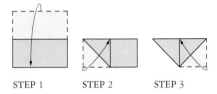

STEP 1   STEP 2   STEP 3

YO-YOS

To determine the cutting size of the yo-yo circle, double the diameter of the finished yo-yo. Thus, for a 1-inch finished yo-yo, draw a 2-inch circle and add ⅛- to ¼-inch seam allowance.

To make several yo-yos the same size, make a plastic template. You can trace onto fabric once, make three or four layers of fabric, and cut several at one time. The sharper your scissors, the more layers you can cut.

To sew the yo-yos, thread quilting thread on a needle, and knot the end. Turn and stitch a ¼-inch seam.

Yo-yos are not the place for dainty stitches as they will put too many gathers in the circle and make the center hole too big.

Stitch very close to the edge of the fold to avoid a belly-button effect in the center of the completed yo-yo.

End sewing near the point where you began. Pull the thread firmly to draw the yo-yo closed. Secure with a few stitches.

MITERED BORDER CORNERS

Pin a border strip to one edge of the quilt top, matching the center of the strip to the center of the quilt top edge. Sew together, beginning and ending the seam ¼ inch from the edge of the quilt top (see Diagram A, *below*). Allow excess border fabric to extend beyond each edge. Repeat with remaining border strips. Press the seam allowances toward the border strips.

Overlap the border strips at each corner (see Diagram B, *below*). Align the edge of a top border. With a pencil and triangle or ruler, draw along the edge of the triangle from the border seam to the outer corner. Place the bottom border on top and repeat marking process.

Right sides of adjacent border strips together, match the marked seam lines and pin (see Diagram C, *below*). Beginning with a backstitch at the inside corner, stitch exactly on the marked lines to the outer edge of the borders. Check the right side of the corner to see that it lies flat. Trim excess fabric to leave a ¼-inch seam allowance. Press the seam open. Mark and sew each corner in this manner.

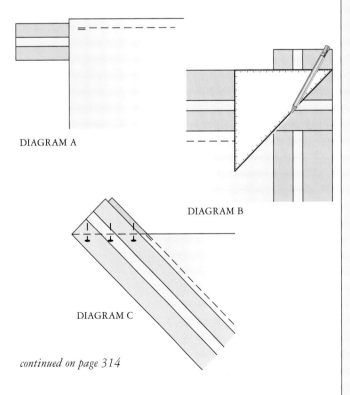

DIAGRAM A

DIAGRAM B

DIAGRAM C

continued on page 314

TIPS&TECHNIQUES *continued*

FINISHED QUILT SIZES

Finished size is important in selecting a project and using or purchasing fabric. Finished quilt sizes can vary with the quilt design and fabric, personal choices, and bed style. For examples, beds with solid, high footboards have no need for extra length at the foot of the bed and platform-style beds and four-poster beds require less width for drop than old-fashioned styles. Additional considerations include whether to combine the quilt with a dust ruffle or whether to provide length for a pillow tuck or use pillow shams.

Mattresses have standard length and width surface measurements, *below*. When measuring for a quilt, include the depth of the mattress and determine the length of drop to cover a box springs or side board, as well as the distance between the quilt and the floor.

STANDARD MATTRESS SIZES:

Crib	27×52"
Youth	33×66"
Twin	39×74"
Full	54×74"
Queen	60×80"
King	78×80"

STANDARD COMFORTER SIZES:

Twin	66×86"
Full	76×86"
Queen	86×88"
King	102×88"

STANDARD BEDSPREAD SIZES:

Twin	90×108"
Full	96×108"
Queen	102×118"
King	120×118"

AVERAGE DIMENSIONS FOR THE FOUR MOST POPULAR QUILT SIZES:

Twin	67×87"
Full	82×97"
Queen	88×103"
King	106×103"

CALCULATING SIZES

To calculate finished size for a quilt, measure the surface dimension of the mattress. To these measurements add the following:

◆ 8 to 10 inches to the length for pillow tuck; eliminate this measurement if you plan to use pillow shams.

◆ the drop from the surface width of the mattress toward the floor, considering whether to cover a box springs or side board or to allow a dust ruffle to show.

◆ the drop from the foot of the bed toward the floor, or the amount to tuck between the mattress and a footboard.

◆ 2 to 3 inches to the length and width measurements to allow for take-up by quilting.

FIGURING YARDAGE FOR BACKING & BINDING

Unless wide fabric is used for backing the quilt, you will have to cut and piece together yardage. Use the following chart as a guide to figure the amount of yardage to purchase and how to piece the backing. Cut binding strips on the straight grain and seam together lengths for the total length needed. Fold the strip in half, wrong sides together, and press. Sew the raw edge of the binding strip to the raw edge of the layered quilt top using a ¼-inch seam allowance, unless using heavier fabric than 100-percent woven cotton (such as flannel or heavy weaves). Using a walking foot to sew the binding to the quilted project helps to eliminate puckers. Join the ends of the bias strips by folding or stitching them together. Turn the binding to the backing of the quilt and hand-sew the binding in place using blind hem-stitching.

BED SIZE	QUILT SIZE	BACKING	2½-INCH BINDING*
Twin and Full	67×87" 82×97"	5¼ yards; cut in half lengthwise, selvages removed. Seam together the lengths of the cut pieces with one full width of fabric.	¾ yard
Queen and King	88×103" 106×103"	7½ yards; cut fabric into three lengths, selvages removed. Seam together the three lengths.	⅞ yard

cut across the width of the fabric (to finish ½ inch)

STITCH DIAGRAMS

APPLIQUÉ STITCH

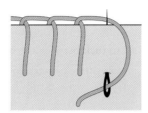

BLANKET STITCH

CHAIN STITCH

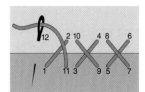

CROSS-STITCH

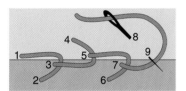

FEATHERSTITCH

FRENCH KNOT

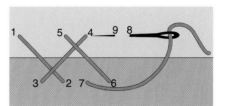

HERRINGBONE

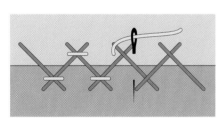

HERRINGBONE WITH COUCHING

LAZY DAISY STITCH

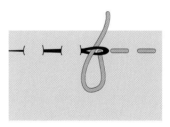

RUNNING STITCH

SATIN STITCH

SMYRNA-CROSS
VARIATION

STEM STITCH

STRAIGHT STITCH

INDEX

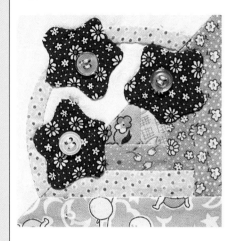

continued on page 318

INDEX *continued*

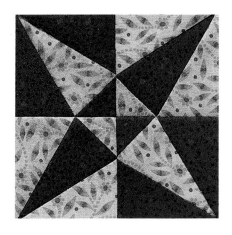

SOURCES & CREDITS

BATTING

MORNING GLORY PRODUCTS / DIVISION OF CARPENTER CO.
302 Highland Dr.
Taylor, TX 78628
www.carpenter.com

MOUNTAIN MIST / STEARNS TECHNICAL
100 William St.
Cincinnati, OH 45215
800.543.7173
E-mail: mountain.mist@
    stearnstextiles.com
www.stearnstextiles.com

FABRICS

BALI FABRIC, INC.— PRINCESS MIRAH DESIGN
800.783.4612
E-mail: batik@balifab.com
www.balifab.com

CLOTHWORKS—A DIVISION OF FABRIC SALES CO.
www.clothworks-fabric.com

FABRI-QUILT, INC.
901 East 14th Ave.
North Kansas City, MO
64116
www.fabri-quilt.com

MODA / UNITED NOTIONS
13795 Hutton
Dallas, TX 75234
www.modafabrics.com

NORTHCOTT / MONARCH
229 West 36th St.
New York, NY 10018
www.northcott.net

P & B TEXTILES
1580 Gilbreth Rd.
Burlingame, CA 94010
800.852.2327
www.pbtex.com

R.J.R FABRICS
Purchased at local
    quilt shops.
To view complete fabric
    inventory visit:
    www.rjrfabrics.com

ROBERT KAUFMAN CO.
129 West 132nd St.
Los Angeles, CA 90061
www.robertkaufman.com

SPRINGS CREATIVE PRODUCTS GROUP
454 S. Anderson Rd. Ste. 400
Rock Hill, SC 29730
www.daisykingdom.com

NOTIONS

**COLLINS & OMNIGRID, INC.
PRYM-DRITZ CORPORATION**
P.O. Box 5028
Spartanburg, SC 29304
www.dritz.com

SEWING MACHINES

HUSQVARNA VIKING SEWING MACHINES
3100 Viking Pkwy.
West Lake, OH 44145
440.808.6550
www.husqvarnaviking.com

WOOD PRODUCTS

WALNUT HOLLOW
1409 State Road 23
Dodgeville, WI 53533
www.walnuthollow.com

GRAPHIC ILLUSTRATION

Chris Neubauer Graphics

PHOTOGRAPHY

Peter Krumhardt
Andy Lyons Cameraworks
Scott Little

PHOTOSTYLING

Carol Dahlstrom and
    Margaret Sindelar
Judy Bailey, assistant
Donna Chesnut, assistant

PROJECT DESIGNERS

Dawn Cavanaugh, pages
27–30, 34, and 44–45.
Ginny McKeever, pages
32–33.
Margaret Sindelar, pages 10,
12–13, 17–21, 23, 25–33,
36–41, 43, and 47–48.
Jan Temeyer, pages 15 and 23.
Elaine Voyce, page 42.
Pat Wood, page 24.
Quilt on pages 20–21
stitched by Linda Beardsley.

QUILTERS & BLOCK DESIGNERS

Ilene Bartos
Linda Beardsley
Dawn Cavanaugh
Ginny McKeever
Margaret Sindelar
Jan Temeyer
Elaine Voyce
Pat Wood